Baby Steps

Claire B. Kopp, Ph.D.

A Holt Paperback
HENRY HOLT AND COMPANY
New York

Baby Steps

SECOND EDITION

A Guide to Your Child's
Social, Physical, Mental,
and Emotional Development
in the First Two Years

Holt Paperbacks
Henry Holt and Company, LLC
Publishers since 1866
175 Fifth Avenue
New York, New York 10010
www.henryholt.com

A Holt Paperback® and ®® are registered trademarks
of Henry Holt and Company, LLC.

Library of Congress Cataloging-in-Publication Data

Kopp, Claire B.
    Baby steps : a guide to your child's social, physical, mental, and emotional
development in the first two years / Claire B. Kopp.—2nd ed.
        p.   cm.
    Includes index.
    ISBN-13: 978-0-8050-7243-3
    ISBN-10: 0-8050-7243-8
    1. Infant psychology.   2. Infants—Development.   3. Child rearing.   I. Title.

BF719.K67   2003
305.232—dc21   2002068808

Originally published in hardcover in 1994 by W. H. Freeman and Company
First Holt Paperbacks Edition 2003

Designed by Katy Riegel

Printed in the United States of America
9   10   8

For my family

Contents

Preface   xiii

Early Development: A Miniguide   1

BIRTH TO THREE MONTHS   23
Preview   25

THE JUST BORN   27
Snapshot   28
Developmental Close-Up
What Does My Baby See?   30

THE EARLY WEEKS   33
Snapshot   34
Images of Development
Perception   35
Developmental Close-Up
Sleep and Wakefulness   36
Motor Reflexes   38

ONE MONTH   41
Snapshot   42

Images of Development

   Motor Control   43

   Perception   43

   Vocalizations   44

   Cognition   45

   Social Development   45

Developmental Close-Up

   Crying   45

   Colic   48

Two Months   51

Snapshot   52

Images of Development

   Motor Control   53

   Perception   54

   Vocalizations and Language   55

   Social Development   55

   Cognition   56

   Emotions   56

Developmental Close-Up

   Emotions   57

Three Months   61

Snapshot   62

Images of Development

   Motor Control   63

   Perception   64

   Cognition   65

   Vocalizations and Language   66

   Social Interactions and Emotions   66

Developmental Close-Up

   Becoming Aware of Others   67

Developmental Hints and Alerts: Birth to Three Months   69

Sharpening Our Focus

Neurons, Neurons, and More . . .   70

Memory   73
Emotion Development   79

FOUR TO SEVEN MONTHS   87
Preview   89

FOUR MONTHS   91
Snapshot   92
Images of Development
    Motor Control   93
    Perception   94
    Vocalizations and Language   95
    Cognition   96
    Social Development   96
    Emotions   97
Developmental Close-Up
    Grasping Abilities   97

FIVE MONTHS   101
Snapshot   102
Images of Development
    Motor Control   103
    Perception   104
    Vocalizations and Language   105
    Cognition   105
    Social Development   106
    Emotions   106
    Sense of Self   107
Developmental Close-Up
    Pushing, Pivoting, Crawling, and Creeping   107

SIX MONTHS   111
Snapshot   112
Images of Development
    Motor Control   113
    Perception   114

Vocalizations and Language   115

Cognition   116

Social Development   117

Emotions   117

Sense of Self   117

Developmental Close-Up

Developing Expectations: The Role of Schedules and Routines   118

SEVEN MONTHS   121

Snapshot   122

Images of Development

Motor Control   123

Perception   124

Vocalizations and Language   126

Cognition   126

Social Development   126

Emotions   127

Sense of Self   128

Developmental Close-Up

Attachment   128

DEVELOPMENTAL HINTS AND ALERTS: FOUR TO SEVEN MONTHS   133

SHARPENING OUR FOCUS

The Baby as Scientist, Genius, Mathematician, and More . . .   134

The Extraordinary World of Babies and Language   136

The Perception of Sounds   141

Vocalizations   143

Comprehension of Others' Words   144

Learning to Produce Words, Learning Labels   145

EIGHT TO TWELVE MONTHS   149

Preview   151

EIGHT MONTHS   153

Snapshot   154

Images of Development

   Motor Control   155

   Perception   156

   Vocalizations and Language   157

   Cognition   158

   Social Development   159

   Emotions   159

   Sense of Self   159

Developmental Close-Up

   Social Play   160

   Social Bids   161

NINE MONTHS   163

Snapshot   164

Images of Development

   Motor Control   166

   Perception   167

   Vocalizations and Language   167

   Cognition   168

   Social Development   168

   Emotions   169

   Sense of Self   169

Developmental Close-Up

   Recall Memories   170

TEN MONTHS   173

Snapshot   174

Images of Development

   Motor Control   176

   Perception   177

   Vocalizations and Language   177

   Cognition   178

   Social Development   178

   Emotions   179

   Sense of Self   179

Developmental Close-Up

   Social Referencing   180

ELEVEN MONTHS   183

Snapshot   184

Images of Development

   Motor Control   185

   Language   186

   Cognition   188

   Social Development   188

   Emotions   189

   Sense of Self   190

Developmental Close-Up

   Parenting: Culture and Development   190

TWELVE MONTHS   195

Snapshot   196

Images of Development

   Motor Control   198

   Perception   199

   Language   200

   Cognition   201

   Social Development   202

   Emotions   203

   Sense of Self   204

Developmental Close-Up

   Emotion Control   204

DEVELOPMENTAL HINTS AND ALERTS: EIGHT TO TWELVE MONTHS   207

SHARPENING OUR FOCUS

The Acquisition of Speech   208

Temperament   212

THE SECOND YEAR: TODDLER TIMES   219

Preview   221

FIFTEEN MONTHS   225
Snapshot   226
Images of Development
   Motor Control   228
   Perception   228
   Language   229
   Cognition   230
   Social Development   231
   Emotions   232
   Sense of Self   233
Developmental Close-Up
   Socializing Children to Everyday Standards of Behavior   233

EIGHTEEN MONTHS   237
Snapshot   238
Images of Development
   Motor Control   240
   Perception   240
   Language   241
   Cognition   243
   Social Development   245
   Emotions   246
   Sense of Self   247
Developmental Close-Up
   Selfhood   248

TWENTY-ONE MONTHS   251
Snapshot   252
Images of Development
   Motor Control   253
   Perception   254
   Language   254
   Cognition   255
   Social Development   257
   Emotions   258
   Sense of Self   258

Developmental Close-Up

Toilet Training   258

TWENTY-FOUR MONTHS   261

Snapshot   262

Images of Development

Motor Control   265

Perception   266

Language   266

Cognition   268

Social Development   270

Emotions   271

Sense of Self   272

Developmental Close-Up

Parenting: Commitments   272

DEVELOPMENTAL ALERTS: EIGHTEEN MONTHS,
   TWENTY-FOUR MONTHS   276

SHARPENING OUR FOCUS

Parenting and Stresses   277

The Child and the Chimp   279

IS MY CHILD OKAY?   285

References   291

Index   303

Preface

Understanding the behavior of babies and young toddlers: this is the primary focus of the second edition of this book as it was of the first edition. The reason for this new edition is to provide ideas about development that have come from new research on infant behavior, on brain development during the early years, and from changing perspectives about the meaning of early behaviors. There is much that is new and thought provoking, and as might be expected, both new and old controversies exist. I describe all of this and more.

However, I have also retained most of the organization and features of the earlier edition. Parents and other readers liked the first book's style.

As you read this book, you will learn about the extraordinary changes that occur from the newborn period to the end of the second year. I describe why babies are able to do certain things and not others, how they think, and what they feel. As you read this book, I hope you'll find that your baby's behavior makes more and more sense. It's been my experience that parents are best able to take advantage of information when they understand when, how, and why their child's behavior changes.

Another reason for helping parents understand what their babies are experiencing is to take some of the hassle and stresses out of parenting. At one time or another every parent has wondered, "Why is my baby acting this way?" Although a baby can't talk to us with words, if we know a few things about development, her behavior can tell us much about her needs and wants. In this edition, I have added a section that speaks to some of the stresses of parenting.

Parents who understand child behavior can be more confident about their ability to handle situations. They know they can figure out how to help their child by accurately interpreting the child's signals for comfort, stimulation, or quiet time alone. With efficient decision making, parents can have more time to enjoy their young child. Some parents tell me that knowing what to expect and what not to expect at any age has not only reassured them about how to care for their baby but also made them feel better about the whole experience of parenting. They like being informed when making decisions. Parents who take the time to learn when, how, and why behavior changes know what they can do to help their young child grow and when they need to seek assistance.

Scientific research helps us to know what kinds of behavior to expect when our children are about one month old, six months old, and so on. That is not to say that babies follow a rigid timetable for growth, but rather that behavior usually develops in a fairly predictable fashion. Every baby develops at his own pace and in his own way, but many babies experience similar patterns of growth. In this book I describe the sequences of behavior changes that most young children follow.

You won't find everything about baby or toddler development in this book. The first two years is a period of rapid change and incomparable growth. If someone wrote a book describing every change, it would be so long that parents would not have the time to read it. Instead, what I do here is to highlight some of the most important changes. In the first year I talk about behavior for every month, and then in the second year I look at fifteen, eighteen, twenty-one, and twenty-four months.

As always, I am indebted to the many parents who have shared ideas with me, and who participated in research. I also extend appreciation to graduate students who have been invaluable collaborators in past research: J. Heidi Gralinski, Ph.D.; Bonnie Klimes-Dougan, Ph.D.; Joanne B. Krakow, Ph.D. (deceased); Irma Röder, Ph.D.; Brian E. Vaughn, Ph.D.; and more recently Susan Neufeld, M.A.; Sheri Coulson, Ph.D.; Leslie Fulgham, M.A.; and Jennifer Wishner, Ph.D.

I also appreciate the many colleagues who have enriched my thinking about early development. There are many but I do want to call attention to a few of them. Michael Regalado, M.D., and I have spent many hours discussing and debating issues of parenting. I greatly appreciate his insights. Nancy Eisenberg, Ph.D., friend and colleague, has fostered my interest in the combined roles of temperament and emotion regulation and preschoolers' behaviors. Although not directly pertinent to this volume, Dale Berger, Ph.D., has helped me relate developmental issues and various approaches to measurement. Donna Bean, M.A., remains a dear friend and incredible research resource.

Lastly, my deep appreciation to Deborah Brody, my editor at Holt, who with scant notice took manuscript in hand and effectively moved it through the publishing process. Deb and her colleagues (copy editor, designer, production editor) are an impressive team.

My husband, Eugene H. Kopp, continues to be an anchor, critic, and supporter, for which I am grateful.

Baby Steps

Early Development

This miniguide defines development, describes how it comes about, and suggests ways to think about your own child's development. Here, and elsewhere in this book, I emphasize scientists' increasing understanding of the early years and also their realization of the variation observed among healthy and normal children and their parents. Yet despite diversity and variability, there are common threads in early development. It is these threads that I highlight in this book, with the goal of helping parents better understand the meaning and significance of the first two years.

Invariably, my descriptions and explanations are couched in a developmental framework on the premise that it is easier to understand a particular behavior if you can see how it fits into the overall scheme of things. Take throwing as an example. Parents of a fifteen-month-old might interpret throwing as a sign of belligerence. It could be, but it's not likely. Throwing at this age is simply an activity the toddler enjoys. It gives him a sense of accomplishment and mastery of an object (a ball) while also developing muscle strength in his upper arm.

Of course there are limits: most parents want to establish guidelines as to where a fifteen-month-old may throw things. If you also look at the broader scheme of things, you can see that this is an age when it is developmentally appropriate to encourage behavior that leads to a sense of mastery. So as a parent, it is just a matter of finding the right toy (a ball), the right place (a yard, a playground), and the right time (when someone can monitor the scene) for the toddler who loves to throw.

✦ DEVELOPMENT AND CHANGE

In everyday conversation, the word *development* has different meanings. We sometimes speak of an event, such as a promotion, as a development. Sometimes we mean a stage of progress; for instance, a child's development as a pianist advanced faster than her music teacher had anticipated. A third use of the word describes a process—how film is changed into snapshots, for example. Which of these definitions is synonymous with what scientists mean when they talk about child development? All of them!

Important changes in a young child's behavior often represent development: the baby's first word and the first step are among the most obvious. Development also refers to certain stages of progress, such as the toddler years or the preschool period. The changes that occur during these times are numerous and dramatic and often have implications for parenting. By the end of the second year, for example, young children often use words to describe their feelings (happy, mad) and to talk about their desires ("I want . . ."). Development also reflects processes that undergo change. An example includes paying attention to one's surroundings. Attention control changes markedly during the first year. In early life, a baby's attention is often captured by a stimulus that has strong contrasts of light and dark. By a year of age babies control their attention for long stretches of time despite unwanted diversions.

⁓

THE STUDY OF BABIES and toddlers' development is the study of change. It often involves observing the behaviors babies display and noting when and how they occur, asking if particular experiences contribute to the growth of the behavior, figuring out how the behaviors fit into the big developmental picture, identifying the amount of baby variability that exists for a particular behavior, and asking if extremes in variability have important consequences for development. Here's an example related to variability: longitudinal research suggests that some babies who are at the high end of consistent irritability have adjustment problems later on, particularly if parenting is inadequate.

Sometimes researchers study emerging behaviors, called "nascent" behaviors, and other times they study how a behavior such as baby's play becomes more elaborate and complex. Researchers are also particularly interested in understanding change as a key to a baby or toddler's ever-increasing competencies: the ability to walk has profound effects on a baby's awareness of space and spatial landmarks (pictures on a wall), or the increasing awareness of one's self leads into budding feelings of pride from accomplishments (completing a puzzle).

When possible, the study of early development is increasingly linked to brain research in which scientists use nonintrusive methods to understand links between the developing brain and developing patterns of behavior. We have known for decades that three-month-olds are more visually alert and socially responsive than one-month-olds. Now, with recent brain research we have learned that visual attention in the first weeks of life is largely due to activation of subcortical neurons. After this age there is an increasing shift to activation of cortical neurons and pathways. The cortex is essential for human thinking, language, emotion control, behavioral inhibition, and more. So this shift is truly important.

Shifts related to increasing activation of brain regions also take place *within* the cortex. A shift in babies' ability to control and sustain their attention, observed toward the end of the first year, has been linked to activation of a specific part of the cortex that is relatively *silent* during the earlier months of life. Here, too, the shift is crucial.

Lately, there's been considerable controversy about offering enriched stimulation to babies as a way to enhance brain development. In this controversy, as in others, it helps parental decision making when parents understand the basic issues. Accordingly, I describe early brain development and its links to behavior in the section entitled "Sharpening Our Focus: Neurons, Neurons, and More. . . ."

✦ WAYS OF THINKING ABOUT DEVELOPMENT

There are so many dimensions of change in the first two years that making sense of them might seem difficult. To some degree this is so because scientists don't always agree about the reasons for change, the relative influences of biology and experiences in early development, and the relation between early brain development and changes in a baby's behavior. I'll mention some of these disagreements every now and then, but for now I'll mostly point out important areas of agreement, which allow us to describe some *ways of thinking* about early child development.

✧ The baby is not a *blank slate* at birth. Our human biological heritage provides newborns with behaviors that are mostly subcortical in origin that

- ✦ improve the odds for survival, should a caregiver not be immediately available. The head-turning response is an example, where the baby reflexively turns his head from side to side if his mouth and nasal passages are blocked by something like a cloth.

+ facilitate the newborn's attention to the world of humans, including their faces and patterns of speech.
+ allow for some kinds of recognizable responses, such as alertness to the social interactions initiated by parents and others.
+ allow the baby an elemental awareness of differences in feelings of distress in contrast to non-distress.

Almost all developmental scientists agree these behaviors give babies a means to engage with others from the first hours of birth. However, there is disagreement about the origins of these behaviors. Some argue for an evolutionary perspective and seek evidence of similar kinds of behaviors among nonhuman primates; others suggest there are specific modules in the brain that specify the launching of these behaviors, and still others state the behaviors reflect learning that takes place from the first hours of birth.

The disagreements about the origins of behaviors also play out in how the behaviors are interpreted. For some, even young babies are intelligent, thinking humans who by two months of age can actively share emotional experiences with their caregivers. Others, including me, believe newborn behaviors reflect *jump-start-responses* to parents' attempts to engage babies in social interactions. The more babies respond to others, the more likely it is that interactions will continue.

Jump-start-responses often occur in social interactions. Many newborns—who are awake and alert—are drawn to speech that has lots of intonation. Parents' bobbing heads and smiling faces are also interesting to babies. In turn, babies respond by being attentive, opening their mouths, and making soft gurglelike sounds. Heightened levels of attention can also be observed when a baby is presented with a visual stimulus that has strong light and dark contrasts. Other newborn behaviors include distinguishing among different tastes (sweet, bitter) and odors (such as a mother's scent) and recognizing the location of particular nearby objects that offer relief when hungry or slightly upset (finding the nipple that is attached to a breast).

◈ A second way to think about development is that biology and *experiences* work together so that every human has a set of physical characteristics and behavioral potentials that we associate with being human. With appropriate experiences, many physical and behavioral attributes emerge in a relatively similar way everywhere. Thus we expect that babies and children will develop

- openness to many kinds of learning experiences
- an upright posture and skill in walking
- fully opposable thumbs for precise movements
- a spoken language, which is open to modifications as a result of learning
- attentiveness to surroundings, with control of attention to suit demands of situations
- affectionate and emotionally satisfying relationships, first with parents and then with others

Some behaviors will require more specific experiences from parents and others for effective development. Language is an example where specific inputs are essential.

✦ A third way of thinking about development involves an understanding that our human species is capable of many kinds of adjustments, such as accommodations to major variations in climate, geographic conditions, and natural resources. Babies born to and reared by Laplanders of northern Scandinavia, Parisians of France, American Indians, Muscovites of Russia, Alexandrians of Egypt, and Pygmy tribes of Africa are all unmistakably human and reveal many, many similarities despite their diversity of social groups and cultural norms.

Along with adaptations to geographic and climate variations, babies and children easily adapt to the different learning environments that typify various social and cultural groups. In the United States we often think of formal schooling as the primary mechanism of teaching information to children as young as three or four years through adolescence. Other cultures, particularly non-Western, provide teaching by augmenting schooling with direct and indirect participation of children in adult chores or wage-earning activities.

Researchers who study child rearing in other cultures have shown us that parents of infants and toddlers use guided participation for teaching—irrespective of culture. The specifics of what is taught differ, but across the street or across the world, parents use a variety of everyday routines (daily hygiene), modeling everyday activities (home care), and direct instruction (use of mealtime implements) to teach. And babies and toddlers learn.

✦ A fourth way of thinking about development has to do with individual differences. Every baby becomes a unique human individual. All of us differ from one another in how we view the world, our personal levels of motivation, what we find interesting and challenging, the kinds of close relationships that we cherish, and more. Three factors account for individual variability: our personal genetic heritage via the genes passed on by one's mother and father; the various kinds of social, emotional, and learning experiences and opportunities provided to each of us during childhood; and the self-selected choices and experiences each of us chooses—even starting in infancy.

Many babies mostly resemble an average, with of course some individual variations on the average. They walk, talk, and show cognitive, social, emotional, and selfhood development around normative average values. Many are fairly even in their temperament style, sociability, and emotional responses.

However, there are some babies where stylistic features point to a wide range of differences. Some babies want a great deal of social company, whereas, at the other end of the continuum, there are others who are mostly content to play on their own and to watch other family members. Similarly, there are some babies who are mostly joyous whereas there are others who tend to be mostly irritable despite responsive parents.

These individual differences are increasingly of interest because of their possible longer-term implications. As one example, Clancy Blair has pointed out that high emotionality during infancy, whether due to a difficult temperament or systemic high states of physiological stress and arousal, can lead to malfunctioning in psychological and physiological regulatory systems. In turn, poor regulatory controls may lead to disorders in cognitive processes such as attention and memory, and then coalesce into inadequate readiness for school entry and subsequent school learning problems.

Blair also cogently summarizes a dictum that has long been obvious: infancy is not destiny. During the early years, it is parents who provide the psychological and physical environment that includes physical care, nurturance, affection, emotional support, and verbal and cognitive stimulation. It is also the quality of parenting that is vastly important in helping babies to learn, to become more social, to control their emotions, and in helping risky babies—those who show high negative emotionality—become far less risky.

✧ A fifth way of thinking about development is understanding that babies are not infinitely malleable. A four-month-old can't learn algebra. A fifteen-month-old may be aware of his mother's sadness and show his concern, but he does not understand why poor health, potential job loss, and financial worries make a person sad.

There is a curious contradiction about babies' ability to learn. On the one hand, human infancy represents the beginning of great potential for learning; alternatively babies' learning is constrained because the infant brain is immature. Babies simply do not have the *brain material* that allows them to learn ideas related to geography, mathematics, history, chess, and a host of other things that older children and adults learn fairly rapidly.

However, immaturity has an important role in helping the baby learn information that is basic to our human functioning. As one example, the young baby's ability to hear sounds is limited so that babies' hearing systems are *biased* to hear certain sounds, particularly those related to human speech. This propensity to hear speech sounds and to learn how to segment speech into words and phrases is one reason that babies can become active participants in language-based communications by the end of the first year of life.

Recognizing constraints also highlights the importance of appropriate, positive experiences for babies. Whether it is language, cognition, or emotion development, babies need meaningful and diverse experiences with parents in order to learn. The exuberance of babies, their pleasure in exploration and interactions with others, is invariably influenced by parents' inputs and supportive behaviors.

◆ DEVELOPMENTAL NORMS AND VARIABILITY

During the last century, developmental scientists began to ask how babies differed as a function of geography, climate, and racial and cultural heritages. One goal was to determine if there were a sufficient number of similarities across many different babies that could be used to evaluate how well an individual baby was developing with respect to his age.

Many thousands of babies were studied, with questions asked about when babies were able to smile, use their hands, sit up, walk, talk, and more. The results of the studies were clear: There are many similarities in early development. There are sound reasons for this. Babies represent new generations, and babies must be given a good chance of survival if cultures are to grow. In a sense, then, biology gives babies a head start with some key survival behaviors and with a ground plan of our humanness. Another factor is that caring for human babies requires similar forms of nurturance from parents and others irrespective of where one lives.

Developmental scientists have used similarities in babies' behaviors and development to record *norms*. Norms simply identify the ages when certain behaviors such as smiling or grasping emerge, how behaviors tend to change over time, and how one developing behavior affects the development of other behaviors. Norms are invaluable guideposts for parents, pediatricians, and researchers, provided they are not employed too rigidly.

However, it pays to remember that babies do differ in some ways as a function of background, culture, rearing styles, and their own individuality. Some researchers have shown slightly earlier motor development among babies of African heritage than those of Caucasian background. Other researchers have compared babies of Oriental heritage with those of Euro-American backgrounds and reported less physical activity among the former. Cultural beliefs often dictate how a baby is carried, the playthings that are provided, the nature of solid food, and more. And, of course, within cultures there is some variability in the way that babies develop because of individual style, parental rearing styles, and personal choices.

Also remember that norms are simply guidelines. While I describe age-related behaviors in this book using the order, the form, and the pace that research and my own experience indicate they most regularly come about, an individual baby or toddler's development will invariably differ in some ways. Sometimes, it is only *extreme* variations in development that are cause for concern. We know that a toddler who is not walking at twenty months of age or a two-year-old who does not engage in play is developmentally *beyond* the normative ranges. Other times, there is a combination of behaviors that is "not right." An example is the asocial, inconsolable, totally noncompliant eighteen-month-old.

An open mind, informed observations, and thoughtful assessments are the keys to the prudent use of developmental norms. Many a child development specialist has said, "Change is a constant in early child development." I use this phrase myself from time to time but I usually go on to say, "And in late infancy and early toddlerhood, individual variability in the pace of growth is one of the most important child development norms."

♦ PATTERNS OF DEVELOPMENT

Growth rates. Some kinds of development move forward rapidly, others more slowly. The baby's thumb-forefinger grasp usually appears around nine months, although the first indications of grasp are likely to emerge at about four months of age. Contrast this five-month period of growth with the longer period of time required to develop a sense of personal identity. At eighteen months, most toddlers show genuine signs of selfhood (concern about a dirty face or embarrassment when introduced to an unfamiliar person are specific examples), but the steps to selfhood start over a year earlier (around three months of age) when the baby first begins to realize that his body is separate from that of another person. Some kinds of development—such as learning that one is a unique person—require a great deal of complex learning, particularly learning that comes from interactions with others. It is in these interactions that each child begins to be aware of the many facets of selfhood and struggles to organize them into a meaningful understanding of personal identity.

Growth patterns. Development of a specific skill sometimes involves a kind of stair-step path, with periods of consistent improvement alternating with phases of relatively little gain. The early growth of speech is a good example of this pattern. Often in the second year, there is a spurt at about eighteen months where the toddler may learn several new words for days at a time. Then weeks go by when no new words appear.

Sometimes we understand why a leveling-off pattern occurs, other times not. In the case of toddlers who are in the midst of learning to walk and learning to talk, it's not unusual to find a slowing down in new word growth. Walking demands all kinds of physical and psychological energy, so there's not much left for words. However, the novice talker needs lots of psychological energy for learning new words and figuring out when to use them. It may be easier to focus on walking—and perhaps more fun at least for a few weeks or so.

Sometimes developmental patterns show another pattern of growth, which is characterized by many new changes in a baby or toddler's behavior. My favorite example is the period from eight to twelve months, when many new or markedly changed behaviors appear, typically leading to more complex and controlled skills. Most fourteen-month-olds, in contrast to eight-month-olds, are aware of their ability to control features of their environments: They gesture to and make eye contact with others to show something interesting, they try to control the action of a fearful toy, they tease parents, and they show definite preferences for those who will receive their affections.

The two other age periods associated with new clusters of behaviors occur at about three months and between eighteen and twenty-four months. I'll describe the changes for you in the appropriate age sections.

Deletions of behaviors. Developmental growth during infancy requires the emergence of time-limited behaviors, which serve as stepping-stones toward achieving a more advanced skill. Once the new skill is in place, the stepping-stone is discarded. Creeping is a good example, as it provides babies with a means to move about independently long before their own bodies are strong enough to maintain a standing position and to walk. Creeping not only provides a bit of independence, it also helps strengthen the trunk and leg muscles that hold the body upright during walking.

Some behaviors simply appear and then disappear. Newborn *developmental reflexes* are an example. They are important in early life; many of them serve (or once served) as survival mechanisms or behaviors that promote social interactions with caregivers. The sucking reflex is a good example: it is active during the newborn period and for several months after birth. Any healthy newborn sucks to take in food. In a short time, the sucking reflex melds into the learned voluntary act of sucking. Developmental reflexes should disappear (or are actually inhibited with brain maturation) between four and six months of age.

Refinement of behaviors. Most of the behaviors that emerge during the first two years emerge in an immature form that, with experiences, gradually become more coordinated (motor abilities), more adept (increase in number of words spoken), more intelligent (use of problem-solving strategies), or more controlled (fewer bouts of crying). Experiences can take many forms, ranging from the thousands of everyday visual and vocal conversations between parent and baby to the seemingly never-ending one-step stair climbing of a fourteen-month-old or the eighteen-month-old's repetition of a word in a dialogue with a parent.

Consolidations of behaviors. There are times during the first two years that new levels of maturity of behaviors or skills emerge at about the same time. The baby practices each of these skills and then suddenly she merges all of them into a more mature act. An example of a newly emergent mature act occurs at about twelve months or so, when parents begin to ask the baby to bring something. "Bring me your shoes," "Bring me your bottle." Three behaviors have to be in place for this *bringing* behavior to occur: (1) the baby has to understand at some level the words *bring me* and *shoe* (or any other object); (2) the baby has to remember the last location of the object; and (3) the baby has to be able to move on her own from one place to another and to carry the object from one place to another. Each one of these requisite skills emerged or became more refined in the months preceding the ability to *bring.*

✦ BEHAVIOR DOMAINS

I've talked about terms used to describe change; however, we are also interested in studying the specific behaviors that babies show. I have grouped related behaviors together into seven domains: motor control, perception, cognition, social development, language, emotions, and sense of self.

Motor Control

During a visit to my infant-development class, a four-month-old and his mother took turns amusing each other. The baby had good head control when held upright. He looked around with an alert expression. When I held a colorful rattle in front of him, he wriggled, gasped, grunted, pumped his arms up and down, opened and closed his hands, and reached again. But he was unable to make contact with the rattle. Pleasure gave way to frustration and he fretted. His mother quickly soothed him by opening his fisted fingers and placing the rattle in his hand.

Despite the baby's inability to take hold of the rattle, he had already mastered some developmentally important motor controls. He moved his head well and kept his head upright most of the time. His shoulder muscles were strong enough to let him raise his arms and reach for toys. We differentiate the baby's body movements into his *gross motor skills*, which include rolling over, sitting, creeping, standing, and walking, and his *fine motor skills*, which include reaching, grasping, and releasing. Using norms, we place the baby's motor development into a general age range.

There's a fairly predictable sequence to the overall pattern of babies' motor development during the first year of life. The musculature related to the head and neck is the first to show marked increases in strength, then strength increases in the shoulders and upper trunk, and then strength increases in the abdomen, hips, and legs. Typically, there's some overlap in increasing muscle strength (upper and lower trunk together, for example), although in normal development a baby's trunk muscles do not get stronger before his neck muscles.

The practical side of knowing about this sequence is that we can see how a baby's motor development is progressing simply by observing his behaviors. The shoulder muscles are strong when he is able to prop himself up when lying on his tummy. When his upper trunk muscles are sturdy, a baby can roll over regularly. As the lower trunk muscles strengthen, he is able to sit by himself. Later, when each part of the trunk and lower limbs is strong, he can support his own weight while standing.

Why is head control a first priority in muscle development? Well, human babies (and children) are best able to take in visual information when their bodies are in an upright position and their heads are upright and stable. Thus, from the standpoint of early learning, it makes sense to have a biological predisposition that fosters "head first."

Another biological bias concerns muscle development from midline outward: a gradual increase in strength first takes place in the shoulder girdle area, then in the arms, and finally in the hands. Arm control (raising, lowering, reaching) depends on a strong and stable shoulder girdle; the effective use of hands depends on strong and stable forearms and wrists.

Most babies follow typical sequences of development, although there are exceptions among perfectly healthy babies. Some babies walk before they crawl, or may not crawl at all. Differences among babies are likely to occur in the timing of motor development, particularly related to very early walking or late walking. Minor variations in sequence or in the pace of motor developments are invariably inconsequential. However, when motor skills emerge far later than expected or the quality of a skill is suspect, parents should seek the advice of a child-development specialist.

Sensation and Perception

The term *sensation* refers to our intake of information from our sense systems, which include touch, taste, smell, vision, and hearing. *Perception* refers to the ability to use the senses to discriminate and recognize objects, people, and events. Visual perception, for example, involves paying attention to a visual stimulus and differentiating it as being similar to (or not similar to) something else (a square from a circle).

In early life, babies' perceptual abilities are linked to the maturity of their sensory systems. The sensory systems that are of most concern in this book, vision and hearing, are relatively immature in the early months of life. In practical terms this means that perceptual discriminations are somewhat limited. Newborns cannot distinguish a pattern made up of threadlike black-and-white stripes from an overall pattern of gray, whereas they can distinguish a pattern of wide black-and-white stripes from gray. They also distinguish a small black-and-white bull's-eye pattern from black-and-white squares.

Babies' visual systems mature quite rapidly, and by three months they see nearby objects quite clearly, and in another few months, as well as most adults. Hearing also matures during the first six months and, at about a year, is comparable to adult hearing. At the same time, both visual and auditory perceptual discriminations improve. Most perceptual abilities (for example, sound differentiation and depth perception) show considerable maturation during the first year. Babies' vision matures, so that, for example, they can see both nearby and more distant objects distinctly, and they can detect fine lines as well as wide ones. Much the same kind of maturing process occurs with hearing. Here the maturation process involves being able to detect soft sounds as well as loud ones, and nearby sounds as well as distant ones.

For the most part, *perceptions are fine-tuned by the experience of living in a social world*. Being held by parents, hearing the sounds of different voices, looking at different faces, touching soft and hard objects such as toys or clothing, playing with objects such as toys, being carried, rolling about in a crib or other kind of bed, creeping, and walking all provide the baby with opportunities to develop visual-perception skills related to variations in depth, size, distance, color, and shape; the auditory perceptions of speech and nonspeech; the sounds of specific letters (*ba, ta, ra*) and words; the sequences of speech; and tactile perceptions related to hardness, softness, fuzziness, bristliness, and more.

When I describe perceptual development in succeeding chapters, I also refer to studies that reveal how babies' sensory systems are changing. Often I'll distinguish sensory growth by spelling out changes that occur in vision and in hearing. I use the title *perception* for these descriptions, and to keep things straightforward I simply refer to *vision* and *hearing*.

Attention. In order to perceive, one has to pay attention with eyes and ears. Attention is crucial to learning, effective social interactions, and emotion control. Paying attention is simply a vital part of living. Given that I often refer to attention in this book, I want to insert a note here about the development of visual attention, which changes dramatically during the first year of life. John Colombo describes attention development in terms of babies' alertness, their ability to attend to *where* things are located in nearby space, their ability to attend to objects including shapes and color, and their ability to control their attention in terms of duration and preferences. Using ideas from Holly Ruff and Mary Rothbart, we can say that in the first year babies learn how to orient their attention and learn to *study* the objects and people they encounter.

The box on page 14, adapted from Colombo's review and an article I wrote, summarizes three periods of attention development that take place after the newborn period. In large part, early attention development is related to perceptual discriminations. Then during the second year, visual attention is also increasingly linked to cognitive activities of learning (attending to and imitating others' actions), acquisition of knowledge of the physical world (exploring toys and other objects), and acquisition of knowledge of the social world (defining people by their attributes and their roles). Individual differences in babies' use of controlled attention are increasingly being studied for potential influences on later learning and social interactions.

Cognition

Behaviors that are classified as cognition include memory, attention, problem-solving skills, comprehension, and learning. In effect, *cognition* is the shorthand word for knowledge, how knowledge is acquired, how our thought processes transform knowledge, and how we remember what we have learned. Consider, for example, that babies and young children gradually build a store of knowledge about their parents, including what they look like, how they speak, what they wear, when they are most happy and most angry, how they provide love and affection, why one or the other or both leave in the morning and come home at night, and more.

Cognitive development includes acquiring information in a relatively efficient way, learning associations between two acts such as a parent's appearance and being picked up, learning to remember, understanding categories of things such as animals versus trucks, and developing insights about cause-and-effect relationships. Specifics of learning include knowledge of people and how they look and respond, knowledge of objects including their functions, awareness of time, and awareness of causality in that one event causes another.

The overall growth of cognitive skills moves rapidly from three months

BIRTH TO 1 MONTH	2 TO 3 MONTHS	4 TO 6 MONTHS	9 TO 12 MONTHS
Minimal alertness, but increases at one month; *sticky* attention due to difficulty disengaging from strong stimuli.	Increasing alertness; engages in spatial orienting; pays attention to objects and their features; better able to disengage from stimuli.	Better control of spatial orienting; increasingly sensitive to form and color of objects; coordinates visual attention with reach and grasp; looks to source of sounds; initiates social interactions with visual attention.	Still better control over spatial and object orienting; locates landmarks; sustains attention; engages and disengages at will; uses attention for social exchanges; engages in joint attention.

on, albeit there are times when cognitive growth just seems to burst forth. One of these times seems to occur between six and twelve months, and another takes place between eighteen and twenty-four months. These latter two periods have been linked to changes in brain functioning. All three age periods are associated with changes in the amount of knowledge babies have, in how they use their knowledge, and in the memories they can retain.

Still another subset of the behaviors in the cognition domain is called intelligence. Basically, *intelligence* is a word that refers to how skillfully and efficiently we use the knowledge we have, particularly when we have to deal with novel and unique situations. Do babies display intelligent behavior? Yes, clearly toward the end of the first year. At about ten months, a baby might recognize that her bottle contains something to drink (even though she doesn't know the word *drink*) and knows exactly what to do when the bottle is handed to her. This cognitive activity demonstrates the baby has acquired some knowledge; that is, she knows what a bottle is used for.

Now, here's where knowledge is used intelligently. The baby is sitting on the floor drinking from her bottle when her big sister approaches with a new doll. The baby drops her bottle and looks at the doll. Accidentally, the sister kicks the bottle and it rolls behind a big stuffed chair. Seeing the bottle disappear, the baby creeps around the chair to retrieve it. She could have cried and done nothing, but she did not. Instead she came up with the solution and an action—that is intelligent behavior.

There has been, and continues to be, considerable controversy about the meaning of behaviors with respect to infant cognitive development. Recent disagreements center on the first year of life and relate to interpretations of behaviors observed in the newborn period and at various other points during the first year. I mention a few of the controversies in the chapter "Sharpening Our Focus: The Baby as Scientist, Genius, Mathematician, and More . . ." However, I mostly don't go into detail about those studies where well-known researchers have major disagreements about findings. Fundamentally, the disputes often center on whether babies are engaging in perceptual discriminations or reasoned cognitive activities. I believe that many of the studies, and the arguments made for them, have few direct consequences for parenting. Just keep in mind that there is a fundamental need for responsive and sensitive parenting in the first few months of life and later. Overall I remain an unadventurous interpreter of babies' early perceptual and cognitive skills. As parents, you must feel free to evaluate research and make up your own minds.

Lastly, cognitive-oriented developmentalists increasingly emphasize the importance of social influences on cognitive development. Parents, other adults, and even older siblings provide many forms of assistance to a baby or toddler as she is trying to understand the toys she plays with. This assistance may take many forms, from simply moving a toy closer to the baby for better inspection to showing how blocks can be stacked on top of each other. This social emphasis on cognition is one that I wholeheartedly agree with.

Social Development

Scientists include many kinds of behavior under the term *social development*: babies' interactions with parents and other caregivers; how babies pick up cues from their parents' *conversations* with them, and how they use these cues to become social interaction partners; how and when babies learn to use others' cues (social referencing); the development of affection; the social skills of babies who are placed in day care; toddlers learning of everyday dos and don'ts; the nature of toddlers' play with other children, and more.

Family practices and cultural conventions influence some aspects of social development, but the basic features of becoming social are similar across cultures. For two-month-olds a social skill involves maintaining eye contact with another person, and matching some of a parent's communicative rhythm in a social exchange. A social skill at six months might entail babbling to someone to "pay attention to me." Toward the end of the first year, social acts often involve a coordinated sequence of behaviors: a baby turns to his father, pulls on his arm, babbles, points to a toy, and then looks back at his father. This group of behaviors, often labeled *joint attention*, is an important milestone in baby and parent interactions. In joint attention, the baby invites an adult to share his interests and his world!

Overall, I repeatedly emphasize how successful social development results from dynamic, ongoing, and varied exchanges between a baby and her parents. The exchanges can take the form of eye contact, vocal communications, or emotional mimicry (smiling to one another). Sometimes the parent takes on the leader role; other times the baby leads.

Professionals who study social development tend to have strong opinions and many debates. Debates about "good" social development have been around a long time. Some contemporary disagreements involve the meaning of attachment (see "Seven Months: Developmental Close-Up"), the implications of early day care, and the meaning of one or another parental behavior for a child's development. I'll mention some of these issues later on.

Language

The development of language is one of the most impressive achievements of the first two years, and it doesn't come easily. In the second year my grandson Andrew began to say his first words. Slowly he discovered that words are labels; he struggled to find the right words after recognizing that he made word mistakes; he gradually learned to associate a picture with a word (he saw a company logo on a truck and exclaimed "cheese"); he discovered the past tense; he realized he could ask for help; he learned to refer to himself as "me." He even realized—and accepted—that he could not always be understood. All of this occurred over the course of a year or so. But Andrew's language development was not remarkable; it was very similar to the language growth of other children his age. What I find remarkable is the extent of language learning that takes place in almost every child within a relatively brief time span.

Young children's primary language challenges are to comprehend speech and to produce speech. Many related behaviors precede the emergence of mature language skills. For comprehension, these include distinguishing one sound from another, discriminating the intonations of language, and learning to associate sounds and gestures with objects and people. Most young children comprehend far more than they can say.

For production, the precursors to speech include vocalizations that include all kinds of cries as well as the nonfretful sounds of coos, babbles, and jargon. Vowel sounds are the baby's first "speech," then the baby learns the sounds of consonants, and still later the baby is able to mix vowels and consonants to produce the familiar "bababa, mamama," and so on. Babies reared in English-speaking families tend to produce more nouns than verbs at first; and when they begin to use sentences, they often say the noun first and then the verb ("daddy tired," "baby cry"). But they might also invert verb and noun and correctly say, "Throw ball."

Around the world, vocalization development occurs in a relatively predictable sequence, with vowels appearing before consonants. In addition, within a linguistic culture, language develops in a fairly predictable way. For example, in English-speaking cultures, children's sentences that include a noun, verb, and object typically reflect a sequence such as, "He hit the ball," rather than, "Hit he the ball."

The process of language acquisition—particularly the beginnings of language—has been sharply debated for decades. One of the arguments basically turns on the issue of whether language development is a separate and independent entity or whether its development is inherently linked to social inputs and exchanges, and learned information about the people and objects in one's surroundings. My intellectual preference is for the second perspective.

I expand on many of these topics, along with an additional focus on developmental changes, in "Sharpening Our Focus: The Extraordinary World of Babies and Language," which follows the Four to Seven Months section, and in another section on the acquisition of speech that follows the "Twelve Months" chapter.

Emotions

Few events in recent memory have seared our consciousness as 9/11. Few events have prompted such varied emotions—fear, sadness, anger, even shame for our remissness in letting such events occur. Fortunately, this wellspring of negative emotions also found some relief in feelings of pride toward the heroic.

Although we could not know if others shared our racing heartbeats and heaving respirations, we knew from others' facial expressions that feelings were reciprocated. Emotionally laden communications flowed with stranger and friend. In time, some measure of emotional equilibrium returned, and plans were made to confront and to protect. All we felt, thought, and acted upon during and after 9/11 represented the complex interplay of our emotions, our thinking, and our motivations. There is nothing comparable in the emotional lives of babies. I say this not to diminish the emotions that babies experience, but simply to emphasize the vast amounts of living that feed into our emotions. Many developmentalists think the young baby's emotions are felt but are not recognized at a conscious or cognitive level until close to the end of the first year. Before then, babies can be in one or another emotional state (pleasure, distress) but not recognize the emotion and its causes or solutions.

Emotion development during the first two years involves the gradual emergence of basic positive and negative emotions. Positive emotions include pleasure and joy, whereas negative emotions include anger, fear, and sadness. Basic emotions have some roots in biology: Anger displays, for example, have links to the facial expressions and physical actions associated with rage responses of attacking animals. Similarly, signs of fear have links to facial expressions and physical actions among animals that have been subdued.

We now know, though, that facial expressions do not tell the whole story of emotional experiences. People can feel great anger, but display a calm countenance. Newborn babies may show facial expressions that resemble anger, but do not experience anger. They have no history of the experience of anger, nor the cognitive skills for interpretation. Indeed, even when we think older babies are frustrated, angry, or fearful, they tend to show a similar facial expression (a cry face). We're better at labeling toddlers' negative emotions because we read their body language along with their facial expressions.

Another group of emotions, sometimes collectively labeled "self-conscious," involve self-awareness and the self in relation to other individuals. In other words, a self-conscious emotion involves a comparison of the self's behavior to the standards of others. The comparison may lead to shame, guilt, or pride. Shame differs from guilt by its association with subjective feelings of undesired exposure and possession of an inherent flaw that is not correctable. Guilt about violation of a standard is correctable in the sense that a person can offer some kind of reparation (an apology). The question of how shame, guilt, and pride are represented in young children has sparked considerable research with toddlers and young preschoolers. One research issue involves how to measure shame and guilt in young children, given their language limitations. Another is concerned with the ages that shame and guilt begin to emerge.

Overall, the countless interactions between parents and babies help babies become aware of their own feelings of well-being compared with feelings of distress. As babies become more cognitively aware and linguistically competent they begin to understand their own and others' emotions, and to apply words to different feelings. As I mentioned earlier, emotion development takes a leap forward during the second year when toddlers begin to define and understand their own selfhood.

In addition to each age period, I discuss in more detail emotions and emotion development at the end of the "Two Months" and "Twelve Months" chapters and in a "Sharpening Our Focus" essay, which contains a time-line chart on emotion development.

Sense of Self

A long time ago I was asked to try to assess the developmental capabilities of a toddler who had a very severe physical handicap. The boy was not quite two years old; he spoke in two-word sentences. As I slowly approached him, he told his mother that I was to stay away. He did not want me to intrude into his personal and psychological space. Frankly, I was in awe of the child's sense of self. I was sure this display of selfhood indicated that his physical disabilities were not restricting his mental development. In time the boy came to trust me, and in the long and slow process of evaluating him, I confirmed my initial impressions of his developmental normality. More important, I came to understand that the boy's strong sense of self and his motivation to achieve blossomed because of the encouragement and enduring support of his parents.

The sense of self is our identity. It is a source of psychological protection and vulnerability as well as a reflection of our feelings, desires, and beliefs. Selfhood first comes about as babies learn that they have a personal physical identity. They obtain this knowledge by exploring their own bodies and then by experiencing their bodies in interactions with objects and other people. A young child's concept of self develops in an orderly fashion: recognition of the body, awareness of feelings and capabilities, and then self-evaluation. The sense of self is barely present at three months, but after the baby's first birthday the development of self is helped along primarily by two factors: parents and the advent of increased language production skills.

Selfhood is a powerful behavioral force by twenty-four months and includes preoccupation with competence and mastery, self-consciousness with strangers, and the word that for a while says it all: "MINE." Parents have profound influences upon the toddler's concept of a good self and one that is not. Research shows that encouragement is supportive of the toddler's sense of self, whereas neglect or outright anger can result in withdrawal or high levels of aggression.

There is no doubt that supportiveness and patience can be difficult as toddlers approach two years of age and forcefully assert their independence and are insistent about exercising their autonomy. These behaviors, though often a trial for parents, are important developmentally. The formidable challenge for parents is to foster the toddler's growth of self while simultaneously helping him recognize the needs of others.

✦ INTEGRATION AND ORGANIZATION OF THE DOMAINS

Although I have classified behaviors in terms of distinct categories, more often than not the baby's behavior reflects the interconnection of the domain categories. A twelve-month-old who plays with her toys, toddles over to her mother to show her a doll, says "da" (doll) to her mother, and then resumes play on her own provides examples of gross and fine motor skills, cognitive activity, language abilities, and social-interaction competencies. All of these skills are inextricably intertwined, and this interdependency of the various domains of behavior is a key feature of development.

The interrelatedness of behaviors in different domains increases as the child ages. This is one reason why it is important for the foundation behaviors in each domain to develop adequately during the baby's first two years. In this context, *adequately* means not only that a behavior has emerged around the time it is expected but also that the quality of the behavior is sufficient to support other developments.

Researchers often specialize in the study of a particular domain of behaviors such as cognitive or social development, but their projects generally incorporate ideas drawn from more than one behavior domain. In this book I discuss many instances where developments in one domain are prerequisites for advancements in another. As an example, a child must have knowledge of an object as a discrete and permanent item (the object does not "disappear" even when out of sight) before he can begin to associate a word with an object.

◆ USING THIS BOOK

I think of this book as a "field guide" to early child development. The book guides parents to an understanding of development by describing behaviors, much like the books used by naturalists watching birds or botanists trying to identify a particular plant. But as a botany field guide does not describe every variation of every plant, so this field guide does not describe every variation of normal behavior. Furthermore, not every baby will display every behavior described in this book. Like most field guides, this book is organized so that a parent may sample it from time to time or read it from cover to cover.

The book is divided into four age groups: birth to three months, four to seven months, eight to twelve months, and the second year. "Previews" introduce each age section and broadly describe developments during the age periods. The developments at a particular age are organized under three headings: "Snapshot," "Images of Development," and "Developmental Close-up." A "Snapshot" is a collection of brief highlights of developmentally significant behaviors at each age. "Images of Development" describes behavioral features at each age in the seven key domains in child development: motor, perception, cognition, language, social, emotions, and sense of self. "Developmental Close-Up" provides a bit more detail about topics that are particularly relevant for the age period. At the end of each age period, I suggest a few hints and mention developmental alerts. If you are concerned about your baby, do consult with your pediatrician. Lastly, following each age period, there is a section labeled "Sharpening Our Focus." This section contains two or three brief articles that provide additional detail about certain domains, such as language development or the essence of major debates going on about development, or that simply let parents know about relatively new research areas that have relevance for early development.

In terms of each chapter's content, I do not spend much time on developmental changes that are explicitly tied to a family's preferences for the way children learn the use of household implements, eating styles, and participation in dressing and bathing routines. Cultural backgrounds and family customs play a big part in shaping the specific form and the pace of development of these behaviors, so it's fruitless to make generalizations about them. I do devote a good bit of attention to cognitive, language, social, and emotional development. And I often mention how play behaviors tell us about a child's developing mental abilities. In addition, I have made a special effort to identify how cognitive skills affect a young child's social interactions, emotional displays, and sense of self. Understanding cognitive growth can enrich parents' time with their child, so I encourage parents to read more about this topic. Also, I include several sections devoted to diverse parenting issues.

To deal with the issue of gender, I sometimes refer to the baby as he and sometimes as she. Sometimes I intersperse both genders within a chapter, other times I refer only to "he" or "she." Every so often I provide examples of the behaviors of babies and toddlers that I have observed or that have been described to me by colleagues or parents.

However you use this guide, this book will be most helpful if you don't lose sight of four basic ideas.

1. *Every child is unique.* The normative behaviors described in this book are illustrative; individual variability is a fact of life.
2. *Guidelines should not be taken too literally.* Your child is not necessarily the normative child described in these pages, and that is all right. Indeed, there are some disagreements among scientists about what constitutes developmental trends in some abilities and just what form they take.
3. *No matter how much we learn about child development, we can never fully explain a baby or toddler's growth.* But the information in this book will help you participate more fully in your young child's development.
4. *Parenting matters.* Parenting babies and toddlers is demanding.

Birth to
Three Months

Preview

The Just Born

The Early Weeks

One Month

Two Months

Three Months

Developmental Hints and Alerts: Birth to Three Months

Sharpening Our Focus
Neurons, Neurons, and More...
Memory
Emotion Development

IT WOULD BE NIFTY if newborns greeted their parents with a broad smile that said, "Hey thanks for bringing me here!" But that's not going to happen. Indeed, newborns are relatively unsociable, which may surprise you. Yet rewards are coming. There are times when your very young baby will look at you briefly with rapt attention, reach out with his arms to touch a part of your body, or even make a few sounds to you. Many of these behaviors reflect behavioral biases that predispose newborns to respond to human faces and smiles, bobbing heads, and human voices. What matters most is that you and your baby can begin to build a relationship from day one! Your baby's response is most likely to occur when she's rested and in just the right state of alertness. If you can't get your newborn to respond, don't worry.

Very young babies are largely unsocial for good reason. Most of their energies must be directed toward adapting to a new environment, the one outside the womb. They must learn to breathe regularly and effectively, to nurse without regurgitating, to stay awake and alert for brief periods, and to have restful sleep periods. These adaptations are called *physiological regulation*, and collectively they are the most important challenges facing young babies. Be patient and provide lots of assistance when your baby needs an extra burp to eliminate gas or additional soothing to fall asleep. You're helping the baby with physiological regulation.

You'll soon be rewarded with the faint but very real social smile of your five- or six-week-old, the rapt attention of your two-month-old as she explores your face and makes eye contact with you, and the broad, consistent smile of your three-month-old as he welcomes your presence with coos and more smiles. The day-to-day interactions you have with your baby contribute to the transition from biologic predispositions to voluntary behaviors.

Once babies' vital systems are working smoothly, they have more total energy, which can be freed for other enterprises. As sleeping and eating become routine, the baby gains increasing control of her motor movements: when held upright her head control is stronger and less precarious than before. As other physical abilities improve—head control, reach, and grasp—

babies increasingly explore their surroundings. As they explore, they learn about their environment.

Social interactions provide the baby with more learning opportunities. She learns that the scent of a familiar person and being picked up seem to happen together, that touching one hand with the other feels good, and that she can produce gruntinglike sounds. By three months, the tissues in her larynx are flexible enough to make vowel sounds. As soon as she emits these cooing sounds, at first accidentally, she sets about learning how to reproduce them. Grown-ups love to hear coos, and babies thrive on the attention that coos elicit!

Overall in just three short months, the baby's vital systems begin to function quite smoothly, her senses are maturing, and the baby can make some controlled head, arm, and hand movements. She has some vocal mechanisms that will eventually lead to speech, she has formed a few associations for events that co-occur, and she has learned that some things make her feel good. Instead of fretful, intermittent sleeping she has acquired the habit of a lengthy nighttime sleep and longer daytime periods of wakefulness. Not bad for only three months work!

The Just Born

+ *all senses are intact and working*

+ *can move head from side to side*

+ *has curled-up body position (fetal posture)*

Birth launches the newborn into a totally new world. The baby has to make accommodations simply to survive, much less flourish, outside the womb. Suddenly he has to breathe on his own, swallow food to get nourishment, lie on a solid surface rather than float in a fluid space, and regulate his own body temperature. A newborn's physiological disorientation is akin to what we would experience if we were suddenly propelled to outer space.

When the umbilical cord is cut, the newborn begins his solo flight. The baby has to keep his plane aloft even though not all of his vital processes were checked out before liftoff and even though he has not been schooled about what to do if something malfunctions. Fortunately, biological predispositions help babies sustain life as they begin their adaptation to a world filled with people and objects and events.

The newborn's survival kit includes reflexes, movements, and the senses. A reflex is a patterned series of movements that occur in response to a particular stimulus; an adult example is the knee-jerk response, and a baby example is the grasp reflex. Reflexes perform many functions for babies. The sucking reflex provides him with a way to take in food now that nourishment is no longer automatically supplied through the umbilical cord. The grasp reflex allows him to hold on to a parent, which can build emotional closeness. Coughing and sneezing keep passages clear for ingestion and respiration.

Beyond reflexes, there are several kinds of movements in the newborn. Some spontaneous movements are total-body actions that are sometimes jerky or writhing and may be accompanied by leg kicks. These movements are due to an immature brain and its connections to an immature neuromuscular system. Spontaneous movements may look as if they are purposeful, such as when the baby stretches, but probably are due to some unobserved internal or external stimulus. Overall though, the spontaneous whole-body movements, whatever their cause, keep muscles toned during the time that a baby has limited means to exercise his trunk muscles and his limbs.

Other newborn movements consist of relatively controlled arm actions. Some of these are survival mechanisms, which are often set in motion by stimuli linked to primitive brain centers. The hand-to-mouth movement is an example: this basic movement allows a newborn to soothe himself by sucking on a hand or thumb under *mild conditions of distress*. Another kind of newborn controlled movement is easiest to observe under precise laboratory conditions and often consists of brief, limited range, up-and-down arm movements as if the baby was getting ready to wave.

The third component of the newborn's survival kit also includes the senses of touch, smell, vision, hearing, and taste, which provide information about surroundings. The baby's sense of touch, smell, and taste are functional, but additional experiences improve the ability to detect subtle variations within these inputs.

In terms of hearing, newborns hear but they do not hear all sound frequencies. Young babies typically detect sounds such as those made by someone who speaks in a normal, everyday voice. They do not detect whispers. By one or two months, infants distinguish some phoneme contrasts (a vowel or consonant), some speech intonations, and speech sounds from non-speech sounds. Yet there are many sounds and variations within a language that young infants do not perceive, and in general they are less sensitive than older infants to duration and rhythm in speech. As with the other senses, both the hearing apparatus and perception of sounds (including speech) improve dramatically in the first six months of life. Experiences and the maturing brain have a major role.

Much of the same can be said about the newborn's visual system. At birth, it is far from fully functional because of the interrelated immaturity of the eyes (e.g., the retina), the visual portion of the brain, and the ability to perceive certain stimuli (e.g., a very narrow band of white and black stripes). The newborn's visual world is often filled with fuzzy, blurry images, even for objects that are nearby. But there is no doubt the newborn sees the overall configuration of faces!

Although newborns differ appreciably from older babies, toddlers, or adults in the quality and quantity of what they take in through their senses, these limitations help them cope with the hustle and bustle that take place in human environments. By seeing less clearly and hearing less distinctly, the newborn is not as likely to become overwhelmed by sensory stimulation. Bear in mind, the newborn cannot move around at will; thus he doesn't have ways to escape bright lights and loud noises.

Overall, the newborn is just a little physical being struggling to exist in a foreign environment. Thanks to biological programs his vital processes can function, and the baby's nascent motor, sensory, and perception skills help him maintain and organize these processes. With parents' assistance, newborns successfully pilot their way through this period of adjustment.

What Does My Baby See?

We've come a long way from the time that pediatricians assured parents that newborns could not see, even though babies' eyes were open wide and they appeared to be looking. Several decades later, Robert Fantz—who had been studying vision in nonhuman primates—closed the book on that myth. Fantz decided to use a variation of his simple observational technique with babies. He showed babies a two-dimensional drawing and then looked for the reflection of the stimulus on the baby's pupil. Surprise! When newborns were shown two different stimulus drawings side by side, the babies' looking patterns revealed their preferences. Contrasts, such as a pattern of wide black-and-white stripes, were preferred over a simple gray background.

Research on infant visual-preference patterns exploded after Fantz's original studies. Still, it's taken a while for scientists to figure out how to accurately measure how well babies see, to identify those parts of the brain that are likely to be involved in newborn vision, and to specify the kinds of visual information newborns can process, at least in some way. Fortunately, advances in measurement technology and the development of sophisticated computer programs have contributed to the acquisition of new knowledge, most of which has come about during the past twenty years.

Let's start with visual acuity, that is, the clarity of a newborn's vision. If 20/20 is normal vision for adults, then the newborn's typical vision of 400 indicates blurred vision perhaps thirty times worse than normal adult vision. However, blurred vision is *developmentally limited*. By this I mean that the young baby's visual acuity improves dramatically, typically by three months of age. At about eight to ten months, the baby's vision is comparable to that of adults who have normal vision.

Several factors contribute to these early visual limitations. For one, the distance between the front and the back of the eye is shorter than it will be later on. The shortened length means there's reduced clarity of a visual image on the retina. Blurred vision is also a consequence of the structure of the retina at birth. The part of the retina called the fovea is associated with recognition of fine detail and color perception. In newborns though, the fovea contains far fewer cones (photoreceptors for detail and color) than are found in adults, and the shape of the newborn fovea makes it less efficient for catching light signals. A third limitation comes from immature neuronal connections within the brain itself and connections from the eyes to the brain's vision centers.

Despite blurred vision, newborns can still perceive many visual stimuli. At birth or soon after, they are able to differentiate a simple geometric shape from another; a moving stimulus from a static one; angles that are wide versus narrow; high-contrast patterns from low-contrast ones; and faces from other stimuli. Faces seem to be particularly attractive to newborns, primarily as a function of certain stimulus properties. Faces contain contrast elements (white eyes, darker skin), relative degrees of contrast (think fair skin and very dark hair), and overall oval shapes. Some researchers suggest that babies also prefer their mothers' faces within a day or two of birth. These findings suggest some form of early learning may take place although its duration is not known. However, other researchers believe there is an innate program that specifies a preference for faces from birth.

Studies from the past decade help us interpret data from some of the earlier vision research. Converging findings from animal and human research suggest that many newborn visual, auditory, and motor responses are largely, but not exclusively, linked to subcortical pathways. Cortical activity is present, but in only limited and selective ways.

The subcortical nature of the young baby's visual responses does not imply these are unimportant activities. On the contrary, other research implies that the earliest forms of visual experiences contribute to the development of cortical pathways. And it is these pathways, which greatly increase starting at about two months of age, that are associated with the acquisition of knowledge about faces, objects, and events in the baby's surroundings.

Improvements in the baby's visual system go along with better control of awake and alert states. During the first three months of life, babies not only increase the amount of awake and alert periods but also are better able to maintain alertness on their own. As a consequence, researchers can more effectively study the kinds of visual stimuli that babies are most attentive to, how long they attend, the stimuli that are likely to distract babies, shifts in attention preferences, and more.

The Early Weeks

- ✦ is most responsive to touch and gentle rocking

- ✦ will look around when awake and alert but vision is blurry

- ✦ can soothe self if mildly upset by sucking on fist or fingers

✦ SNAPSHOT

A few hours after birth the baby's heart and blood systems begin to work effectively, but not all vital processes stabilize this quickly. Even at three weeks of age, respiration, sleep, ingestion and digestion, and modulation of body temperature have still not completely settled into smooth and steady functioning. Nor are all these systems synchronized with one another. Hiccups, slight quivers, fussing, jumpiness, spitting up, and restlessness are body upsets that signify temporary disruptions in the baby's journey toward physiological stability.

Maintaining physical functioning is hard work for the three-week-old. You can sometimes coax her into looking at you, but don't be surprised if she soon tires. The baby just doesn't have the strength for sustained social interactions. However, the occasional wide-eyed alert look she directs your way tells you she's processing something about your interactions.

Sleep gives body processes a chance to function without external distractions and lets the baby recharge his energy. Babies of this age have only a small amount of energy to store and consume large amounts in just a short period of wakefulness. Young babies require a great deal of rest, and they sleep as much as twenty hours in each twenty-four-hour period.

Often, the baby is comforted by caresses and light touches. Light stroking reduces her fretfulness and promotes sleep. Though the young baby's sense of touch is not fully developed, she does seem to feel marked discomfort from significant pressure. Pain associated with pressure is a subjective experience, and a baby may be more or less finicky than other newborns about being accidentally pinched or tightly held.

A two- to three-week-old already prefers sweet formula to all others and easily tells the difference between sour and bitter solutions. The baby is also able to distinguish differences in the smells of things around her; she dislikes the smell of foul substances as much as an adult does. Research also shows that babies quickly learn the scents associated with the people who routinely care for them. Sometimes a familiar scent is enough to soothe mild upsets. Also at this age, the baby may respond to speech by becoming still or sometimes by making startle movements. Vision is still blurry.

Keep an eye out for your baby's responses to your presence and to different soothing techniques. You'll soon discover the ones that typically work best.

Despite their overall immaturity, babies of this age are not totally at the mercy of their surroundings. They have two highly effective means of coping with the world: they can cry and they can sometimes reduce mild forms of distress. A cry indicates that something is not right and summons parents to provide care and comfort. Self-soothing goes like this. As the three-week-old is lying on her side, with her free arm bent at the elbow, her fist happens to rub her cheek, and then her mouth. She opens her mouth to receive the fist, and sucking occurs. She may drop off to sleep.

✦ IMAGES OF DEVELOPMENT

Perception

Vision. At this age babies see objects best when the objects have sharp contrast. A baby's vision is pulled toward her father's mouth: his white teeth stand out against his otherwise blurry-looking facial features. Research shows that when the baby looks at an object she doesn't see all of it. She sees only a portion of what she is looking at, most typically a section of the edge of the item because of its high contrast. So the three-week-old probably sees only a corner of her dad's mouth. That's fine for now.

Babies can't easily coordinate turning their heads to visually track objects that are slowly moved in front of them. However, they can visually follow objects that are moved within a ninety-degree arc, their visual range without head movement. A baby peers at these moving stimuli with jerky, short eye movements that scientists call saccades.

Overall, the baby does a lot better at making visual discriminations when a parent holds her upright and supports her neck so that her head doesn't wobble. Humans have a vestibular mechanism that negates the influence of head movement on vision. At this age the mechanism hasn't quite finished developing. A wobbly head interferes with looking, so that's why a baby's visual discrimination is a bit better when a parent helps her hold her head still.

Hearing. Babies of this age are very responsive to pitch and respond more to sounds that have a high pitch rather than a low pitch. That is why female speech can be more interesting to a young baby than male speech. But this fact shouldn't deter dads from talking to their babies!

Very young babies sometimes exhibit a skill that lets them use sound to identify location. In adults the process is called sound localization. I cannot see a key turn in a lock, but the sound of the bolt moving tells me that the door is being opened. When a baby's parent shakes a rattle next to the baby's left ear, the baby sometimes turns his head to the left. This indicates a nascent ability to respond to an object by the location of its sound. At this age, sound localization seems to be a primed response rather than the sign of coordinated, mature perception. In a few months' time the baby will regularly use spatial perception and hearing skills to locate the sources of sounds, just as adults do.

Studies of fetal learning indicate the auditory system becomes functional before birth. Sounds, or at least vibrations, pass through the mother's abdominal wall and bathe the fetus in communications from the world outside the womb. Toward the end of the prenatal period, around the middle of the seventh month, fetuses actually begin to hear speech intonations (a form of sound vibration) and to differentiate what they hear. Because the fetus hears the speech of one person—the biological mother—more than any other, studies have shown that babies in the first few weeks of life outside the womb not only differentiate their mother's speech but actually prefer it. A reasonable explanation for this preference is that familiarity attracts the young baby, and the speech of his biological mother is the most familiar speech sound in his new world.

◆ DEVELOPMENTAL CLOSE-UP

Sleep and Wakefulness

During the first weeks and months of the baby's life the topic of sleep—the parents' as well as the baby's—dominates parents' consciousness. On a six-times-a-day feeding schedule, parents don't sleep much, and like the dieting person who craves food and fantasizes about eating luscious desserts, parents hunger for sleep. Despite vast differences in an individual parent's tolerance for lack of sleep, most parents of young babies report they never get enough.

Like so much of newborn activity, the baby's ability to sleep soundly and consistently has to become synchronized with the patterns of the outside world. This synchrony takes place while babies are also establishing daytime periods of awake and alert states. Fortunately for parents, these two processes are intertwined and often do not take long to establish. For most babies sleep and alertness evolve into predictable time patterns within two to three months. Some babies take longer and others take only a few weeks. Of course, if you're a parent of a young baby, even a month of disturbed sleep can seem like a lifetime.

At first most babies have little in the way of awake and sleep routines. Upsets in physiological processes contribute to early sleeping irregularities. As physiological processes stabilize at around six weeks, many babies begin to establish a rhythm of two to four hours of sleep, a short time of wakefulness, and then another few hours of sleep, and so on. This pattern is determined in great part by the baby's need to have food at relatively frequent intervals.

In addition to the number of hours slept, the characteristics of the baby's sleep change over the first few months. A few weeks after birth a baby has periods of sleep and alertness and an interim transition state where he is neither awake nor asleep. When the baby is actually sleeping, he experiences periods of quiet sleep and active sleep (this is also called REM, for "rapid eye movement," sleep; rapid eye movements occur only in this sleep stage). During quiet sleep the baby's heart rate and respiration are even, his face is relaxed and eyes motionless, and his muscles have tone. In active sleep, the baby's respiration and heart rate are irregular. Muscle tone is also markedly reduced, and this accounts for body twitches, facial grimaces, and rapid movement of the eyes under his closed eyelids. Facial grimaces are sometimes mistakenly interpreted as frowns and smiles in a sleeping baby. No, the baby is not having a pleasant dream or a nightmare. As the baby's sleep patterns stabilize, the proportion of REM sleep decreases and quiet sleep increases. REM sleep is considered essential for brain maturation.

Around the third or fourth month babies begin to sleep in patterns that replicate adult sleep. At that time babies tend to have a long period of wakefulness during the daytime and as long as a five- or six-hour sleep period at night. These developments in sleeping hours and sleep states are largely a function of brain maturation that influences more effective operation of neurophysiological mechanisms, but environmental influences play a role. Studies show that the sleep of babies can be influenced by variations in room temperature, sounds, ambient light, cultural patterns, sleep arrangements such as co-sleeping, where mother and baby sleep on the same bed, and the style of caregiving, including breast- versus bottle-feeding. As one researcher said, sleep is primarily biological but it takes place in social contexts. It's not surprising that sleep experts suggest that "sensitive caregiving" can help very young babies establish orderly, restful sleep routines.

The regulation of sleep differs from the developmental change involved in establishing a day-and-night pattern. What this means is that babies can have a relatively long period of nighttime sleep, but the sleep is not necessarily uninterrupted or a sound sleep. Babies often have one or more awake periods at night and can go back to sleep on their own. However, more often than not nighttime waking leads to intense crying. Parental sleep assistance takes the form of feeding, reinserting a lost pacifier, or a combination of feeding and various kinds of soothing techniques (e.g., rocking, sounds). Consistently poor sleep in a baby can affect her daytime arousal regulation, such as attention, and her irritability. Thus there's good reason for parents to intervene.

What can you expect? In one study, almost all three-week-old babies needed some care during the night. When they were three months old, only half required some night assistance to return to sleep. Data from a large Australian study show that when young babies needed parental help to go back to sleep, help was mostly needed once or twice a night. Fortunately, less than 10 percent of parents reported three or more sleep interventions per night. Some parents have elected to co-sleep with their young babies in order to lessen nighttime sleep disturbances. Co-sleeping is controversial: check with your pediatrician.

Most sleep researchers emphasize the variability among babies and parents in terms of sleep patterns and sleep needs. Another point worth remembering is that babies have ups and downs in terms of sleep regulation: they may have sound nighttime sleep for a while, and then have a period of sleep disturbance. Sometimes the problem can be pinpointed, other times it cannot. Overall, I'm not a member of the "just let her cry it out" school, whatever the age of the baby.

Lastly, there are unconfirmed reports that young babies tend to sleep less soundly when placed on their backs than on their tummies. However, guidelines from the American Academy of Pediatrics emphasize the need for parents to place babies on their backs or on their sides for sleeping. This recommendation is based on data that suggest back- and side-sleeping postures reduce the incidence of Sudden Infant Death Syndrome.

Side sleeping, with the baby's sides supported by firm diaper rolls that prevent the baby from turning to his tummy, is worth a try if your baby does not sleep well on his back. Swaddling the baby, but not tightly, in a small blanket often helps as well.

Motor Reflexes

Human genetic heritage endows the baby with many motor reflexes. Long ago, all these reflexes had survival value, but today only a few are important adaptations to living outside of the womb. While no longer serving the purpose of survival, some of these reflexes are useful in other ways. Some help babies and their parents get to know each other. A few are used by physicians to evaluate the baby's nervous system.

The motor reflexes that disappear over the baby's first six months are called developmental reflexes. Some, such as the grasp reflex, are ultimately replaced by voluntary actions that enable a baby to respond to more various and more complex demands. Other reflexes such as the palmomental reflex (mouth opens when pressure is applied to the palms) are not replaced; the maturing brain inhibits them.

Six developmental reflexes are especially interesting. Two that serve survival functions are the head-turning response and the sucking reflex. The former is "insurance" providing the baby with the ability to breathe by evoking a turn of her head whenever her nostrils are accidentally covered. The second reflex allows the baby to take nourishment because it fosters automatic sucking when a nipple—or blanket or fist—is placed in her mouth.

Among the reflexes that don't seem to serve a survival function, the Moro reflex somewhat resembles an adult's startle reaction to a surprising or fearful event. Physicians often use this reflex to evaluate a newborn's neurological functioning. A pediatrician elicits the reflex by holding the baby up in both of his hands. One hand supports the head and shoulders while the other supports the back and bottom. The legs dangle. Using a controlled but sudden movement, the doctor lets the head "drop" an inch or two. The drop elicits the Moro: the baby looks as if she is about to hug someone. If the baby's response is hardly noticeable or very pronounced, the physician will conduct tests to ensure that the atypical response is not signaling an underlying neurological or physiological impairment.

When the baby lies on her back, the tonic neck reflex makes her assume the posture of a miniature fencer in the *en garde* position. Her head turns to one side and the arm on that side moves in front of her face and bends at the elbow. The other arm lies straight alongside her body. This position is fairly pronounced in the early weeks and gradually becomes inhibited (disappears) by the time babies are six months old. If a baby regularly assumes this position after six months, a thorough neurological examination is warranted.

Two reflexes promote an emotional bond between the baby and her parents. The rooting reflex stimulates the baby to turn her head toward a parent when a corner of her mouth is touched. Parents interpret this head turn as a sign of the baby's interest. Being "welcomed" like this invites a parent's reciprocal interest and spurs more interaction.

The grasp reflex occurs when a baby's parent opens her hand and touches her palm with a finger. The baby's hand closes protectively around the parent's finger. This act of physical bonding promotes the development of mutual affection and fosters interest in continuing interaction.

One Month

- body movements are constrained by reflexes
- is alert when talked to
- differentiates speech from other sounds
- tends to late-day irritability

◆ SNAPSHOT

Behaviors that most obviously set one-month-olds apart from newborns are better head control, longer periods of visual attentiveness, and greater sensitivity to human voices. At this age, babies are also beginning to have more regular sleep patterns. Overall, however, one-month-olds are still struggling to satisfy basic biological needs and are most content when fed, talked to, and then allowed to fall asleep in a quiet spot.

One of the most pleasing changes in the baby's behavior is his growing power of observation. When fully awake, babies might now and then gaze intently at nearby shadows on the wall, or glance around when picked up. Also, if fully awake and lying on their tummies, many babies can briefly raise their heads to look at brightly colored toys. These periods of attention are often accompanied by a wide-eyed expression of alertness, as if babies have discovered that nearby objects are interesting to look at. Sounds too are increasingly appealing: babies often strain to listen closely to sounds, with barely a muscle moving.

A baby's newfound attentiveness is a delight for parents. However, attentiveness at this age may go along with an increase in irritability, particularly late in the afternoon. Irritability occurs because some sights and sounds capture the baby's attention for seconds or minutes at a time, and yet babies don't have the capability of turning away when they've had enough input. As a consequence, overload in the form of sensory fatigue sets in, which leads to crying. Overload can build up relatively silently, so that you're not aware of it. But by the end of the day it can be fairly intense for the young baby.

It's difficult for parents to predict which visual stimuli capture a baby's attention; for one six-week-old, it was one of the toys that hung on the side of her crib. Totally mesmerized by it, she studied it repeatedly and then became overaroused and worn out by early evening. Instead of falling asleep easily, she fretted even when held and rocked. Fortunately, late-day irritability tends to last only a few weeks. It often declines when babies learn to control their attention by looking away.

Sleep is very important for one-month-olds, and they still sleep a large part of every twenty-four hours. Although sleep periods can be unpredictable, this inconsistency will change soon. By five or six weeks of age, some babies begin to show a day-night sleep cycle in which a longer sleep period is part of the nighttime routine along with added wakefulness during the day. Day wakefulness gradually settles into a pattern with three or four hours of sleep, a wakeful period, and then three to four hours of sleep again.

✦ IMAGES OF DEVELOPMENT

Motor Control

At one month the baby's head is usually turned to one side when she lies on her back. One arm is usually stretched out straight while her other arm is bent at the elbow. This posture is usually associated with the developmental reflex called the tonic neck reflex. The developing brain inhibits this reflex; in fact, you'll barely see evidence of it in a matter of weeks.

There's an underlying rhythm to the baby's spontaneous arm and leg movements. However, arm movements may become jerky when the baby is excited. Then both arms straighten out and they are thrust in front of face and chest.

If a baby is placed on her tummy—when she is awake and alert—she may lift her head momentarily an inch or two off the mattress. When her head drops, she turns it to one side. While lying in this position her legs spontaneously move, and she looks as if she's trying to crawl. Babies have a bit of control over these movements, and the repeated bending and straightening of their legs is not forceful enough to propel their bodies forward. Although babies of this age cannot roll over or crawl on their own, they can roll as part of a reflexive-type movement. For this reason, you do not want to leave your baby alone on a bed.

When a baby is propped into a sitting position, the back is rounded like a big C because trunk muscles are weak. Most of the time the baby's head droops forward; in fact, everything droops—head, shoulders, back, hips, and legs—when babies are tired.

The hands of one-month-olds are usually closed into fists because of the grasp reflex. But this reflex is not as strong as it was in the newborn period, and if someone else opens the baby's hands, she can hold onto a rattle momentarily.

Perception

Vision. The one-month-old shows a variety of looking behaviors, gazing with interest at his mother's face or a bright toy. Sometimes he looks at an object for minutes at a time; sometimes he looks around with eyes that have a vacant, vague expression as if he were daydreaming; and he switches back and forth between attentiveness and vacant staring, like a light bulb going on and off. He tends to switch off when he's tired or trying to look at something that he isn't able to see clearly. Many parents have intuitively discovered that babies see best when held snugly and upright. Even when a baby is in this position and fully attentive, his face can be expressionless.

On his back with his head turned to one side, a baby can visually follow a bright object when it is moved slowly from his side up toward the middle of his chest. When his head is not turned, he will keep his eyes on a bright object that is rotated in a small circle. Already he has learned how to coordinate head movements with the direction of his gaze.

One of the distinguishing features of one-month-olds' vision is their tendency to see only part of a toy or a mobile that hangs over the crib. They can take in only a portion at a glance; most of the time they look at part of the outline or edge of the toy. A baby will look toward the center of a toy if it has high contrast and also moves. A mobile that has a red ring with a bright ball suspended in the middle is a perfect target for visual attention.

Faces continue to appeal to babies of this age because they have high-contrast features: Lips are darker than teeth, foreheads lighter than hairlines and hair. The mouth region, because of the contrast of skin color, lips, teeth, and tongue, draws the baby's attention like a magnet. Eyes also have big appeal.

Hearing. At one month, babies are now more responsive to human sounds (speech) as distinct from noises in general. They become still and turn their heads when speech is directed to them. Babies like to listen to the sounds humans make as much as they like to stare at their faces. This attraction to human speech is important for it will prompt the baby to listen to the sounds produced by the people (you!) who care for her. In time, attention to speech helps your baby develop her own communication skills.

Research shows that babies of this age also begin to differentiate the specific sounds of speech. In addition to discriminating the speech sounds of *pa* and *ba*, one-month-olds discriminate some vowel contrasts and are sensitive to contrasts in intonations that occur in everyday conversational speech. It has also been shown that shortly thereafter babies begin to detect the difference between two-syllable contrasts such as "dada" and "baba." As with vision, auditory perception shows considerable change at about two months.

Vocalizations

This month the baby takes his first steps toward becoming a vocal partner. Initially, the sounds he makes are like the soft noises we produce when clearing our throats. Then at about six weeks, one or two of his vocalizations become distinguishable. These sounds are soft and pleasing and are like the vowels of "ah," "eh," or "uh."

The ability to make various sounds is associated with changes that occur in the parts of the throat associated with speech. The larynx, for example, is becoming more flexible and mobile so that it is physically possible to produce discrete and distinguishable sounds apart from cries. At first, the baby doesn't plan to make vowel sounds; these noises are accidentally emitted. Soon he learns how to reproduce the sounds he has generated, and by two to three months he repeatedly utters these soft vowels.

Cognition

Taste and touch senses are fairly mature at birth, and signs of early learning are often observed in these senses. During the first month, for example, many babies quickly learn to differentiate nipples, their own fingers, and pacifiers. Now when hungry they will turn away from pacifiers and seek the nipple associated with food.

Social Development

You'll notice that your one-month-old is more socially responsive than she was during the newborn period. There are more times during the day when your baby looks alert when spoken to and looks longer at your face. Then there are other times when you'll have to coax her to look at you. In other words, the baby is not quite in the "right state" to be receptive to your vocal or visual bids but with a little help from you—high-pitched talking, singing, touching her face—she can respond. Sometimes too, at this age, babies show the faintest beginning of a smile or they may vocalize a little. But at this age, they cannot simultaneously smile and make sounds because that takes a degree of visual and vocal coordination that they do not yet have.

At about six weeks or so, a baby's behavior signals that she's learning about social interactions. She begins to modify her behavior—by being very quiet or looking more alert or even breathing rapidly—when she is picked up, changed, or fed. This type of behavior tells us that she is aware of a difference between social and nonsocial events. This recognition is an important early step toward sociability and becoming a partner in social exchanges. The baby's behavior also signifies cognitive activity: she's learning about her everyday social world.

✦ DEVELOPMENTAL CLOSE-UP

Crying

Parents often have three questions about crying. Are babies, particularly newborns, really unhappy or angry when they cry? How does crying change across the first year? How should parents react to a baby's cries?

Newborn crying. Babies' cries in the first month or two of their lives relate to *physiological upsets* as opposed to psychological upsets. That is, a baby is having difficulty digesting food and feels pain, she's hungry, hiccups are disturbing her sleep, she's in need of warmth, or she simply is in need of the gentle swaying that is similar to that experienced in the womb. As far as we know, babies of this age are unaware of feeling the psychological states of boredom, anger, or fearfulness, no matter how much we tend to associate crying with sorrow and distress. Whatever the cause of crying, bear in mind that a little crying goes a long way! So respond to your baby as rapidly as possible.

Developmental trends in crying: the first year. On average very young babies might fret (mild sounds of discomfort) or cry an hour or so a day. An increase to about two hours often occurs at about six to eight weeks of age, most particularly during the early evening hours. As I mentioned above, this surge is often linked to overstimulation, which occurs because babies are more aware of sights and sounds in their immediate surroundings. At the same time, babies of this age do not have many options for disengaging from stimuli that bother them. At most they turn their heads, close their eyes, and cry for help. Soon though you'll observe behaviors that signal a new level of maturity. Three-month-olds often turn away from bright lights or turn toward an object or person that is less fatiguing to look at.

On average, in the next month or so, crying decreases to about an hour a day. Moreover, crying becomes less tied to upsets due to physiological distress or stimulus overload and is progressively more related to psychological needs. A baby's cry may signify boredom and the need for a new toy or mobile to look at, a desire for company, or just a desire for a change of scene. Parents intuitively learn how to decipher these psychologically based cries by evaluating how the baby responds to attempts to soothe her. As parents develop expertise in understanding cries, so babies become clearer in sending their cry messages.

By six months babies tend to coordinate their cries with looking toward a parent as if saying, "I need *you*." Along about eight months, many babies fret when an unknown person gets too close for their comfort level. This *wary* response is often a sign that the baby really distinguishes familiar faces from those that are unknown and reflects cognitive growth. By the time a baby reaches a year of age, its cries, looks, and gestures tend to go together. A gesture may be used with cries to point specifically to something the baby wants. Still later, when babies have become walking toddlers, cries are often accompanied by tugs that pull the parent toward a specific toy that's wanted. In general, babies tend to cry less as they become more mobile and are able to move around and pick up toys they want.

The group trends, which I've described above, may not reflect an individual baby's experience. Babies differ in how they cry, when and why they cry, and the frequency of their crying. Some babies cry as if their hearts were breaking, while others barely whimper even when a favorite toy disappears. There is no denying that the babies who get upset easily and who cry intensely can be hard to deal with.

Parents and their crying baby. Crying is the only way that young babies can communicate their needs. Basically, a baby's cry tells you that "something is not quite right." Learning to understand the baby's cry is a little like learning a new language; it's terribly confusing at first. Even so, many parents are able to distinguish their own infant's cry from those of other babies just a few days after birth. Within a short time, most parents become skilled interpreters of cries. By the age of one month, parents usually recognize a pain cry, a cry associated with hunger, and cries signaling general discomfort. Later on, parents also discover that cries associated with the baby's fatigue and boredom are often short and more like frets than hunger and pain cries.

There are many points of view about handling a baby's crying. What to do depends upon your beliefs about parenting, the baby's age, her general well-being, her temperament, and the specific situation. One certainty about crying is that it's the baby's attempt to say that things are not right. In this context, I find it difficult to subscribe to the idea that parents should mostly let a baby "cry it out." This approach could hamper the social and emotional bond babies and parents are establishing. And as a practical matter, letting a baby collapse from the sheer exhaustion of continued crying may only prolong the problem, since sleep that follows fatigue tends not to be restful. Overall, research has shown that tending to babies' cries, even those of older babies, does not spoil them but rather in the long term makes them more contented.

Overall, cultural groups place few restrictions on types of soothing techniques parents use. The only guiding belief is that soothing should be given in a nurturant way. A tour around the world would show that some Finnish mothers gently stroke the crying baby's cheek and neck. In Eastern Europe crying babies are wrapped snugly and rocked in cradles, many African women still carry their babies in a sling across their backs, and here in the United States babies are placed in kangaroolike snugglies that provide both soothing and warmth. Effective soothers for young babies often involve movement, stroking, and warmth, whereas for older babies effective soothers involve distractions such as a toy, a move to a new view, or simply the watching of ongoing family activities. Interesting laboratory studies on soothing—research by Elliott Blass, for example—may in time provide additional insights that are helpful to parents.

Colic

Some young babies have prolonged, intense, high-pitched crying, despite the best intentions of their parents. This kind of crying, typically called *colic*, starts at around two weeks, reaches a peak at about eight weeks, and declines dramatically a month or two later. Colic is terrifying and exhausting to parents, because they feel they're doing something terribly wrong. Some pediatricians and psychologists think that poor parenting is at fault. However, recent studies have shown that colic can occur when family situations are optimal and when parents are sensitive.

Sometimes it is thought that colicky babies simply have difficult temperaments—that is, they're just biologically predisposed to being somewhat irritable. However, this point of view has less credence these days because so often the so-called temperamentally difficult two-month-old becomes an easygoing six-month-old. An increasingly accepted view of colic is that it represents a transient age-related phenomenon that is probably tied to two factors. One is a baby's abrupt and high sensitivity to fatigue (or hunger), which leads to a very high state of arousal (intense crying). The arousal is so forceful that the baby's regulatory mechanisms don't work as well as they should. The second factor in colic relates to a baby's lessened ability to respond to soothing and to recover relatively quickly. With increasing maturation—particularly the brain and behavioral growth that occurs around three months of age—the colicky baby's reactivity and regulatory abilities improve. Studies have found that, for the most part, months after the colic episode the parents of colicky and non-colicky babies are similar in how they stimulate and respond to their babies.

There are times, however, when prolonged and intense crying continues for a number of months. One estimate suggests this may occur with about 10 percent of babies. In these instances, there is likely to be a problem unrelated to the quality of parenting. Intolerance to formula is one factor, with others linked to the mother's use of street drugs during pregnancy, the prescribed medications a nursing mother might be taking, an infection the baby has, and certain kinds of developmental anomalies. Fortunately, the most serious biologically based causes of intense crying are relatively rare.

Crying that is long-term, and crying that is always intense, need careful attention.

Your baby. Recognize that a week or two of increased crying is not necessarily colic. Rather, it could be a sign of a need for more food intake, an unrecognized change in the baby's surroundings that leads to heightened stimulation that he can't handle, or a minor variation in routine that the baby is trying to adapt to. Sometimes babies become accustomed to changes when they have additional soothing time, for example, being carried in snugglies. However, intense and prolonged crying that does not respond to various kinds of soothing does need attention. Insist upon help and advice from your baby's health care provider.

Two Months

+ lifts head and shoulders above mattress
when on tummy

+ stays awake longer during day

+ makes eye contact with parents

+ responds differentially to vocal intonations

+ smiles weakly

After the baby has had two months of living outside the womb, its physiology works fairly well. Sucking on the breast or bottle is accomplished without too much dribbling, hiccups are less frequent, digestive upsets are decreasing, and sleep is becoming less of a problem for the baby—and for you. As the baby's body comforts increase, there is more energy and attention for other things, such as being social. She starts to make eye contact with her parents and, when alert, shows visual attentiveness to toys. Occasionally she smiles. She coordinates her head and eye movements without much effort and holds her head up higher and longer, when placed on her tummy, than she did a month ago.

At two months the baby's awake period may extend to two or three hours at a time and, fortunately for parents, often occurs during daytime hours. Then at night, there may be a stretch of sleep that lasts four to five hours. For some babies, this long stretch begins about 10 P.M., but for others it starts about 1 or 2 A.M. In any event, the extended day wakefulness and extended night sleep means the baby is making progress toward a predictable day-and-night cycle.

Most babies' surroundings are filled with interesting patterns and colors, and the two-month-old is able to scan nearby objects and sometimes gaze at a particular pattern or object that intrigues her. Now her attention is less likely to be glued to the point of fatigue on something very bright and colorful; rather, she can turn away on her own. Neuroscience research suggests that changes in alertness, scanning, and orientation to objects are due to increasing activation of cortical visual pathways. What this means in terms of behavior is that babies will gradually gain more control of their attention.

Do keep in mind though that two-month-olds are still novices when it comes to maintaining their visual attention. At times, they struggle to keep their focus on a particular toy or a person. Fortunately, you can help. If your baby is alert but her gaze is wandering as if out of control, hold her in your lap facing you. Lightly support her head. Now talk with an animated voice, smile, and bob your head. Together, these work wonders.

Motor Control

Muscle strength is one way to tell the two-month-old from the younger baby—if the baby has spent some periods of wakefulness lying on his tummy in addition to sleeping on his back. If this has occurred, the baby is likely to be able to lift his head and shoulders several inches above the crib mattress and rest on his forearms. When his energy runs out, his head and shoulders slump down to the mattress; but after a brief pause, he picks up his head and repeats the routine. While on his tummy, the baby's legs are bent, but he actively straightens them out again and again and makes crawlinglike movements. His body may shift around because of leg motions.

As you may know, pediatricians routinely advise parents to place babies on their backs for sleeping as a precaution against Sudden Infant Death Syndrome. This sleeping position has been associated with a slightly later onset of head control for some babies. There's no evidence this slightly later onset has any long-term consequences.

Generally two-month-olds have more upper-trunk strength than they did a few weeks earlier. You can see some tension in his back muscles when you hold your baby in a seated position. You'll also notice the baby's back is becoming less curved, and he briefly supports his own head when braced against your shoulder.

When your baby is awake and on her back, you'll notice her arms are often raised above her head, making a U shape. This position is a hint that the baby is moving toward a symmetrical arm posture. Soon she will be able to move both arms to her sides or in front of her body, and each arm will be able to assume a position that is a mirror image of the other. This postural adjustment is enormously important and will soon be followed by reaching. As humans, we need to be able to have both hands in front of us so we can use utensils, operate tools, and play musical instruments. The two-month-old's progression to arm symmetry is a tiny step toward using two hands. Now, you're likely to see your baby make tentative arm swipes at one or two objects in his field of vision.

At two months, the grasp reflex is also weakening considerably. When the reflex was strong, the baby's fingers could close tightly around a rattle placed in his hand. Now his fingers generally open as they touch a rattle. If he momentarily manages to hold a toy, he tries to bring it toward his mouth. In a couple of months or so, your baby will be capable of holding a toy, moving it into his field of vision, and looking at it—but he's not there yet.

Perception

Vision. This month there is definite improvement in how effectively a baby surveys his surroundings and in the accuracy of his ability to look directly at a person or object. Now both eyes often work together, and this helps the baby see better. Improved vision makes a two-month-old look more alert than a younger baby.

Better head-eye coordination makes possible faster and more coordinated visual scan. At this age, a baby can systematically follow a bright object that is moved back and forth from one side of his head to the other and tracks the object in one movement rather than the series of starts and stops that characterized a one-month-old's scan. He will also follow a toy that is moved up and down in a vertical track.

When a two-month-old looks at a face, her gaze sometimes rests on the hairline area, lips, or eyes. If she's alert, she usually maintains eye contact. Of course, the baby doesn't know yet that eye contact is important for interpersonal communication; she is merely responding to the movement and the light-and-dark contrast of the other person's eyes. Yet babies' increasing interest in faces and their fascination with moving objects suggests that the dynamo duo of a talking and animated face is an endlessly intriguing stimulus. Not surprisingly, the attraction to faces often leads to babies' recognition of faces of people who care for them on a regular basis.

Researchers have systematically charted the improvement in two-month-olds' ability to look at visual targets. When babies of this age are given a two-dimensional drawing of a triangle, they are more accurate than one-month-olds in finding the outline of the triangle. They also scan a greater portion of the outline. When presented with the outline of a square that has a dot inside, they are more likely to look beyond the outline and attend to the dot than a month earlier. Researchers have documented that at two months babies have many visual-discrimination skills, including being able to distinguish shapes and contours, light-and-dark contrasts, movement, red or deep blue from white, and some familiar people and toys. These refinements in visual sensitivity point to increasing activation of cortical pathways.

Hearing. The two-month-old can hear a variety of nonhuman and human sounds that differ in pitch, intensity, and intonation. We know this because babies of this age tend to stop moving when they hear a bell ring, a simple melody, or a person speaking. A common feature of all these sounds is some sort of variability. A ringing bell consists of high-pitched sounds that start and stop. Melodies contain variations in tone. Voices contain rising and falling intonations.

In speaking to babies, parents often use exaggerated intonations, as in

"HI, baby!" Babies are particularly responsive to the emphasized "hi." For the most part, exaggerated intonation is a behavior that mothers (and others) use intuitively with the aim of eliciting a baby's attention; this kind of speech is sometimes called "motherese." Because of the baby's natural attraction to sounds with variation, motherese usually produces the desired result—it gets the baby's attention. Studies show that motherese-type speech is similar around the world.

Vocalizations and Language

There are two significant changes in sound production at two months. The first is what scientists call a vocal volley. In a vocal volley the baby imitates a string of sounds that are made by an adult, for example, "AAH, aah, aaah." Because at this age the baby can reproduce only sounds that are already in his vocal production repertoire, and since almost all of his sounds are vowels, he can only echo an adult's vowels. Another change in the baby's vocalization is that his "speech" sounds show some of the distinctive intonations of adult speech such as *rise* and *fall*.

Social Development

Being social demands a lot of psychological effort from one-month-olds. At two months, being social has less competition from bodily functions and takes less available energy. Increased wakefulness means more periods of alertness, and parents often try to direct some of this alertness into social interactions with the baby. Most two-month-olds are decidedly interested; however, there are limits to a baby's ability to engage in social activity for long periods. You'll recognize overstimulation when the baby repeatedly turns away, closes his eyes, or frets.

Periods of social alertness allow parents to bring their baby into a nascent form of conversation. It goes like this: A mother makes eye contact, smiles, and talks to her baby in short sentences, speaking with exaggerated intonation. Then the mother stops talking, and to her surprise the baby starts in. He makes animated sounds and even produces a faint smile to show pleasure, and he is quiet. The parent starts talking again, now raising her voice just a bit in order to hold her baby's attention. The "dialogue" continues for several minutes, ending only when the baby gets tired. This conversational game brings pleasure to parents as well and is an important step in emotionally uniting parents with their baby. As a mother of a two-month-old said, "Everything was worth it when she started to smile, talk, and play with me."

Studies show that toward the middle of the third month, the baby begins to initiate actions when a person moves out of his line of vision. These actions may include visually following the person, becoming quiet, or showing a change from a smiling to a neutral expression. Such behaviors indicate not disappointment over being left alone but rather an awareness of and fascination with the most interesting object in the baby's range of vision. It is fortunate for parents and their baby that the fascinating object is most often a person.

An advantage of the two-month-old's vastly improving skills is increased responsivity to soothing that relies on speech directed to the baby. Provided the baby is fretting gently or, at most, crying softly, talking can now be as effective as rocking.

Cognition

The ability to voluntarily direct one's attention is a prerequisite for learning about events, objects, and people. From time to time, babies of this age work really hard to focus their attention, and as a consequence they begin to develop some rudimentary cognitive skills. There is, for example, elementary learning particularly at feeding time. A bottle-fed baby occasionally stops crying just at the sight of the bottle, or a breast-fed baby might stop crying when positioned on his mother's lap for nursing. Because of these kinds of responses, we know that at two months babies are already beginning to associate two events that occur close in time.

If one event is typically followed by another, babies tend to develop nascent forms of *expectations* about the paired events. Babies often form expectations from a parent's voice and associated caregiving (being picked up), and being dressed or covered in certain ways (swaddling for sleep time). You might find it fun to try to discern your baby's expectations; but recognize, they're easier to observe under laboratory conditions than at home. In any event, associations and expectations are basic building blocks for cognitive development.

Emotions

With the onset of the social smile, the baby's face now shows something akin to an expression of outright pleasure. She breathes heavily and squirms when a familiar toy is shown to her, demonstrating that she is pleasurably excited by this event. At this age her facial expressions also reveal discomfort. However, most of the time her face shows little at all in the way of emotion. Her still somewhat neutral stare means that lots more development will occur in cognition, vision, and even facial muscles.

Emotions

A lizard mother does not suckle her newborn; she has no vocal system to call to her young; she does not play. The lizard baby is on its own from the moment of birth. Mammalian mothers, whether cat, dog, monkey, or human, suckle their young; send and receive vocal messages; and engage in playful behavior. Sandra Scarr once wrote that primate infancy is an elaboration of the mammalian pattern, in that years of parental care are devoted to a small number of offspring. Human infancy is a *further* elaboration of primate infancy. The increased period of parental care goes along with the evolution of a more open program of learning and adaptation on the part of young humans.

Brain material differs for reptiles and mammals; reptilian brains do not have structures related to the limbic system. It is these limbic structures, says Paul MacLean, which evolved over aeons, that led to the *honing* of emotions "that guide behavior." Brains also differ among mammals. Primates have a larger percent of brain material devoted to cortex, and humans have the largest proportion of cortical neurons in their brains. Humans compared to other mammals, as well as to nonhuman primates, have a large neocortex relative to the size of our brains along with a well-developed frontal cortex that we use for anticipation, planning, evaluation, and empathy. Emotion behaviors shared by mammals include aggression or assertiveness, protectiveness, dominance, and physical closeness; however, humans are unique in their ability to override these and other emotions. We label emotions, reflect upon and evaluate them, decide if we want to act on them, and plan emotion-laden events. Of course, under certain conditions emotional arousal can adversely influence cognitive processes.

During early infancy, babies don't have the cognitive capabilities for thinking about their emotions, much less for evaluating them. So initially emotions, rather than cognitions, prime the baby's behavior. Awake, alert, and feeling emotionally secure while cuddled in his parent's arms a four-month-old soaks up information. This baby's learning opportunities differ considerably from the baby left alone for hours, and whose cries are often ignored. Emotionally bereft, there is little motivation to learn. Later on, the first baby will likely use his acquired knowledge to appraise a situation, and that appraisal can lead to an emotion. Consider the nine-month-old who is suddenly greeted by an unfamiliar adult; the baby's storehouse of knowledge does not include information about this person. The unknown makes him fearful, and he cries.

Sometimes emotions are described as primary and secondary (or social or self-conscious). Primary emotions include anger, fear, and pleasure, and chiefly involve the deep, older structures of the brain. Primary emotions typically surface quickly with moderate to strong physiological responses. Afterward, cognitive interpretations take place. Remember how your heart raced the last time you saw a highway patrol officer suddenly appear in your car's rearview window. Speeding? Traffic ticket? Car insurance rates? Thoughts would have followed your awareness of heart pulsations.

The self-conscious emotions usually begin with cognitive appraisals that involve introspection where we think about our own behavior in terms of others, and evaluate our behavior according to family, social, and legal norms. If norms are ignored, the violator feels shame or guilt. When norms are met with exceptional skill, there is a sense of pride. Guilt occurs when a sibling forgets to call a brother who had a serious operation. Guilt though can dissolve after the phone call is made. In contrast, shame inhabits the world of the child, who is endlessly teased about his gawkiness. He feels unworthy and humiliated because of an inability to improve his athletic skills. Shame, some theorists hold, becomes so ingrained in our psyches that it is difficult to modify.

What does all of this have to do with human babies? First, emotion development takes a long time to mature. Babies' emotions are not fully developed at birth nor during the early months of life nor even by the end of the first year. Many neuronal connections have to be made. The growth in babies and toddlers' cognitive understanding will be essential for their growing understanding of their own and others' emotions. Similarly, the growth of comprehension and spoken language facilitates the labeling and control of emotions.

Second, babies may produce facial expressions that resemble the facial expressions of nonhuman primates or nonprimate mammals. These facial expressions are likely to be part of an evolved bias for acquiring emotion responses. However, facial expressions do not tell the whole story of emotions. Studies of young babies, for example by Linda Camras, reveal that expressions typically associated with one emotion (such as an expression of pain) can occur in situations where the emotion is not likely to occur (mom and baby are happily cooing to each other). Years later, smiles are often used to mask annoyance. Many of us believe that an emotional facade has great value in the maintenance of social relationships.

Third, emotion development has to do with learning opportunities. Basically, babies and toddlers learn about emotions from their interactions with parents, siblings, and others. One kind of learning has to do with expectations about the events and social experiences that make a baby feel good, and those that lead to distress. This learning occurs long before babies understand emotions and the labels we use to define them. If a baby's physical and psychological needs are met, he will be alert and open to learning and exploration. Susanne Denham reports that happy mothers tend to have happy toddlers. In contrast, if needs are inadequately met, children may withdraw into themselves and feel forlorn. Another kind of learning involves the culture's language of emotions and norms about emotion expressions. Even at eighteen months, toddlers process some information about the causes of emotion.

In terms of emotion development, babies have the biologically based potential to acquire both basic emotions and those related to self-consciousness. A part of what we used to call the limbic system, specifically the amygdala, is associated with emotions such as anger. In time, as connections develop between the deep structures of the brain (for example, the amygdala) and the cortex, babies will be able to associate emotions with expressions and language that describes the emotions. Still later, with increasing activation of frontal cortex pathways, babies can begin to exercise control over some emotion states such as mild fear. Of course, I have oversimplified a process of development that goes on for decades.

Three Months

- *when alert, follows movement, gazes at others, smiles, and coos*

- *brings arms to midline of body and plays with hands*

- *head is bobblingly erect when held upright*

- *anticipates everyday routine, such as opening mouth at appearance of nipple*

At this age babies' behaviors suddenly seem wonderfully coordinated. When fully awake, the fourteen-week-old holds her head up and focuses her eyes. She looks intently at toys, pictures on the wall, and anybody that approaches. Last month the baby had a little smile that she directed to anything, to anybody, and sometimes to nothing at all. This month her smile is big, and she specifically directs it to people and to toys.

At this age, the babies' microworld is endlessly intriguing to them. They look at a suspended mobile for minutes at a time and sometimes visually explore the entire surface of an object. They also visually follow moving objects, whether it is a toy that a parent moves across a tabletop or one that is held at the baby's eye level and moved slowly from side to side. Sometimes a baby's eyes and arms operate in tandem, with arms tentatively extended as if reaching for objects that she sees. There is no mistaking a baby's genuine pleasure in these experiences.

In addition to pleasure, babies show the emotions of interest and boredom. A new toy elicits attention, cooing, smiling, and pleasurable wriggling, but old toys may be greeted with yawns, averted gazes, and fretting. Babies' smiles tell us they like to be entertained. Toys and mobiles are fun, but now people are their favorite source of pleasure. If you find yourself responding to your baby's smiles, you're not alone. Researchers who have studied the emotional responses of babies and their mothers have found a third to a half of mothers actually mimic their babies' emotions.

In an impressive display of early independence, many babies of this age begin to create their own amusements by playing with their fingers. Accidentally, at first, and then purposefully, they raise both arms and hands in front of their eyes, touch their fingers, move their hands apart, and touch their fingers again. Seeing and feeling their hands move is so compelling that babies prolong this game. This activity staves off boredom and tiredness when there's no one else around. It's also a wonderful example of babies controlling their own attention in the service of cognitive growth.

By three months babies have active memories, possibly remembering some of their most familiar experiences for minutes and possibly for days if there are sufficient visual cues and reminders. A baby moves with pleasurable excitement when she sees her bottle and may open her mouth in anticipation of a soon-to-happen feeding. The bottle signals food! She may also recognize simple, sequential associations; for example, a door opening is usually followed by the sounds of footsteps. If a delay occurs in a schedule that she has come to recognize (like feeding), she cries to let us know that she's not happy that something is amiss.

Overall, so many distinctly human mental and social behaviors emerge at this age that three months is a major transition point in early infant development, which is increasingly linked to cortical activation of behaviors. Babies are increasingly thought of as *psychological beings* with likes, dislikes, and pleasures. Moreover, many of the baby's reflexive, biologically based survival behaviors are being replaced by experience-driven functional skills related to motor, perceptual, and social domains. Indeed, motor skills change rapidly from this point on. It is amazing how quickly babies continue to shift from being almost helpless beings to relatively adept individuals.

✦ IMAGES OF DEVELOPMENT

Motor Control

This month unmistakable changes occur in the baby's head position and control, arm movements, and body control. Her head is held higher and for a longer period of time. Her arm movements are directed at things in a purposeful though largely uncoordinated manner. Her shoulder muscles are stronger and her shoulders straighter.

The baby gives all kinds of signals that her body is getting prepared for rolling over, crawling, creeping, and eventually standing. When she's on her tummy, she holds her head up for minutes at a time at an angle between forty-five and ninety degrees above the mattress surface. She kicks actively and purposefully when on her tummy or back. When she's held upright, her legs support a fraction of her weight.

Remember the tonic neck reflex? It's less and less noticeable. The baby's head is mostly held in the midline when she's lying on her back. When she's alert and quiet, her arms are mirror images of each other; if one arm is lying at her side then the other is also in this position. When she's resting, both arms usually lie on the mattress at shoulder level with elbows bent and hands near her head. The baby looks as if she has been surprised and thrown her arms up in exclamation.

Now that she can keep her head in midline and arms in symmetry, the baby can visually attend to things that are straight in front of her. Her new skills also include bringing her hands into eye range for visual inspection and play. This begins a wonderful collaboration of eyes and hands and new opportunities for learning.

At three months, reaching movements are often weak and unsteady. But the baby keeps on trying and does her best at reaching when lying on her back. In this position, babies do not have to strain to keep the head upright and shoulders stable while simultaneously trying to reach for a toy.

Grasp continues to mature into a more useful tool. In a propped position, a three-month-old often opens one hand if a small toy is presented to her. But she can hold onto the toy only briefly. Her grasp does not yet involve her thumb, and at this point she primarily uses her palms and fingers. Importantly, fewer spontaneous body movements occur when she attempts to hold onto something, so her grasp is less disrupted by unwanted activity.

Babies seem to have an inborn awareness of the unique value of their fingers. When a small toy is held in front of them, they briefly and unskillfully move their fingers over it like miniature space probes. Occasionally they can manage to use their hands to carry a toy to their mouth. This hand behavior is not necessarily guided by vision; rather, it is simply an elaboration of the more basic, largely reflexive hand-to-mouth activity. Still, these hand behaviors mark another important step because babies are beginning to learn how useful their hands can be.

Perception

Vision. Acuity, the ability to see objects clearly, is better now, and three-month-olds can attend to details that they missed in earlier explorations. In the laboratory, researchers have learned about developmental changes in accommodation, which is the process that helps babies of this age see objects clearly that are nearby or at a short distance. The rapid adjustment of the curvature of the eye's lens assures that a baby's visual focus is good regardless of distance. Just how well does a three-month-old see? Well, she can now differentiate faces that have smiles from those that have frowns. In fact, she smiles to a smiling face and rarely smiles at someone who is frowning.

Babies of three months also discriminate different shapes; that is, they can tell a bottle from a stick or a ball from a person's head. This ability is called form perception. A baby even briefly remembers the configuration of simple forms or shapes, an ability called shape constancy. A bottle-fed baby can recognize that her bottle retains the same basic shape, the bottle shape, whether it's upside down or sideways and whether the light is dim or bright.

Spatial perception is clearly improving. In laboratory studies, babies respond differentially to variations in spatial orientation and to spatial scenarios that involve making distinctions between *above* and *below*. Also, around this age babies distinguish red from green and blue/green from white. It is possible that different colors influence their psychological state.

Hearing. Measuring how well a baby hears different speech sounds and how well she hears loud and soft noises is far more difficult than measuring different responses to facial smiles and frowns. Research and common experience show that her hearing is getting better. Other research also tells us that considerable improvement takes place in her processing of sounds between six and twelve months. And by twelve months, babies' hearing is close to that of adults.

Cognition

More and more the baby's mind takes on the qualities we associate with human cognitive functioning. For example, at this age babies often become still when something interesting comes into view, and they remain quiet in order to give the object of interest undivided visual attention. Research studies have documented the kinds of learning three-month-olds are capable of and the particular circumstances in which their memories form. Given appropriate cues some memories last for a week.

At this age, babies increasingly learn from their own play, which is helped along by their growing skills in moving their arms and hands and their ability to maintain attention. Many times this early learning starts out with an accidental discovery. Consider the colorful mobiles that parents often hang in their baby's crib. Most mobiles contain objects in bright, contrasting colors, and a few of the objects make sounds when they move. A three-month-old is lying in her crib: she's awake and alert, and is moving her arms up toward her head and then down again toward the mattress. The baby accidentally hits the mobile, and it moves. There's a sound as well. This unplanned event is intriguing, but the baby does not know she caused the mobile to move. Perhaps an hour later or the next day, the baby's arms again happen to touch the mobile. Then this occurs again. One day as the baby's arm hits the mobile, she begins to associate her arm with the mobile's movement. She repeats the activity over and over, all the while reinforcing her knowledge of objects and her own activities with them.

Other experiences contribute to learning. The baby touches a cuddly toy and over time discovers that it feels different from her rattle. We know that at this age, babies' psychological functioning builds upon their ability to be attentive, their growing purposeful use of their arms and hands, and the discriminations made by their own perceptual systems. A baby repeats her exploring and play activities because they are pleasing to her, and with every repetition, she learns a little more about her body and her surroundings.

More so than earlier, social encounters also provide numerous opportunities to learn. A baby of this age is often able to discriminate between the way one person holds her and the hold of another person. She may stiffen somewhat if an unfamiliar person holds her. This is not the expression of concern about strangers that we see later on at about eight months. Rather, it's simply a reaction to newness. To be able to recognize that something is new means the baby must have learned the characteristics of something that is familiar.

The notion of recognizing the familiar has ramifications for changes made in the baby's care and schedule. When a three-month-old is introduced to a new regime of care (for example, a new babysitter), she may show periodic upsets for a few days. This does not mean she is spoiled; it's just her response to unfamiliar people and/or routines. Holding her, talking to her, and comforting her make adjustments in routines easier because these familiar sensations are reassuring. As new settings and people become more familiar, she once again shows pleasure with her surroundings.

Vocalizations and Language

Until this month the baby's sounds were mainly squeals, hiccups, and cries. Cries could be used to register distress, but the baby didn't have a sound that indicated she was experiencing pleasure or enjoying something that was interesting. Now the vocal system has developed to the point that different vowel sounds can be regularly and voluntarily produced. These sounds are called coos and sound like *ooh, aah, uuh.* When a baby discovers that she can make these sounds, they soon become one of her favorite pastimes and she coos repeatedly. Babies are particularly fond of cooing when they are content, amused by a toy, or captivated by a parent's voice. They may even coo when they see a familiar person come into view.

Hearing coos is itself exhilarating for most parents, but there's an added benefit. Babies begin to engage in reciprocal imitation: They respond to coo sounds, and their parents make similar coos. This is called vocal tennis, and it is a sign that the baby is tuning in to parents. At three months the overriding limitation to vocal tennis is that the baby can only echo sounds that are already part of her repertoire. If a baby can produce *ooh* but not *uh,* then she'll imitate *ooh* but not *uh.*

Social Interactions and Emotions

In this section, I connect emotion and social behaviors because of the profound effect the baby's smile has on parents' and babies' interactions. Prior to ten or twelve weeks of age, many babies smile every so often to people or to objects, but often not consistently. But at three months, babies do not have to be coaxed to smile; they generate a spontaneous smile, which is often labeled "the social smile."

Several factors contribute to the gradual emergence of the social smile. Babies sleep better, and thus during the awake periods they tend to be more alert to their surroundings. As I noted earlier, babies are better able to pay attention to things that interest them. In other words, they are more cognitively engaged than ever before. This has ramifications for social and emotional growth.

From early in life, faces and speech have had great appeal to babies. Now the baby can seek out faces to look at, attend to facial features, and listen to everyday speaking voices. Another person's smile and lilting voice resonate to her, and she can actively respond. This is the scenario. The three-month-old's growing psychological awareness includes feelings of pleasure and some recognition that she is a separate *being*. Most important then, the baby is able to respond by producing a social smile because of her converging skills: She can process at some level the meaning of her parent's behavior and evaluate the behavior also at some level, and she has an elemental awareness that she herself can produce an emotional response that is appropriate to the other person. The converging skills are basically linkages among cognitive processes, emotions, and control of facial muscles. Together, these represent an enormous developmental growth.

With the social smile, barriers to social exchanges melt away. The baby is besieged by people competing to be the recipient of her warm smile. They tickle, they babble, they laugh, and they cajole. This competition provides the baby with a first-class schoolroom for exercising social skills. While it is often the case that initially babies smile almost indiscriminately, beaming at most everyone who smiles to them and who speaks soothingly, they soon begin to make distinctions about familiar people as opposed to less familiar ones. When these distinctions become more clear to them, babies begin to direct smiles to the people who are most often around and who make them feel good.

In addition to pleasurable feelings, babies of this age also show behaviors that more clearly indicate they experience displeasure or annoyance. Babies cry when they are bored. These cries of displeasure sound different from cries that have a distinctive physiological origin such as tummy upsets. Some of these psychological cries may, at first, be puzzling to parents. But the puzzles are solved when parents begin to associate different cry sounds with cues from the baby's activities. Just as parents readily respond to smiles, there is good reason to respond to the baby's signals of her psychologically based needs, wants, and displeasures.

♦ DEVELOPMENTAL CLOSE-UP

Becoming Aware of Others

The psychological growth of babies is often apparent in their interactions with others. Babies' behaviors show they clearly enjoy being with others. And their responsiveness acts like a magnet to parents. The more these pleasant interactions occur, the more babies enjoy them. Both baby and parent get an emotional lift from each other. The negative side is that babies of this age may cry when they are left alone. This is not a sign of being "spoiled"; it's an indication that the baby likes social contact.

Although babies don't have to be taught to enjoy social interactions, they do need help in learning how to modulate their pleasures and displeasures. A three-month-old easily becomes overexcited and frets. Parents often intuitively know how to handle this, by becoming more subdued and by talking softly. When the baby is quiet, parents make attempts to reinstate smiling by raising their voices, making more animated facial expressions, and exaggerating their body movements. Parents' distinct sequences of arouse, soothe, arouse, soothe are one way babies get practice in how to control their emotions so that they can maintain social interactions.

Parents also have a profound influence on the baby's continued interest in social interactions. As early as three months babies are bothered when parents' smiles are replaced by frowns or other unhappy expressions. An example is a mother who now looks worried because of family troubles when previously she often smiled at her baby.

Ed Tronick, who has studied mother-and-baby interactions, asked mothers of three-month-olds to be unreactive and still faced instead of animated. Typically, the babies initially cooed to their mothers but gave up and turned away when they saw that their mothers were not responding. In another study, mothers were asked to briefly simulate a depressed state by not touching their babies, by speaking in a monotone, and by otherwise being inactive. Babies of three months responded to these behaviors by crying and looking away.

Does all this mean that a three-month-old has a sense of a caregiver's habitual mood or even the sequence of a daily routine? Possibly. In a recent study, investigators reported that more actively emotionally engaged mothers tended to have more actively emotionally engaged babies. What seems to be happening is that a three-month-old is capable of building associations between behaviors emitted by himself and behaviors of another, and vice versa. This kind of responsiveness is called *contingent*. A smile should beget a smile, and a cry should bring a parent's soothing response. Smiles greeted with neutral expressions or frowns are unexpected events and are probably unpleasant to the baby. She reacts the only ways she can, by dampening her own emotional responses, by turning away, or by crying. However, don't worry if the baby frets once in a while when you are having a bad day and are not as responsive as you ordinarily are.

But do know that babies of mothers who are chronically depressed tend to show reduced levels of pleasure in social interactions. What seems to be occurring is that depressed mothers do not respond contingently to their infants' bids and they do not offer as many pleasurable activities to their babies as do nondepressed mothers. These kinds of parent behaviors have potential ramifications for later development. So, if you're a parent who typically feels downhearted and blue, it is important to obtain assistance.

DEVELOPMENTAL HINTS AND ALERTS:

BIRTH TO THREE MONTHS

How to Be Helpful

+ Do not overstimulate your baby. She'll sleep better if you keep intrusive inputs to a minimum. Use pastel-colored sheets. Use one or two toys or mobiles as opposed to a cribful. Avoid bright lights. Keep TV volume low.

+ Cuddle and carry your baby when she cries in distress. Use a snuggly on those days when she seems especially tired.

+ Talk and sing to your baby whenever he is alert.

+ Try to find space for a rocking chair. It's a great way for you and your baby to relax and to spend some quality time together.

When to Seek Help

+ If your baby cries most of the time, check with your pediatrician about food allergies or other physical problems.

Don't hesitate to seek advice about your baby's health and development if by three months your baby

+ does not lift his head at all

+ does not respond at all to social overtures

+ shows no facial expressions

+ is largely inattentive

+ does not respond to sound

SHARPENING OUR FOCUS

NEURONS, NEURONS, AND MORE . . .

This thing that you've seen on a shelf in a museum, resting in a bell jar, looks like an inert vegetable but it's an old brain. That's what it is. But don't let this desiccated thing fool you. At some point, that brain was pulsating and active in somebody's head, just like your brain is active right now! The brain, all few pounds of it, is a marvelous organ composed of threadlike neurons, other kinds of brain matter, electrical pulses and activity, and chemical actions. The brain works directly and indirectly with all parts of our bodies. It allows us to think and dream and love. It is the organ, state A. F. Kalverboer and A. Gramsbergen, that "senses the environment and ultimately governs, orchestrates, and modulates" our reactions to a sometimes unpredictable environment. Let's check out the brain, focusing on its early development.

Neuroscientists have made enormous strides in documenting the dynamic nature of the maturing brain and some of its linkages to behavior. Often animal studies have contributed to our understanding; a good example comes from animal studies that have documented periods of the synaptic growth and pruning of neuronal connections. This is a normative developmental progression, which makes neuronal connections more efficient.

Careful application of animal research and new studies of human infants' brain functioning have provided informed perspectives about early brain development. In turn, the brain research has facilitated our understanding of the links between brain and behavior. These links can be examined further by coordinating data obtained from noninvasive procedures such as electroencephalograms (EEGs), which record brain wave activity, and, researchers' observations of infant behavior. Research collaborations between neuroscientists and developmental psychologists have produced impressive results. Richard Davidson and Nathan Fox have linked differential activation of the frontal lobes with variations in older infants' emotion expressions. Michael Posner and Mary Rothbart coupled the year-old baby's ability to not touch a toy until he has visually inspected it to the increasing activation of a specific region of the brain (anterior cingulate gyrus).

In general, we know from animal and human studies that brain development *during the early years* has these characteristics:

✧ A period of dramatic growth in nerve cell connections occurs, in which one neuron begins to transmit information to a nearby neuron or to one that is farther away (in another part of the brain). These connections take place via axons and dendrites that come from one neuron and go to another neuron; the area of neuronal connection is called a synapse.

The efficiency of neuronal transmission is substantially aided by a covering—called myelin—that begins to envelop individual axons. The formation of myelin is also a developmental process: over time myelin increasingly covers neurons, and in turn neuronal conductivity becomes faster and more efficient.

The growth of neuronal connections leads to comparable growth in the folds of the cortex, which is the outer layer of the brain that contains neurons associated with uniquely human activities. At birth, the cortex is relatively smooth. The more connections, the more the cortex has to fold over on itself in order to accommodate the increasing neuronal activity.

✧ A marked overproduction of neuronal connections (the synapses) occurs during infancy and early childhood. At some point after this period of synaptic overproduction, a pruning process begins to take place. Pruning eliminates those synapses that are rarely activated. Overall, the system becomes more efficient when the *excess material*—unused synapses—is removed (by dying off and dissolving).

✧ Brain development also involves an increase in the activation of highly complex neurochemical processes, which occur as neuronal signals cross the *synaptic space*. In addition to providing readiness for sending and receiving messages across the synapse, neurochemical processes (for example, serotonin is a neurotransmitter) also regulate a neuron's *receptivity* to a signal, contribute to alterations in the brain's operations, and bias some kinds of behavioral responses.

✧Neuronal connections, synaptic overproduction, and synaptic pruning do not simultaneously occur in every part of the brain at the same time. Rather, there is a process of differential timing in which a particular part of the brain begins growing many new neuronal connections, overproducing connections, and pruning at one point in time while another part of the brain starts this growth process at a somewhat later time. The density of neuron growth across the brain areas associated with the visual system begins earlier than the density of brain growth in frontal lobe areas that are associated with behavioral inhibition, the ability to plan, and conscious memory activities.

✧In general, a baby's initial behaviors seem to be largely subcortical. Then, at about two months, there is a shift that involves more neuronal connections with cortical portions of the brain. The end of the first year is associated with increased connections and firing of neurons within the frontal lobes, and sometime during the second year, the lateral prefrontal lobes and the temporal areas are increasingly activated. Neuroscientists are fairly certain that the frontal lobes show development well into early adolescence.

Some Features of Early Brain Development

AGE	BRAIN (CORTEX) FUNCTIONING	EXAMPLES OF ASSOCIATED PERCEPTUAL/COGNITIVE BEHAVIORS
Birth–1 month	Primary motor and sensory areas	Attention
1–4 months	Motor and sensory	Anticipation, recognition, memory
4–8 months	Sensory and sensory association areas	Responds more quickly to changes; develops expectations
8–12 months	Additional association areas; frontal lobes increasingly activated	Problem solving; increasing evidence of recall memory; beginnings of behavioral inhibition; signs of working memory by end of first year
12–18 months	All cortical areas functioning; functioning of association areas still evolving	Trial-and-error learning; increase in imitative acts; improved spatial awareness; improvements in problem-solving skills
18–24 months	Cortical areas functioning and maturing; connections between cortical areas still forming	Increasingly thinks in terms of ideas; increasingly remembers without cues; begins to think in terms of cause and effect

◆ Although biology more or less dictates the overall architecture and functioning of the brain, especially the cortex, it is the multitude of human experiences that ultimately shape and organize brain functioning. Experiences matter during infancy and the toddler period and for the rest of life. Indeed, the famed neuroscientist John Allman has suggested that interactions with others and playful behavior may be essential for the development of the forebrain.

The bottom-line message is that babies' brains are precious. Brain development matters. Caring and responsive parenting is important. But parents should avoid thinking about every activity in terms of their baby's brain and neurons and synapses. This just isn't necessary.

MEMORY

What would our lives be like if we could never remember an event, a favored memento, a loved one? It's difficult to imagine. Many of our memories are incredibly detailed and tied to a multitude of experiences, which we remember via thoughts and words. We also hold vivid memories that are linked to experiences involving a scent or taste. In the springtime, a common flowering bush exudes a dreamy scent: when I happen upon one, memories emerge of the bush-strewn path I took to the local beach when I was a schoolgirl.

Very young babies seem to have memories of scents such as the scent of a mother's body. They also remember events that repeatedly occur in tandem: the sight of a bottle and being fed, a father's touch and being hugged. And like us, young babies rely on recognition (or cued) memory such as the sight of a face seen before to retrieve information. However, many of the baby's early memories fade over time because they are not tied to ideas and words that the baby uses consciously.

For a good many years, we thought that young babies relied primarily on recognition memory for retrieval, and then months later their recall memory system, which did not rely on cues, emerged. Nowadays we have a more comprehensive understanding of infant memory, thanks to clever researchers, innovative technology used to measure infant behaviors, recent brain research, and a greater understanding of the parts of the brain that are involved in memory. Drawing from the ideas of some of these researchers, specifically Patricia Bauer, Mark Johnson, and Charles Nelson, I will describe a few ideas about infant and toddler memory.

To start, there's a new terminology. The newer views of memory include two major subdivisions; one is labeled *implicit* and the other is called *explicit*. Implicit memory does not need conscious awareness. An example is memory that is embedded in a series of actions such as using dining utensils or riding a bicycle—once the skills have been well learned. Some implicit memories can be brought to consciousness given a particular circumstance: as a long-time bicycle rider, I've recently become more conscious of braking for a stop because of a change from toe clips to clip-on pedals.

In contrast to implicit memory, explicit, or declarative, memory operates with consciousness and depends on the use of words or ideas to retrieve names, places, and episodes from our recent or longtime past. Examples include responses to: "What did you do yesterday, after work?"; "Tell me the most memorable experience from your childhood."

Current views also suggest that implicit- and explicit-memory systems are interrelated: both have beginnings early in life and expand over time into more complex systems. However, the development of explicit memory takes considerably longer to mature than does implicit memory. One other difference between implicit and explicit memory pertains to its neural bases. In general, subcortical and cerebellar pathways are associated with implicit memory, whereas cortical areas such as the temporal lobes and prefrontal cortex are associated with explicit memory. Both implicit- and explicit-memory systems encompass different memory processes. I've summarized these in the accompanying diagram, which also shows how each memory process relates to babies. The table is brief, so it may help to read the examples that follow.

◆ BABIES' MEMORIES

Implicit

Expectant. This kind of memory is reflected in studies that look for evidence of anticipation. In the now classic study by Marshall Haith and colleagues, 3½-month-olds were presented with a series of visual stimuli (for example, schematic faces, geometric shapes) at the right or left of a viewing screen. Subsequently, the stimuli were presented to each baby using a series of pre-determined sequences, which were either alternated as to right and left, or were random, right, right, and so on. Babies showed a quicker and a greater amount of anticipation for the right-left sequence. Presumably they had learned the sequence and utilized some form of mental processing that allowed them to *forecast* the sequence of the learned event when it occurred. The babies remembered the sequence for subsequent presentations that were similar.

Conditioned. This kind of memory involves pairing two different stimuli. A well-known example involves a colorful mobile that is hung over a baby's crib, with a ribbon connecting the mobile to one of the baby's legs. The baby is allowed a certain amount of time to learn that moving his leg jiggles the mobile (leg kicking and moving the mobile *are paired*). The researcher records the number of kicks when the mobile is present or absent. Two, five, seven, or ten days later when the baby and mobile are reunited, memory is measured by comparing the ratio of kicks that occur after re-presentation of the mobile to the kicks that occurred before the mobile was removed. If the baby remembers, he should begin to kick at a higher rate as soon as he sees the mobile. At three months, babies' kick rates rise when they are re-exposed to the mobile. However, there are too few longitudinal studies of babies' implicit memories to be able to state with certainty how long memories last.

Explicit

Proto-explicit. This is the term I use to describe an emergent form of explicit memory where recall seems to take place, but because of the immaturity of the baby's language development, memory processes cannot be based on the conscious, word-based retrieval system used by speaking individuals. I list three kinds of babies' memories under *proto-explicit*, all of which seem to suggest babies use heightened levels of awareness for memory retrieval and they may use some kind of image as a retrieval mechanism. Recognition memory, which often relies on visual or auditory cues for retrieval, is one process. Some researchers suggest newborns show recognition memory. Cross-modal memory is another example that is typically studied in laboratory settings. A baby is allowed to touch and manipulate an object (the target), but is prevented from seeing the object she is touching. Later, when the baby is visually presented with several objects including the target, the baby shows a preference for the target. The action suggests the baby is actively processing information gleaned from touch and transferring the information to the visual system.

Early forms of problem solving also suggest examples of proto-explicit memory. A mother brought her twelve-month-old daughter to our laboratory, where the child squirmed and generally seemed wary. After a minute or two, the twelve-month-old suddenly reached into a pocket of her stroller and retrieved a small photo album. She slowly turned the pages and looked at the photographs of family members. She closed the album; she handed it to her mother. At that point she looked at us and smiled. The child seemed to remember how she could make herself feel better, and she drew upon these memories in a situation that was stressful.

Explicit. Bauer suggests that elicited imitation is an instance of nonverbal recall of events. Elicited imitation is examined in the laboratory setting, where props are used to demonstrate a set of actions to the child. The child

MEMORY: THE EARLY YEARS

TYPES:

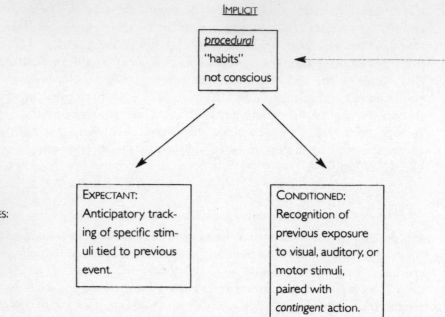

IMPLICIT

procedural	
"habits"	
not conscious	

SUB-TYPES:

EXPECTANT:
Anticipatory track-
ing of specific stim-
uli tied to previous
event.

CONDITIONED:
Recognition of
previous exposure
to visual, auditory, or
motor stimuli,
paired with
contingent action.

CHARACTERISTICS:

Learning tends to be
slow; memory often
tied to specific con-
tent and not prone to
error.

PROBABLE AGES: 2–3 MONTHS   1–3 MONTHS

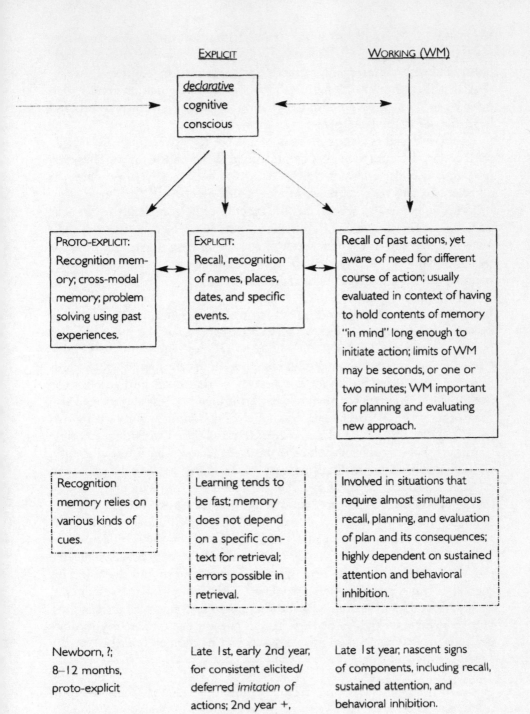

declarative
cognitive
conscious

PROTO-EXPLICIT:
Recognition memory; cross-modal memory; problem solving using past experiences.

EXPLICIT:
Recall, recognition of names, places, dates, and specific events.

Recall of past actions, yet aware of need for different course of action; usually evaluated in context of having to hold contents of memory "in mind" long enough to initiate action; limits of WM may be seconds, or one or two minutes; WM important for planning and evaluating new approach.

Recognition memory relies on various kinds of cues.

Learning tends to be fast; memory does not depend on a specific context for retrieval; errors possible in retrieval.

Involved in situations that require almost simultaneous recall, planning, and evaluation of plan and its consequences; highly dependent on sustained attention and behavioral inhibition.

Newborn, ?;
8–12 months,
proto-explicit

Late 1st, early 2nd year, for consistent elicited/deferred _imitation_ of actions; 2nd year +, words used for recall.

Late 1st year, nascent signs of components, including recall, sustained attention, and behavioral inhibition.

permission from Johnson and Nelson. Appreciation to C. Nelson for his suggestions.

is given an opportunity to imitate the actions, at which point measurements are taken of the child's spontaneous and exact imitations. At a later point, and without intervening practice or modeling, the child is again presented with the props. Memory (the amount of information retained) is inferred by comparing the child's behavior when first given the props and her behavior at the later measurement time.

Imitative recall is clearly evident by twelve to thirteen months of age, with retrieval of imitated acts extended by eight months or so. However, imitation is considerably better by older toddlers than younger ones. In addition, Bauer's research reveals that the effectiveness of recall using imitation is influenced by several factors, including the complexity of the acts to be imitated, how well children can engage in problem solving on their own, and in some cases the amount of speech children have. It is interesting that many of these factors are also responsible for variations in recall memory among older children and adults.

Working memory. Playing bridge or chess are everyday examples of working memory. Both games require memory of past moves by the self and other players, careful consideration of the current state of the board or card table (for example, where the remaining chess pieces are located or which cards remain in play), and a plan for the next move that takes into account the potential implications of the move. Expert bridge or chess players may also have other skills, such as fast-paced analytical reasoning, facility with visual rotation tasks, and a talent for numbers, that help their working memories.

Clearly, babies can't play chess or bridge. However, an interesting task, which has elements of working memory, has been devised for babies between eight and twelve months of age. An attractive toy is hidden under one of two felt pads (A, B) that are laid out on a table. At about eight months, babies typically reach for the A pad when the toy is hidden under the A pad; however, when the procedure is changed and the toy is hidden under the B pad, babies still tend to look for it under the A pad. At about twelve months, babies successfully reach for the correct pad to find the toy. This success is linked to behaviors associated with frontal-lobe development, including memory, behavioral inhibition, and a change in activity: the baby remembers which A or B pad hides the toy, simultaneously inhibits the tendency to reach where the toy was first hidden, and reaches for the toy under the pad where it was last hidden.

✧ Although memory processes continue to develop throughout childhood and beyond, the first year sees major growth in our human memory system. Three months marks a major turning point because the implicit aspects of memory are clearly functional at this age. Researchers have also demonstrated that some memories of three-month-olds may last a week or more. Under some circumstances, memories can be reactivated. We are uncertain about how much three-month-olds actually remember in their everyday lives. However, we are certain that from the third month onward memory abilities grow rapidly, and this growth provides the basis for the development of other cognitive and social skills.

Perhaps the most profound change in memory occurs with the transition to language. Consider the implications for consolidating memories as you read the following words said at various occasions by a twenty-month-old. Remembering is reflected in the word *broke*, in terms of how broken things look; *fix*, such that a toy that is broken can be repaired; *mess*, in terms of a memory about general state of messiness or messy clothes; *stuck*, with respect to no movement; and *mine*, with respect to one's personhood and one's own possessions.

EMOTION DEVELOPMENT

Our emotions are invariably linked to our social interactions. Partners, friends, children, employers, acquaintances, and even the driver in the next highway lane can make us feel good or angry or fearful. Of course, physical events also influence our emotions: gorgeous sunsets, a shimmering mountain lake after a storm, wildflowers swaying in a spring breeze evoke joy; lightning, earthquakes, hurricanes breed fear. Of course you know this, but indulge me as I make a point. You know about emotions because you understand the words that I have written, and you can easily conjure up memories or scenarios of the scenes that I describe.

Babies, as you well know, have neither the words nor the memories to understand emotions. Mostly, they rely on social interactions to recognize when they feel content and when they feel distressed. A soft, warm body and gentle words go along with contentment, whereas being alone, being screamed at, or being handled roughly go with distress. It is the baby's everyday social experiences that bring about emotions and fine-tune emotion development.

In the chart that follows, I show a development progression for emotional development. You'll note that social interactions and other skills precede the columns on emotion development. Also note that almost every age has an associated entry for babies' facial expressions. In contrast, entries for emotion understanding come in at various ages, as does the baby's ability to control his own distressful negative emotions. These patterns reflect the relatively spread-out changes that occur for both of these components of emotion development.

Do keep in mind, the descriptions below are representative normative trends that may not fit all aspects of your own baby's emotion development.

AGE	PROMINENT FEATURES OF BABY'S INTERACTIONS WITH OTHERS OR IN PLAY	SOCIAL DEVELOPMENT
EARLY WEEKS	Occasionally looks alert to others' speech: has difficulty maintaining attention to others; does not look around for others	Predisposition to be social; visual attentiveness to such contrasts as found in human faces
1 MONTH	Alert more often when talked to; changes behavior slightly—quiets, breathes rapidly—when picked up.	Differentiates the speech of others from nonsocial sounds.
2 MONTHS	Vocal dialogue (baby listens to other, coos when other is silent; visually follows other person	Makes eye contact; smiles faintly.
3 MONTHS	Smiles, coos to others with contingent response; generalized excitement; smiles to toys; follows another with eyes; anticipates— opens mouth at sight of nipple	Distinctly social being who shows enjoyment when with others
4 MONTHS	Directs social smile to familiar people; initiates social bids with eye contact and coos	Has nascent expectancy about others' behaviors; shows elemental associative learning re others' activities
5–6 MONTHS	Lots of babbling vocalizations to others; becomes silent in unfamiliar settings	Social bids with tentative, idiosyncratic gestures; recognizes general configuration of familiar people

EMOTION DEVELOPMENT: Expressions	EMOTION DEVELOPMENT: Understanding	EMOTION DEVELOPMENT: Control of Distress
Generalized distress responses represented in cries that range from mild frets to screams; when not crying, expressions are mostly neutral		Can self-soothe with nonnutritive sucking, if not too highly aroused; most effective soothers: rocking, touch, white noise
Differentiated cries (e.g. hunger) emerging, mostly related to physiological upsets; increase in irritability late in the day		
Nascent signs of pleasure, occasional smile		More sensitive to soothing techniques involving voice.
Pleasure emerges; boredom emerges as a nascent form of a negative emotion		Turns from nonsmiling face; can distract self when bored by focusing on visually interesting sight
Laughter emerges, most frequently to tickling and other physical activities	Begins to distinguish facial expressions	
Turns head away from disliked food	Begins to match emotion expressions to those of other individuals	

AGE	PROMINENT FEATURES OF BABY'S INTERACTIONS WITH OTHERS OR IN PLAY	SOCIAL DEVELOPMENT
7 MONTHS		Greets others with babbling; pick-me-up gesture; attentive to simple social games
8 MONTHS	Nascent comprehension of words and phrases	Affectionate to specific people; makes social bids clearly; wary of unfamiliar individuals; requests social games
9 MONTHS		Makes specific affectionate displays; tries to "be like" others (e.g., wants to eat same food)
10 MONTHS	Begins to look at others' faces as possible cues for ambiguous situations	Social referencing
11 MONTHS		Affectionate to greater number of individuals; increased interest in agemates; more coordinated participation in social games
12 MONTHS	Shows toys to others; imitates simple behaviors; enjoys practicing "taking turns"; relies on one or more key individuals when upset; points when wants to call attention to something	Attachment; use of gestures

EMOTION DEVELOPMENT: Expressions	EMOTION DEVELOPMENT: Understanding	EMOTION DEVELOPMENT: Control of Distress
Shows evidence of fear and anger		
Increased individuality of emotional expression; laughs as participates in social games		
Frowns; seeks comfort from selected others when fatigued or fearful; may shake head—precursor to "no"	Beginning responsiveness to "no" and sharp tone of voice	
Shows intense positive and negative emotions to very specific people, objects, and events	Modifies actions based on others' facial expressions	May rock body when upset
Temperamental style more evident in emotional responses		
Shows nascent form of jealousy; aroused by others' distress; engages in activities for "sense of mastery"	Some awareness of others' emotion states	In some instances, stops crying when senses "in control"; can distract self

Age	Prominent features of baby's interactions with others or in play	Social Development
14–15 MONTHS	Exhibits checking back behaviors to be sure of caregivers' presence	Includes parents in play; explores on own but visually scans for parent; imitates others' everyday actions
18 MONTHS	Spurt in word growth; comprehension may exceed word production; engages in pretend play	Aware of others' disapproval; responds to some dos and don'ts; says no; recognizes things have a characteristic appearance; aware of gender-related activities; peer play periods extended slightly, with more imitation of peers
21 MONTHS		Increase in verbal/physical exchanges with peers; more finicky and exacting behaviors
24 MONTHS	Separation "worries," clinging; has good memory for many everyday activities and some past events; speech often includes "I," "me," "mine," nouns, pronouns, and verbs	Takes interest in family routines; offers to help; awareness of others' everyday roles; makes excuses to others; may try to deceive when engaged in prohibited activity; increase in demands for independence; more pretend play with peers

EMOTION DEVELOPMENT: Expressions	EMOTION DEVELOPMENT: Understanding	EMOTION DEVELOPMENT: Control of Distress
Increase in empathic responses; slight increase in irritability from previous months	Seems to delight in *teasing* parents, as if testing	
Signs of self-conscious emotions: shows coy behavior; shows nascent forms of guilt; increase in annoyance when thwarted; may insist on own way; offers empathic responses to others when observes upsets; peak period for incidence of temper tantrums	Begins to use words to define own emotion states (e.g., "mad")	Uses transitional objects to soothe self; occasionally seeks parent when senses that can't do an activity such as a puzzle
Decline in irritability; shows affection to selected peers	Uses words to define others' emotion states	
Intense emotional responses—heights of pleasure, deeply felt anger; shows considerable pleasure when succeeds in activity; increase in disputes with peers over toy possession; can be contrary, but also appropriately contrite	Reads others' moods; understands when a self-action has hurt another and may spontaneously apologize	If has adequate words, apologizes for willful action; may try bargaining to get way, and to avoid self distress; more rapid intentional help seeking when can't operate a toy or solve a puzzle on own

Four to Seven Months

Preview

Four Months

Five Months

Six Months

Seven Months

Developmental Hints and Alerts: Four to Seven Months

Sharpening Our Focus

The Baby as Scientist, Genius, Mathematician, and More . . .

The Extraordinary World of Babies and Language

DURING THIS PERIOD BABIES celebrate the emergence of a whole new dimension of being: Their physiological processes are complemented by more capable psychological processes. These changes transform the baby from a primarily physical person with a few hard-earned motor and social skills into a more mentally alert, sociable individual who is busy "doing, thinking, and feeling." Curious, attentive, and often happy, babies seem to revel in their ever expanding mental abilities. Being able to initiate social interactions also delights them, and they try to keep these exchanges going.

Improvements in the baby's visual perception make many of these cognitive and social developments possible. A particularly important advance is that visual acuity now moves more closely to adult levels. Now babies can actually see quite clearly, and they find many things in their surroundings they want to examine more closely. Better sight helps guide reach so that, in fact, a baby can take hold of and investigate objects that are of interest. Improved perceptual abilities also help babies distinguish familiar people, and this leads to more developed preferences for their own caregivers.

The baby's fine motor skills develop to the point that she can pick up many objects although small items elude her. By the end of this period, she can easily hold a toy. Gross motor skills are coming on-line rapidly, and by the time she's seven months of age, she can sit unassisted, stand with help, and occasionally crawl for a few moments.

By and large, throughout this period the baby is an enthusiastic explorer, and as she approaches the end of this phase of development, she becomes more receptive to social games. Actively investigating her surroundings and playing games with caregivers help advance her nascent mental abilities in several ways. Attention improves. Increased sensitivity to her surroundings helps her develop additional expectations about events. She displays basic communication skills, that is, she is getting better at coordinating gestures and vocalizations to indicate that she wants to be moved or needs something to eat.

Babies of this age can anticipate certain events. The sound of a door being slammed and a shout of "I'm home!!!" signal the appearance of an older brother. The experience of anticipation and the excitement of fulfillment (when the brother actually appears and touches her cheek) reinforce the baby's pleasurable memories. Sometimes, though, anticipation leads to disappointment: the expected event does not occur, or a favorite plaything is beyond reach. Then delight gives way to tears. Sometimes, too, during these months changes in everyday schedules provoke irritability because the baby has gotten used to a pattern of sameness. It's helpful when parents keep in mind the cognitive abilities of a five- or six-month-old and recognize that their baby's crying can have psychological causes (boredom). Sensitivity to this fact makes soothing so much easier.

Overall, these four months are an exciting time for baby and parents. Being able to do more things with her hands, briefly experiencing the thrill of self-locomotion, developing knowledge about everyday happenings, participating in entertaining social events, and having the ability to get attention when she needs it bring pleasure to the baby. In turn, parents are often delighted with the psychological and physical growth of their baby.

Lastly, it's helpful to know that many babies start to teethe at this age, and teething often goes along with increased crying. Be prepared to give extra soothing; your baby will appreciate it.

Four Months

- rolls from tummy onto back

- reaches tentatively

- hears soft sounds

- initiates smile to familiar people

Among the changes that occur this month, four stand out: the baby is more energetic; she uses her hands more and more; she holds miniconversations with people and with her toys; she shows nascent signs of an emotion similar to anger every now and then.

The baby's general peppiness is particularly evident in interactions with people. She stares alertly when talked to, responds with coos, then stops cooing and waits to be talked to again. She's keenly interested in some of her toys and coos to them from time to time. The baby's increased energy and animation result from consistently improving sleep habits and digestion, better vision and hearing, increasing freedom from constraints imposed by reflexes, and greater strength in neck, shoulder, and chest muscles.

Whereas hand play and exchanging social smiles captured the baby's interest last month, attempting to reach for toys is the passion this month. When the four-month-old is propped in her infant seat, her arms lie still at her sides. Her father brings her a small toy rattle and slowly shakes it. Her arms pump up and down, her lips open, she breathes heavily, she coos and gurgles, she kicks her legs, and her arms reach out with big, fast movements. She's working out! Her hands touch the rattle every so often.

A month ago, the baby was perfectly content to be held and talked to for hours on end, but now her behaviors show that she wants to do other things as well. While being held, she suddenly squirms, trying to make contact with a toy. It is clear that at this moment she wants to touch a toy while being held. Now that people and toys are both important to her, you can help your baby's explorations by providing her with a few interesting playthings and a bright, quiet corner, where you can be nearby. She doesn't want to be left alone.

Increasingly, developmental changes assume growing importance. This month a baby's new behaviors reflect specific developmental advances such as reaching: the advances also support the growth of other behaviors. Because reaching is more proficient, the baby's awareness of nearby space becomes more precise, she learns more about her own body and its actions, and she experiences more pleasure due to successful toy encounters. In other words, skill in one area of behavior is a stepping-stone for others.

Here's another example, which concerns how head control and visual attention begin to work together and thus improve each skill even more.

This month the baby's head control is quite good, whereas before she really had to work to prevent her head from sagging. She doesn't have to expend as much effort keeping her head up, so she channels this energy elsewhere. Some of the energy goes toward visually exploring more distant objects in her room. The baby looks intently and repeatedly at the table, a chair, and the windows in the room. As she looks, she's beginning to learn more about the shape and color of the objects in her surrounding space.

Because the baby can hold up her head relatively well, her visual perception gets better. She looks around longer, clearly sees objects that are across the room, and becomes able to distinguish additional shapes and forms. Turning her head this way and that exercises her neck muscles and helps reinforce head control. This cycle of feedbacks continually improves the baby's motor and visual skills. But something else is also happening. She is taking in new information; her cognitive skills are improving along with her motor and perceptual skills.

Despite all these behavioral advances, every once in a while four-month-olds remind us that they are still very, very young. They become overloaded with sights and sounds, and they wear themselves out working so hard to reach their toys. And then they become irritable. Some days they can't seem to maintain their alertness, they don't smile and coo very much, and sleep doesn't come easily. Being held is the only thing that reduces their discomfort, and some nights an extra feeding helps.

◆ IMAGES OF DEVELOPMENT

Motor Control

Overall, four-month-olds are much stronger than they were just a month ago. Back muscles are more active, legs are beginning to show some sturdiness, and arms move vigorously when reaching for a toy. In fact, the baby is strong enough now to roll over.

Neck muscles that were so fragile a short time ago are stronger this month, and head control is often sustained whether the baby is on his tummy or his back or held upright. If placed on their tummies, many babies can raise their head to a ninety-degree angle to the mattress and hold this position for minutes at a time. When a baby is on her back and her arms are gently pulled to raise her into a sitting position, she tries to help by lifting her head and shoulders just a bit.

The baby's trunk muscles are strong enough for her to roll over from her tummy to her back. The first rolling over can happen any time now, so the baby can't be left unattended on a bed. Like most new behaviors, rolling over just happens one day. The baby likes the feel of this new activity and tries to repeat it. After she has repeated it once, she soon gets the hang of it and rolls over often. But once she gets on her back, she's stuck; she doesn't have enough muscle strength to roll over from back to tummy, and this irritates her.

Her back is also too weak to maintain an unsupported sitting position. Her fetal posture is gradually disappearing, but just below the shoulder girdle, her back is still gently rounded. She needs a bit more lower back strength for unpropped sitting.

At four months the baby shows that she is keen to get on with moving all parts of her body on her own. She stretches her legs out when she is lying on her tummy, and she makes slow steplike movements when she is held upright. These stepping movements are far more controlled actions than the reflex movements she displayed as the younger baby.

The baby's reach is guided by her vision: she looks at her hands while they move toward a toy. Later on she will bypass looking at her hands and look directly at the toy she wants. For now, she's taking the time and practice she needs to make her hands and eyes work together efficiently. You'll notice that your baby's reaching movements are often circuitous at this age.

About half the time the baby approaches toys with both hands; the other half, with either the right or left hand. If she successfully grasps a toy, it may be for just a few seconds. Sometimes she can bring the toy close to her eyes for inspection and then move it to her mouth to suck on. Other times she holds the toy with one hand and fingers it momentarily with the other, looking all the while at the toy. At this age she needs to direct all of her visual attention to hold onto the toy. If she is distracted from her goal, she drops the toy. But she tends to be persistent and tries again, and in a month or two this persistence will pay off. She will be able to hold onto two toys at the same time, although very briefly.

Even though the four-month-old's grasp is still immature, it is good enough for her to hold onto a one-inch-cube or a small rattle. She primarily uses her palm and cupped fingers. Smaller objects, such as pellet-sized pieces of cracker, still elude her. At four months her fingers are not very flexible and her thumb is not yet mobile: it does not move independently of her other fingers or hand. Despite these limitations, she scratches the tabletop, clutches at a cloth or a part of her body, and rubs her head with her fist. But when she touches and grabs a part of her body, it seems as if she mistakes her body for another toy; she does not seem to understand that it is she who causes the touch.

Perception

Vision. At two months it was necessary to coax the baby into an attentive state in order to get her to look at a toy. Sometimes the enticement worked; other times it did not. Now attention is rapt and sustained for minutes on end. Sometimes attention is so intense that the baby seems to be trying to commit a view to memory.

Looking behavior with toys differs from visual attention to people. Toys elicit sustained concentration, whereas attention to people involves repeated sequences of looks and turning away. There's a reason for this difference. A toy has a finite number of stimulating attributes: color, shape, possibly movement, and perhaps a repetitive sound. The baby's visual skills handle these stimuli without any difficulty.

People, on the other hand, represent a complex spectacle made up of ever changing stimuli. Heads bob up and down, faces smile or frown, mouths show teeth or are closed, and voice sounds are variable—soft, loud, shrill, deep. Even a person's trunk and limbs move periodically, and fingers move constantly. Inadvertently, people can present a brief information overload for four-month-olds. As a result they turn away for a few seconds simply to take a break from all this sensory stimulation. Once they regain composure, they return to look intently. For the baby a person is the equivalent of a complicated, flashing neon sign that is fun and exciting to look at. But even adults must turn away momentarily from the intensity of neon's color and movement.

A baby of four months is aware of different primary colors, differentiates shapes, distinguishes sizes, and detects movement, and now begins to recognize differences in texture. She sees little objects that are nearby and bigger objects that are at a distance. And she seems to prefer red and blue to other colors.

Studies of babies' visual perception show that while four-month-olds see distinctly, they focus on parts of an object rather than on the whole. Babies might be mesmerized by the head and hair of a rag doll and totally ignore its body or feet. The doll for the baby is the head and nothing else.

Hearing. This month the baby is better able to hear some soft sounds. She hears tiptoe steps and the rustle of paper being crumpled. She's curious about sounds and will turn to look at the place where a noise came from.

The baby is a keen listener to human speech and behaves as if she were suddenly aware of the nuances of spoken language. Studies show that she is more responsive to infant-directed speech than to the typical conversational speech adults use with each other. Most of us talk to babies using exaggerated intonations and changes of pitch, which is a sure way to get their attention.

Vocalizations and Language

The baby now coos often and plays with sounds as if they were toys. She repeats sounds over and over sometimes with minor variations in intonation. This month consonants appear in the baby's speech, primarily *m, k, g, p,* and *b*. There is nothing magical about these letters—they are just the easiest for the baby to produce. Sometimes the baby will combine a consonant with a vowel: "Aah, gaa."

Two well-known language researchers, Roberta Golinkoff and Kathy Hirsh-Pasek, report that starting at about four months, babies' vocalizations sound as if they purposefully manipulate their speech sounds, sometimes whispering, other times seemingly shouting. Moreover, babies' vocalizations sound more like real speech when they interact with adults than when they vocalize to toys.

Although crying doesn't disappear, on balance four-month-olds cry less than younger babies. One reason is that they are visually and motorically more competent and so are better able to distract themselves. They do cry when bored, when they want attention, and when they are just plain overloaded with sights and sounds. Many babies of this age have clearly different cry sounds now for hunger and sleepiness, so it is easier for parents to respond to crying. Whimpers substitute now for coughs and grunts as a means of attracting attention, and seeing mother may elicit a whimper simply because it brings her to the baby.

Cognition

This month, not only does the baby reach out to touch toys, she also begins to use her hands to investigate anything she can touch. Her probes are tentative; she just barely touches the fingertips to a toy. (It will be another four months or so before she engages in self-controlled sustained play.) As slight as these finger movements are, they help the baby make more discriminations about toys. Touching also benefits her visual explorations because touch and vision combined help her sustain her attention. Toy play gives daily practice to the baby's nascent cognitive skills.

Last month the baby showed signs of anticipation when familiar and regularly scheduled events occurred. This month these skills get better. Often babies show anticipation as soon as they see a cue for an everyday occurrence; they might open their mouths upon seeing their mother's breast or a bottle. They may make wriggling movements when first propped for feeding as if they can't wait to eat!

Social Development

This month the social smile becomes even more social. The baby consistently smiles in response to another's smile and frequently initiates a smile to a familiar person. When smiling becomes selective, the baby shows that she recognizes the distinctiveness of some people, which is a milestone in social awareness. The first step in feeling close to another person is the ability to distinguish this one person from others, and a second involves defining the person's action in some way that leads to feeling good. Next month this might include being held a particular way. Babies of this age also signal their feelings about others with various cues: they might whimper when a favored person leaves their line of vision, subtly raise an arm an inch or two *asking* to be picked up, or even engage in playful vocal interactions.

Social interactions also include baby-initiated games. The baby rolls over from tummy to back but can't roll in the other direction on his own. He cries. The baby's mother comes to his rescue, rolling him to his tummy. The baby smiles and immediately rolls over to his back. He looks at his mother and smiles again. She turns him over. And just as soon as he's on his tummy, he rolls over again. He looks at his mother and smiles again. Okay, she's gotten the message—he wants *her* there—and she plays the game for a while.

Emotions

The baby's range of emotion skills is expanding. He laughs at certain sounds such as *cluck-cluck*, laughs when tickled, and gurgles a throaty sound with anticipation. A laugh is a glorious sound that signals genuine pleasure. Some of the most effective ways to elicit a laugh are to play peekaboo or to gently tickle the baby.

There is evidence from laboratory studies that starting at about four months babies discriminate among facial expressions of others and more easily discriminate faces that represent an extreme emotional state. This developmental growth suggests that babies are increasingly sensitive to the perceptual configurations of faces and thus learn to discriminate different facial expressions. Does this mean that babies of this age understand the meaning of a facial expression? This is unlikely; however, there is disagreement about this among developmental researchers.

◆ DEVELOPMENTAL CLOSE-UP

Grasping Abilities

Most of us don't think consciously of our hands as tools, but tools they are. Hundreds of times each day, our hands serve us: they make our bodies presentable to others, assuage our hunger, commit our ideas to paper, play chess, knit a sweater, set a table, and give love. Although we share with nonhuman primates the ability to grasp, we are the only species that has a truly opposable thumb, a thumb that can move in an arc around the palm, and a thumb tip that can meet the tip of any one of our other fingers. These movements provide the extraordinary hand precision that is a characteristic of many of our everyday activities. We button the tiniest of buttons, pick up the crumb of bread dropped on the floor, and take hold of the strand of hair that has blown across our eyes.

Let's look at the baby's development of grasp. The story begins with precursor arm reaches observed during the newborn period. However, the baby's development of a voluntary and controlled grasp starts with a strong body foundation that can support the baby's arm and hand. This often occurs at around four months when babies' shoulder girdles and upper trunks stay firm when the baby reaches out (against gravity) for a toy.

Reaching and grasp develop somewhat separately. Reaching involves the arm unit, which must become coordinated before grasp can be used effectively. Claes von Hofsten in his studies of babies' reaching movement has found that effective and coordinated reaching depends on a baby's ability to produce a fairly straightforward reach trajectory rather than a reach that is composed of several trajectories. This means that a successful reach involves only a small number of discrete reaching movements. Of course, as Esther Thelen reminds us, effective reach and grasp also involve babies' awareness of an object that is reachable and graspable. Vision will play an important role, at the very least in giving feedback to the baby about the necessity of *correcting* a reach or grasp.

At four months, the development of reach and grasp is aided because of the inhibition of the grasp reflex: The baby now has more control of his fingers. Thus, when toys are dangled in front of him, he reaches out as best he can and, if able, moves his fingers over the objects. His fingers with their sensitive nerve endings provide inputs about the characteristics of things he touches: This thing is soft, that thing is hard. This kind of feedback helps the baby learn about the properties of objects and how they should be held.

Initially, when the baby holds a toy, it is his palms rather than his fingers that do most of the holding. And it is primarily the little finger side of the palm that is involved. This palm grasp is precarious, not very accurate, and requires a great deal of baby energy to use. Gradually the baby's grasp begins to involve more of the thumb side of the palm, and after several weeks the baby actually holds a toy between thumb, palm, and base of the index finger.

But this first thumb, palm, and index finger grasp looks a bit like the grasp of a chimpanzee: the thumb makes contact with the side, rather than the tip, of the forefinger. This is called the "scissors grasp," and it is useful and functional but not perfect for our human activities. Try picking up a small safety pin with a scissors grasp!

The true fingertip grasp is the most precise grasp of all, enabling us to engage in very precise and delicate tasks. This wonderful fine motor skill, one of the last steps in biology's contribution to grasp development, comes about when the baby's thumb rotates away from his hand, and his thumb and forefinger tips can meet, making a letter O—at about ten to eleven months. Now the baby needs practice to become really skilled in using the fingertip grasp, and he gets it every day by playing with toys and learning to pick up a bit of food and bring it to his mouth.

The development of grasp takes about half a year. As the baby approaches his first birthday, grasp will be accompanied by the ability to release objects voluntarily. These two skills, grasp and release, prepare the baby for learning specific hand skills, such as holding a spoon, cutting with scissors, and building a sand castle. When you look at the dexterity of a four-year-old as he constructs a toy robot, it can be hard to remember the four-month-old who struggled so hard to take hold of the mobile in his crib.

Last, researchers have shown that the development of reach and grasp is not a lockstep process that is identical for all babies. While it is a given that all healthy babies learn to reach and to grasp—after all this is part of our human heritage—it is also true that babies differ in their paths to grasp. Some babies are more coordinated than others, some make many movement detours as they try to grasp, and some find more enjoyment in large muscle activities than in fine motor actions. These variations, though interesting, do not appear to have major implications for the overall development of a baby's grasp. What does seem to matter in the long term is what we do with our hands—as tinkerer, woodworker, musician, painter, knitter, baseball player, computer designer, or average Joe/Jane—our brains, and our goals.

Five Months

- wiggles on tummy

- makes incipient crawling movements

- follows another's gaze

- imitates caregiver's vocal intonations

- smiles at self in mirror

The five-month-old is an explorer, sensitive to and interested in his surroundings. He goes beyond simply looking and touching; he carefully and systematically observes faces and toys. He is equally interested in his own and others' sounds, and he stays quite still so that he can listen closely to the speech and the other sounds that surround his space.

The baby's curiosity extends to learning about his body. He closely watches his hands and fingers as he grasps, rubs, and strokes toys. He purposefully moves the back of his head back and forth against his mattress as if confirming the existence of a body part that he cannot see. His legs particularly captivate him, and he repeatedly raises one leg and then the other when he is held in a standing position. Lying on his back, he sometimes tries to bring his feet toward his face. He might reach out and grab a foot, and struggle to bring the foot to his mouth. Once in while, he might actually be successful and nibble his toes. You'll notice that in a couple of months, having had lots of practice and obviously enjoying the control over their own bodies, babies become quite skilled in foot-to-mouth play.

At five months, babies are becoming less distracted by intrusions. Until now their activities could be at the mercy of the comings and goings of a family member or visitor, and a disruption often meant the end of self-initiated play. Now a baby handles interruptions fairly easily. He might be reaching toward a mobile when his sister thrusts a teddy bear in front of his face. Although he turns toward her and the bear, he can also smile at her, and easily turn back to his mobile. He can ignore the distraction because of his improved ability to focus and to control his attention. Learning becomes easier with controlled attention.

Babies of this age seem to sense their expanding abilities, and now, when they can't do something, they clearly indicate frustration. Mentally willing but physically unable to crawl, they are sometimes thwarted in their efforts to get nearer to interesting things. In a valiant effort to get to an interesting toy, they perch on their tummy, elevate their arms and legs, and "swim" rapidly. But this physical exertion is all for naught, and they often break out with a loud "Aaaaah." Everything about these actions says, "I want!" Help your baby in situations like these. You'll be contributing to a happy baby.

When a five-month-old is relatively calm, he is more skilled at sending signals to others, and at these times he simultaneously seeks eye contact and makes noises (grunts, laughs, coughs) as if to say, "Come here, please!" He is learning that gestures combined with sounds other than cries work well at getting another person's attention. At this age, gestures to parents are mostly subtle, so it's helpful when parents consciously tune in to their baby's arm and hand movements and the sounds their baby produces—in relation to specific situations. Parents are often delighted when they detect consistency in their baby's new signals.

Babies of this age often seem so capable that it is easy to imagine that they have all kinds of mental abilities. They don't. Watch when something appears in a new guise: a five-month-old can be thoroughly bewildered. It takes him a while to realize that his father is the same person even without his mustache or that his sister is still his sister, though her long, straight hair is now a mass of frizzy curls. After drinking orange juice exclusively from a bottle, a baby can be surprised when he is given orange juice in a baby cup. He seems amazed to discover that orange juice is orange juice, whether it comes in a bottle or a cup.

✦ IMAGES OF DEVELOPMENT

Motor Control

At this age, the baby's neck, shoulder, and upper chest muscles are sturdy, his back is almost fully straight from head down to hips, and his abdominal muscles are firm to the touch. When the five-month-old lies on his tummy, these strengthened muscles help support the upper part of his body.

The baby rolls over from tummy to back and back to tummy. He makes incipient crawling movements, precursors of the conventional crawl that will appear at about seven months. Sitting on his own is still difficult, because he still doesn't have the required trunk strength and postural control. On rare occasions he does manage to sit alone momentarily, but soon flops over.

Around five months of age, reaching is most often accomplished by one arm, although two-arm reaches do still occur. Overall, the baby's reach is less variable this month, in part because it is now almost always visually guided. He may still fling his arms now and then because he is not always able to anticipate the minute arm adjustments that are required for a precisely guided reach. Amazingly, though, when he reaches toward a rolling toy car, he is usually fairly adept at adjusting the pace of his reach to the toy's speed. The baby is increasingly coordinating the act of reaching with the desired goal of taking hold of a toy.

The five-month-old typically approaches most toys with a push-pull scraping action, with palms and fingers cupped as he attempts to adjust his hand to the shape of a toy. He grasps as well as he can and is undeterred by failures. He has considerable difficulty with small objects (a bit of cracker), and although he repeatedly makes scratching movements, his attempts are usually in vain. Uncoordinated finger movements are the reason he cannot pick up small items.

At five months, babies are sufficiently skilled in handling toys to free up attention that previously went to monitoring the acts of reaching and grasping. When they succeed in grasping a toy, they visually inspect it, smile and vocalize to it, and then mouth it for a short examination with their lips. If the baby has two toys in front of him, he manages to hold one while looking at the other. However, this is the limit of their coordination of attention and grasp: if a toy is placed in each of their hands, they invariably drop one.

Late in the month, babies begin to transfer a toy from one hand to the other and to lift a cup by wrapping a hand around it. Considering that they only gained control of their hands a short while ago, these actions are quite an achievement and demonstrate the growth of hand-eye coordination.

These hand activities are important preludes to actual toy play. In about two months the baby will purposefully and gleefully fling toys from a table-top. Another month after that he will studiously examine a toy by turning it over and over in his hands.

Perception

Vision. Vision is still getting sharper and clearer, and the baby begins to pay attention to smaller and less obvious things, such as a little piece of paper lying on the floor or a particular facial feature such as a parent's nose. The baby continues to be fascinated by movement. In fact, movement so intrigues the five-month-old that, given the choice between an interesting or motionless toy and a less interesting toy that moves, the baby invariably chooses to look at the moving toy.

The baby's perception of depth is also improving, as is his perceptual differentiation of colors. Babies even show preferences for specific colors, often preferring objects with clear versus mixed hues. They tend to prefer blue over violet, yellow over orange. In general, red is a favorite. Other studies show that the baby recognizes a face, whether he observes it in a right-side-up position or upside down. When the baby is able to recognize an object regardless of its spatial orientation, scientists say that the baby has acquired a skill called *form constancy.*

Hearing. The five-month-old listens quietly to others' conversations, and his attention is easily captured by baby talk that is addressed specifically to him. He also distinguishes between phrases that reflect approval and those that signify disapproval. He invariably reacts with signs of pleasure to positive speech and becomes sober at the sound of negative speech. His different facial expressions reveal that he is discriminating sounds and sights in his surroundings.

Facial responses to different sound qualities may reflect a primitive understanding of emotions or they may simply be a genetically programmed reaction to the more melodious sound features of positive speech. Scientists do not agree about this. In any event, the five-month-old's attention to the details of speech helps him become familiar with the language used by people in his culture.

Vocalizations and Language

Consonant sounds (*agu, grr*) are more varied and more frequent this month. The baby's vocalizations also show a drift toward the language of the baby's cultural environment; that is, his intonation and the relative length of his utterances sound more and more like those of his caregivers.

Although the changes in the baby's early vocal production are strongly influenced by a biological game plan, the shaping of the baby's actual sounds largely depends on the speech he hears. In other words, without conscious awareness of what he is doing, the baby shapes his vocalizations so that they resemble the rhythm of the sentences spoken by his caregivers. At five months of age, a baby reared in the United States by English-speaking parents and a baby reared in China by Chinese-speaking parents both make consonant sounds, but the melody of their vocalizations already differs.

Cognition

An interesting behavior emerges this month, in which the baby visually follows an object that moves out of her line of vision. This behavior is seen quite often in the baby's play. When a baby plays with her rattle and it falls out of her hand, she turns her head to watch the rattle descend to the floor. This visual-pursuit behavior, which seems so simple, suggests that babies understand that a moving rattle is still a rattle. This intuitive understanding of the constancy of an object when in motion and when still probably helps the baby become more sensitive to specific features of objects and people. We cannot say for certain that this is one value of visual pursuit, but it is true that this behavior emerges at the same time recognition memory time is lengthening. In fact, some studies suggest that babies now remember certain illustrations, such as pictures of faces, for as long as two weeks.

Social Development

A social counterpart to visual pursuit appears now: the baby follows another person's gaze. The baby sits on her father's lap, and they are looking at her cereal bowl. The father talks about the bowl, and, while talking to her, he glances away from her to look at the bowl. Watching her father's eyes as he turns to view the bowl, the baby slowly shifts her gaze in tandem with his. Gaze following demands attention, and thus it helps the baby practice controlling her visual focus. Gaze behavior also introduces her to the idea of using her vision to secure information from her caregivers. In a few months babies look toward a caregiver's face as if seeking cues about how to respond to new situations.

When a five-month-old matches her looking behavior to that of her caregiver, she signals to others that she can be influenced in a new way. Parents notice this cue and intuitively make adjustments in their own actions to facilitate the baby's learning. Parents may hold the baby so that she can look in the same direction as they are looking. They glance more often to an object they are talking about to assist her in making associations between the words they are saying and the object.

One additional social development occurs this month that is important in the overall scheme of things. Now a baby easily recognizes a few differences between familiar and unfamiliar people. She sometimes becomes quiet and sober at the sight of strangers, although she does not actually cry. In another two or three months, distress around strangers often intensifies, and negative responses are more intense. But for now, the baby simply signals that something is not quite right by being more silent than usual.

Emotions

Last month laughter materialized, and this month unqualified glee appears. The joy is unbridled when a baby plays with toys or with his parents. It is rather fun to sit back and observe your baby laugh at a teddy bear, at a mobile, and even at the leaves of a tree swaying in the wind.

Intense pleasure can go along with intense negative emotions, which might appear when babies sense their own limitations. When on his back, a baby sees something fascinating come into view and tries to reach it. He wriggles and tries to turn over, but he can't, so he kicks his feet and whimpers. This is the turtle frustration fret, so named by one of my assistants. The baby looks like a turtle that has somehow turned over onto its back and can't right itself again. Everything about the baby's actions communicates, "I want to, but I can't." A little bit of disappointment is okay, but too much leads to a sad baby. Keep an eye out for signs that help is needed now rather than later.

Sense of Self

A baby of this age now smiles at her image in a mirror. Psychologists have different ideas about why this happens. Some say she is simply reacting to another face. Others suggest that she perceives the face as a familiar person (or object) and this brings on her smile. But some scientists regard this display as a precursor of the development of a sense of self: the smile registers the baby's nascent awareness of her own body.

While not everyone agrees about why the baby smiles at her self-image, scientists do agree that a nascent form of self-awareness is the cause of a primitive form of resistance observed at this age. Resistance behaviors tend to appear in two ways. One involves pushing-away hand movements; a baby does this when she is offered food she does not like. The other occurs when a baby clamps her mouth shut and turns her head from side to side after tasting something that doesn't appeal to her. Don't let these resistant behaviors irritate you. They truly reflect the baby's growth as a person.

✦ DEVELOPMENTAL CLOSE-UP

Pushing, Pivoting, Crawling, and Creeping

I sometimes suggest to my students that one way to gain a sense of the baby's world is to get down on all fours and creep. When students actually do this, they invariably comment about how restricted they feel and how glad they are to be able to walk upright! That's a good sign: humans are meant to walk. Creeping is simply not convenient for us: eye contact is difficult to maintain, transporting objects is a real challenge, and the pace restricts how far and fast you can go. However, creeping is wonderful for babies for it brings them freedom to move around on their own. And they love it!

Creeping comes on-line in a series of developments. First it is an abdomen-elbow movement; in time, this matures into a position where the abdomen is off the floor and the arms are straight. The various styles of creeping are called wiggling, which occurs at about five months; pivoting, at about six to seven months; crawling, at seven to nine months; and creeping, at nine to eleven months. Babies vary considerably in the age at which they begin any of these stages, but most children crawl at around seven months and begin creeping about two months later. But do be aware that some babies these days start creeping somewhat later. This seems to be the case for babies who spend most of the day on their backs and of course sleep on their backs for safety reasons.

Wiggling occurs when the baby, lying on his tummy, inadvertently moves his body because his legs kick out and his arms move. In contrast, pivoting is a circular kind of movement the baby makes while lying with much of his weight supported by knees, abdomen, and chest. The pivot point is under the abdomen, and it is the baby's vigorous kicking movements that cause him to move in a roundabout fashion and occasionally forward or backward. Pivoting is not efficient, but it does let the baby move his whole body a short distance. More important, pivoting is a purposeful movement that occurs when the baby wants a better view of something.

A month or so after pivoting appears, tentative signs of crawling materialize. Crawling labels the motion in which, with abdomen touching or lying slightly above a supporting surface, the body pushes along as a function of alternate, reciprocal movements of elbows and legs. There is a commando version of crawling in which reciprocal movements of the elbows pull the body forward. In contrast to pivoting, crawling produces appreciable forward-and-backward activity.

In creeping, the baby's hips are bent, his knees are tucked under the lower abdomen, and his straight arms hold his chest and shoulders well above the level of the floor. The baby moves with hands and lower legs touching the floor. (Some babies creep with their buttocks up in the air and with only their hands and feet touching the floor; they look like an inverted U.) Creeping requires good shoulder strength as well as trunk and hip strength to hold the body above the floor in a stable position. Most babies need some practice in the creeping position before they actually begin moving about. Typically, babies try out the creeping position between nine and ten months and start to creep about four weeks later.

"Wait a minute," you might be saying to yourself, "I learned that creeping comes before crawling." Yes, some writers do say that creeping precedes crawling. I follow the terminology of the foremost experts of developmental norms, Arnold Gesell and Nancy Bayley, who long ago described crawling in terms of the baby on his tummy and creeping with the baby on all four limbs (tummy off the ground).

Over the years a mystique has arisen about crawling and creeping, probably because these are the baby's first forms of independent locomotion. Some professionals claim that crawling/creeping and reading or crawling/creeping and learning are linked. They assert that babies must crawl in order to avoid later problems with cognitive skills. However, there is no scientific evidence supporting an association between crawling and later educational achievement. In fact, a few babies never crawl, and some hitch around on their buttocks. They are just fine developmentally.

Some parents tell me they've been advised that babies who do not crawl or creep in a certain way may have a serious motor disorder. It is true that a markedly peculiar style of crawling (such as using only one leg for propulsion and dragging the other) may indicate a serious motor problem. But there would usually have to be signs of other developmental lags in head, shoulder, and/or trunk control for a crawling style to be a sign of permanent impairment.

However, don't hesitate if you think something is not quite right. In fact, not too long ago I saw a baby who had a subtle drag in one leg as he crawled, and a slightly unusual walking stance. After he made a couple of visits to our laboratory, where I still observed these unusual patterns, I suggested his parents check with a pediatric neurologist just to be sure that motor development was okay.

Scientists have recently become interested again in crawling, creeping, and walking. Their renewed research efforts show that all of these forms of self-produced locomotion are important sources of learning. Babies learn about their bodies as they move around in different postures, positions, and situations. These various experiences also force babies to obtain new information about their surroundings; for example, about space and objects (furniture) in space. They begin to pay attention to the rigid boundaries of a table leg in the middle of the floor or the space beneath a table. Often they monitor distance to people and to toys, which translates into the ability to gauge how to avoid bumping into walls. They learn about surfaces that feel good to crawl on (low-pile carpet) and those that are uncomfortable (sidewalk). A whole new world of textures and tactile sensations opens for babies.

Crawling and creeping are tools that help babies learn about their surroundings, particularly space and spatial landmarks, and about their own bodies. These actions also provide them with a nascent sense of mastery, independence, and pleasure, which grows even more when babies start to walk.

Six Months

- briefly sits without support

- transfers toy from hand to hand, and bangs toy

- develops expectation about familiar event

- touches and vocalizes to parent

Every now and then, development takes a giant step forward, and the baby suddenly seems far more capable than before. This month is one of these times. There is all-around growth in the baby's skills. These are some of the achievements often seen at this age:

- ✦ rolls over easily and inches forward when on belly
- ✦ sits alone momentarily
- ✦ supports most of weight in a standing position, when assisted
- ✦ distinguishes between male and female voices
- ✦ makes sounds that bear resemblance to speech
- ✦ learns the behaviors that characterize familiar people
- ✦ sees almost everything with good vision
- ✦ emits specific whines for attention

This impressive list of behaviors is ample evidence for labeling this month a pivotal age in early development. One example of the baby's new competence is her increasing precision at sending messages about what she wants. She not only recognizes what she wants, she demonstrates from time to time that she can figure out what she needs to do to get what she wants and does it. Here's an example. A baby is sitting on her mother's lap; she looks directly at her mother, then at the toy her mother is holding, and then she lightly touches her mother's hand. The baby is telling her mother that she wants the toy. When her mother responds to her gestures by offering the toy, the baby may smile broadly as if recognizing the success of her communication. The son of a former student showed how he wanted to hear the song "Itsy-Bitsy Spider." While his mother held him, she sang the song. And when she was finished, the baby looked at his mother, made *eh, eh* sounds, and raised one of his hands ever so slightly. His gesture was subtle.

Sometimes the timing of babies' messages is slightly off. But it is pretty amazing that they use gestures, eye contact, and nonfretful vocalizations to make their wants known, when just a few months ago the only way they could communicate was to cry.

These examples nicely match Barbara Rogoff's research. She and her colleagues systematically studied the various ways babies *use* their mothers to have their wants met. In a series of studies, the babies ranged in age from five or six months to past the first year. By six months, babies often used rudimentary gestures (something like a point), or looked at their mother's face or hands as a way to get their message across.

This month also marks a period of important and far-reaching changes in the baby's perception of sounds, especially speech, and in the baby's vocalizations. Parents are most likely to notice a more speechlike quality to the baby's vocal productions. Instead of producing isolated vowel sounds, babies begin to vocalize a string of babbles, which is a change due in part to the maturing of the baby's vocal musculature. There are all kinds of small muscles in the throat that contribute to different speech sounds. These muscles develop with everyday use.

Overall then, this is an age marked by significant growth in the number and complexity of the baby's abilities. I particularly like Sybil Escalona's summary of six-month-olds, written decades ago. Six-month-olds, she said, "make things happen." They show anticipation such that when a parent has outstretched arms, the baby expects to be picked up; they show intentionality by producing incipient gestures; they engage in elementary problem solving by looking at falling objects; they show resistance to things they don't like; and they are eager to be part of social interactions.

Escalona also reminds us that as more and more behaviors develop, the degree of variability in babies increases. Six-month-old babies vary in many ways including how they play with toys, how they respond when tired, and how active they are. A highly active baby in one of her studies was "boisterous," loved movement along with social interactions with his mother. His vocalizations were frequent and infectious. In contrast, a highly inactive six-month-old was most content playing with toys in his crib. It was his mother who encouraged him to join in social play. Both of these babies were similar in the level of their developmental skills.

Escalona invariably encouraged parents and professionals to recognize a baby's individual style and to offer caregiving that is sensitive to that style.

✦ IMAGES OF DEVELOPMENT

Motor Control

At six months, the baby's trunk is strong enough to support his rolling over from back to tummy. He also has the strength to sit alone momentarily, provided he leans forward and plants his arms on the floor to maintain his equilibrium. By the end of the month, his balance improves and he sits straighter and for longer periods of time, sometimes even holding a toy, without falling over. He stands with assistance and supports most of his body weight on his legs. If he feels secure while he is being held upright, he bounces up and down and makes gleeful noises.

Grasp now requires less conscious effort. The baby reaches eagerly for toys, and his efforts invoke fewer extraneous body movements. He will make anticipatory adjustments of his hand so that his grasp accommodates the size and shape of objects. Sometimes though, he miscalculates where he should be reaching but tends to persist in his efforts until he is able to grasp the object he wants. Babies of this age can now hold onto a toy in each hand and easily transfer toys from one hand to the other. This is a delightful activity to watch, because babies truly seem to enjoy hand-to-hand transfer.

At the beginning of the month, grasp primarily involves holding a toy between the first and second fingers and the palm. As the month progresses, babies begin to use their thumb in concert with their other fingers, but small objects still elude their grasp. Babies resort to scooping at small objects with the whole hand.

As a baby's hand coordination improves, he is even more inclined to try to bring objects to his mouth. While this creates parent concerns about safety, mouthing is a source of many learning experiences. The lips and tongue have sensitive nerve endings, and the baby can get to know the finer features of texture and shape by mouthing objects. Since the baby attempts this maneuver with anything he can grasp, parents have to take special precautions to see that small objects are out of his reaching range.

Perception

Vision. For a while now, six-month-olds have been able to discriminate the boundary of a toy (the outline of a teddy bear) visually as well as some of the toy's characteristics (teddy's ears), but they have had difficulty taking in both kinds of information at the same time. Studies show that babies of six months easily do this, and researchers infer from the behavior that babies are now beginning to form whole pictures of objects.

With ever increasing visual skills, babies recognize familiar people more clearly. Accompanying this development, mild fretting is displayed if a stranger approaches too closely or too quickly. This negative response is often quite brief.

Depth perception has increasingly become better; babies of this age readily respond to stimuli as a function of object size and distance. Studies also reveal that babies are skilled in figuring out the orientation of objects (up, down, or sideways). And in a display of both perceptual growth and memory, researchers have found that six-month-olds can distinguish one visual pattern from another in a matter of seconds and store this information for periods as long as a few weeks.

Equally impressive is the six-month-old's ability to combine different kinds of information. The baby makes a connection between the input she receives when looking at an object and the information she gets by touching the same object. In one study, babies were given a small square block, but they were prevented from seeing the block in their hand. While they were holding the block, they were shown drawings of a square and a circle. The babies looked more often at the drawing of the square than the drawing of the circle, suggesting that they recognized that this image resembled the object they held. From a functional standpoint, this coordination of vision and touch means that the baby no longer always has to look at the things she holds in her hands.

From a neuroscience standpoint, cross-modal processing suggests some frontal-lobe activation: that is, babies retain information obtained from one sensory system (touch) and then transfer the information to another sensory system (vision).

Hearing. At six months, babies have a keen interest in a variety of sounds. Babies seem most attuned to loudness, intonation, and other acoustic cues. Because music has complex sounds, babies tend to listen intently to nursery songs, music on the radio and TV, and the sounds of instruments. The baby also distinguishes male and female voices; she expects a female voice to go with a female person and a male voice to go with a male person. If this doesn't happen, she registers surprise. The six-month-old is also remarkably good at identifying the *vocal signatures* of the people who are most often around her.

This sensitivity to everyday sounds has developmental implications for language. The baby's hearing is becoming fine-tuned in a manner that makes her most receptive to the speech sounds of her family's language. For example, if a baby lives in an English-speaking family, she hears people around her say words such as "cat" and "tack." The baby is not exposed to people speaking Arabic words that include the sound of *tca*. At around six months, this lack of exposure has an effect on speech perception. If we studied the baby's response to sounds, we would find that she is losing the ability to discriminate the sound *tca*, a sound she had the potential to recognize in earlier months. This fine-tuning progression happens with babies around the world. Japanese babies, for example, become less able to discriminate *r* sounds because *r* is not a sound in the Japanese language.

Vocalizations and Language

Losing the ability to hear certain sounds also fosters the baby's responsiveness to the sounds of his own family's language. This transition in auditory perception occurs gradually and is a function of the multitude of times each day that babies hear words that have certain speech qualities (*cat*, not *tca*).

It is from these repetitions that the baby will learn to produce sounds that mimic the intonation qualities of the family's language. Later on, the baby's speech will also reflect the family's language.

The "talk" of babies of about six months is called *canonical babbling*. It consists of vowels and consonants in a sequence such as *da-da-ga-ga*. The consonants most often used at this age are *g*, *k*, *l*, and *d*. Each syllable in a string of babbles is clearly defined and articulated. Babies babble no matter where they live!

Babbles sound like adult conversational speech in both intonation and "sentence" length, and this indicates that the baby is definitely listening to the speech around him. As far as we can tell, babbles do not have any meaning, but obviously babbling is one way for babies to practice forming sounds. Some scientists believe that babbling prepares the baby for speech production by helping him become better aware of his own sounds and how he can make his sounds vary.

Cognition

Years ago there were arguments about how babies learned, with some arguing for hands as instruments of learning and others for vision. We now know that long before hands are functional, babies take in information. However, hands have an important role in learning, if only because holding onto a toy fosters the baby's attention to the object and its characteristics. In my view, six-month-olds demonstrate active mental activity as they go about holding, transferring, and banging toys. Indeed, babies of this age seem to take more control of their own learning.

Taken together, a number of studies suggest six-month-olds construct some kind of representation of a whole person, which includes more than one or two surface characteristics. They may know a parent by a combination of his appearance, walk, voice, touch, and scent. The baby reveals this knowledge with signs of greeting such as smiles and special babble sounds, and these occur even when the parent is dressed in jeans, a suit, or a bathrobe and whether the parent is smiling or frowning.

There's a decades-old study that was done in a hospital setting that supports the changing cognitive skills associated with this age. Babies of various ages were in a hospital for a variety of illnesses, none of which were life threatening. The researchers were interested in studying how parental leave-taking (that is, separation) affected the babies; not surprisingly, they found that most babies cried when their parents said their good-byes. However, within a relatively brief time span the hospital staff could often console the babies who were younger than six months. Not so the older babies; these babies tended to be inconsolable for long stretches of time. The inconsolable responses suggest the babies had formed an emotional and social bond with very specific individuals, a bond that was most likely based on knowledge and memories of their nurturing parents.

Social Development

At five months of age the baby visually followed another person's gaze to an object held in a hand, and now at six months he follows another's gaze to an interesting object that is farther away. This activity is the beginning of the development of joint attention and is made possible by the baby's ability to pick up and utilize cues from another person's gaze. Joint attention paves the way for more efficient learning and for sharing more social experiences. "Look at the car," you say to the baby while you point to a car. Your familiar voice causes the baby to stop and pay attention, and now the direction of your head tells him where you want him to focus his gaze. You don't have to move the baby physically to the car so that he will look at it.

The age of six months also marks the onset of an elementary form of social imitation. If you bang a toy on a table, the baby will bang a toy. (Babies of this age love to bang toys.) If you smile and move your body toward him, he moves his body ever so slightly toward you. Mimicry behavior develops rapidly over the next six months, and all of it evolves from these first tentative efforts by the baby to be like you.

Emotions

The baby is now beginning to match his emotions to others' emotions. If the mother is sad, then the baby is likely to project sadness. The baby probably doesn't know what it means to be sad, but he can perceive and reciprocate the facial expressions associated with this emotion. This coordination of behavior is another example of the baby's overall mental development: he can integrate what he perceives about others' feelings with how he acts.

In terms of a six-month-old's own emotional displays, he is characteristically a happy little child and wonderfully responsive to people who please him. He shows his pleasure with glee (rocking back and forth, smiling, and laughing), performing solely to make his favorite people also laugh. His ability to distinguish familiar people clearly makes him a bit more wary of strangers. By and large, though, he doesn't fret in the presence of strangers as long as the situation he's in is familiar or family members are present.

Sense of Self

The baby's self-awareness gets a boost with his focus on lower body parts. He might kick his feet and look at his legs while they move. Or he holds a foot up in the air and carefully inspects it. All the while, his attention is intense, as if he is creating an internal model of his own body.

◆ DEVELOPMENTAL CLOSE-UP

Developing Expectations: The Role of Schedules and Routines

When a sequence of events occurs regularly, we begin to anticipate a particular order for these events. Most of the mundane events in our lives—waking up, bathing, dressing, mealtimes, the drive to work—occur within a well-established sequence and predictability. A sequence often represents a routine that we create in order to carry out certain tasks. The routine is an organizational tool for us, but this routine also reduces our cognitive efforts. If need be, the freed mental energy can be directed to other tasks.

In contrast to routines, schedules are time-based limits we impose on our lives. We establish times for waking up, going to bed, work, and recreation. We utilize schedules for each day, for a period of a week or longer. A schedule represents predictability and consistency. The use of schedules also reduces cognitive effort because we don't have to spend time wondering about what will happen next and when it will happen.

Some of our schedules come from the natural world, and others from our social interactions and the experiences we create for ourselves. We expect that day will follow night, when we work there will be compensation, and when we play we will experience pleasure. If our expectations are violated consistently, we become inconvenienced and downright upset.

Schedules and routines help babies in innumerable ways. Most of the young baby's expectations develop from the world caregivers create for her. In other words, when parents provide sameness in the baby's day—for example, recurring and consistent periods of physical care, play, and rest—they facilitate their baby's physiological and behavioral functioning. One neuroscientist suggested that all *systems*—you can read that as all *humans*—need stability for effective functioning. Similarly, when parents structure the baby's immediate living area into places to sit, lie down, and move about, they pave the way for the baby to learn expectations about the consistency of space and the predictability of many events that occur in each niche of living space. And, of course, parents help the baby develop social expectations when the parents are consistently available for play or when they regularly provide soothing in times of fatigue and hurt.

Routines introduce babies to another kind of learning. Routines actually impose restrictions on babies' experiences. One neuroscientist suggests that routines reduce uncertainty and confusion because they mark boundaries that facilitate learning and memory. Parents often use routines for the baby's bath, for dressing, and for preparing for trips to the grocery store or elsewhere. Even more important is the parent's use of the *language of routines* as a teaching device. Long before babies understand language, parents mention a planned activity: "When you wake up tomorrow, we'll first go . . . , and then we'll. . . ."

In addition, routines are pervasive in the socialization of toddlers and older children: parents typically familiarize their children with family norms by describing and actively monitoring routines involved in early-morning personal hygiene, putting toys away, and engaging in family chores. Daily routines of this nature contain a built-in reminder to the child to pay attention to *this* set of actions and *this* sequence of events.

Routines also have central roles in parenting in the contexts of child safety. Here parent-initiated routines are meant solely to govern their own actions that have direct consequences for baby and child. Safety routines involve consciously thinking about objects or experiences that could harm the child, and taking a series of steps to limit the child's exposure to these hazards (e.g., finding ways to restrict child access to floor-level cupboards, free-standing bookshelves, audio equipment).

Developmentally, studies suggest that at six months babies recognize brief everyday routines. Mother, for example, fills the tub with water, gets a towel, assembles fresh clothes, and then puts the baby in the tub. When an infant is able to remember the sequence of an event—bath time—on the basis of a cue that starts the sequence (water in the tub), the next step for the baby is to anticipate the event and to form some kind of memory for the routine. Babies do show they remember: they expect to be fed by certain people and in a certain way, to see certain people when they wake up, and to see caregivers react in certain ways to the babies' own actions. If expectations are not met, the baby will likely show a behavior akin to disappointment.

It is unrealistic to expect that a baby's schedule and everyday routines can be adhered to each day. However, when major changes in the baby's schedule are necessary, do try to ease them in slowly.

Seven Months

- crawls

- distinghishes specific facial features

- exhibits "focused" listening

- investigates toys by dropping them from heights

- enjoys social interactions

- enjoys familiar caregivers

In terms of family activities, at seven months babies are well on their way to new levels of sociability. This change is due to the accumulation of social skills that occurred in earlier months.

- ✦ At two months, your baby made eye contact with you every so often.
- ✦ At two to three months, his social smiles blossomed forth.
- ✦ At four months, he often stopped crying as soon he saw you.
- ✦ At five months, he showed he wanted attention by coughing or grunting or using body language.
- ✦ At six months, his social bids tended to be more specific. He might have looked at you, touched your hand, and perhaps looked again at your face. More than in any previous month, he showed delight when you laughed and played with him.

In the next few months these foundation behaviors are combined and used to create richer forms of social interactions. Playing social games is an example. At around seven months many parents try out new activities and games with the baby such as pat-a-cake, "horsey," and "where are you?" Gradually, the seven-month-old understands that a social game such as pat-a-cake is different from just sitting on his father's lap and playing with his father's fingers. The baby might stare at the new game, make barely perceptible movements, and utter a few sounds as his father coaxes him to play pat-a-cake. He doesn't quite understand the game and his role. In another two months, he'll be a veteran. He delights in "I'm gonna getcha!" The eight-month-old laughs, tugs at his parents' hands or clothing, and babbles away hoping the games will continue. He gets better at participation and also shows other signs of sociability, such as initiating a wave for good-bye and throwing kisses.

By seven months most babies are quite adept with their hands, and they readily reach for anything that seems graspable, particularly if the graspable thing is on a parent. Eyeglasses, a lock of hair, nose and ears, jewelry, clothing, wristwatches, and more become ready prey! Understandably, parents get a bit annoyed and try to change the baby's behavior. A firm "No, that hurts," while briefly holding the seven-month-old's hand begins to get the message across that pulling Mom's hair hurts. Of course, although babies are too young to understand *hurt*, they'll get the gist of the idea.

These attempts to teach babies how to behave are examples of how parents try to socialize their babies to family norms. Basically, socialization involves parents' inputs to children about acceptable kinds of behavior (dos and don'ts). It's helpful to keep in mind that socialization is arduous for parents and baby. Babies don't come equipped with a built-in sense of family norms! Parents soon learn that patience, and then more patience, helps, but so does an understanding that babies of this age are not malicious. They just don't know any better.

Seven-month-olds do have several cognitive and emotional resources that help build their awareness to firm voices and negative facial expressions. One is the baby's growing emotional bond to a parent: he wants smiles and games, not disapproval. Another is his ability to distinguish a happy facial expression from one that is negative (a frown, for example). So even though the baby does not comprehend speech, he can readily associate his action and his parent's negative response. In the months ahead, the baby's ability to "read" faces will improve dramatically and will help him learn which behaviors are acceptable and which cause distress.

The social arena is not the only domain where important changes are occurring. Some form of crawling often appears this month. The baby, tummy touching the floor, propels himself clumsily forward using arms and legs. Babies love the sense of moving on their own. Even though they may only be able to crawl a distance of three or four inches before collapsing, they determinedly practice crawling for minutes, even hours, at a time. The practice pays off. In a matter of weeks they easily cover the length of a room.

Crawling opens up new adventures. Cupboards, furniture, and table legs become accessible. So do electric cords, low shelves, the dog's dish, the garbage pail, and house plants. Here too is another new concern for parents. The only solution is baby proofing floor space. Be watchful.

◆ IMAGES OF DEVELOPMENT

Motor Control

At seven months the baby's shoulders, chest, abdomen, and hips are sturdy enough to support sitting alone and crawling. She is not quite ready to stand on her own because her body is still bent slightly forward at the hips. But the baby's legs are developing strength, and already her legs support her full weight when she's held in a standing position. Not only is the baby stronger now but also her body is remarkably flexible. She easily grabs hold of a foot and puts a toe in her mouth.

If a seven-month-old is placed in a sitting position, she is likely to maintain the position for minutes at a time. She sometimes leans forward on her arms and hands to stabilize her balance. Soon she'll try to get into a sitting position on her own but is not adept enough to move from lying on her back or tummy into a seated position. This movement involves a complicated sequence of maneuvers that are still beyond her.

One new aspect of behavior is the baby's tendency to use one hand instead of both when reaching or grasping. A one-handed reach means the other hand is free: all sorts of opportunities open up. A baby might hold a toy doll in one hand and stroke the doll's head with her other hand. As she does this, she begins to understand that hands are tools. One hand stabilizes an object while another performs actions on the stabilized object. Once again, a stepping-stone effect is in action: improvements in the baby's use of her hands as tools also promote cognitive development and vice versa.

At seven months, this grasp involves mostly the baby's thumb and the first or second finger. This type of grasp permits picking up small objects (pellet size), which seven-month-olds do relatively quickly and easily. However, the baby still isn't able to bring the tips of her thumb and first finger together like adults do; instead, she grasps by using her thumb against the side of her forefinger. In a matter of weeks, play with toys will have strengthened the baby's fingers, and the adult grasp will increasingly materialize. But for now, the challenge is to get the grasp down pat. Parents help by providing small pieces of cracker for practice in self-feeding skills, which coincidentally also improves grasp.

There is occasional clumsiness in the seven-month-old's grasp. She may drop the toy she is holding, yet reaches for it again and again. She is unabashedly enthusiastic in her play and obviously enthralled with the idea that her arms and hands are terrific tools. Between crawling and working with their hands, babies keep very busy.

Perception

Vision. The baby's ability to perceive more subtleties in visual stimuli takes several steps forward at this age. Researchers have demonstrated that the seven-month-old can distinguish between male and female faces, detect the difference between a smile and a frown, recognize a distinctive feature of a face such as a bushy eyebrow or a crooked nose, and remember faces. All these skills help the baby identify familiar and unfamiliar faces and thereby assist in the process of socialization.

Babies of seven months are so intrigued by what they see that they sometimes stop playing to stare at a face. Their gaze is intense, as if trying to etch a face into memory. The baby's visual attention is also intense when playing with toys. He keenly observes how a wheel moves if it is touched or that a toy drops if he pushes it off the table.

Studies also show that the baby is now sensitive to spatial layouts. We can see this at home as a baby crawls. He detours around a box left in the middle of the room and rarely bumps into furniture. He also seems to have a good sense of the path from his room to another nearby room.

Hearing. This month represents yet another key time in language development, primarily in terms of sound perception. The baby listens more selectively to often heard words such as "mommy" or "daddy." She may hold her body very still or change her facial expression to register her attentiveness. In laboratory studies, babies show they can remember a particular word that is embedded in a few brief sentences even if they don't know what the word means. This kind of focused listening, along with memory for a few words, prepares the baby for understanding the link between the sound of a word and a gesture. The fruits of this exertion will be exhibited in a month or two when the baby waves as someone says, "Bye-bye."

When babies begin to remember words, this must mean they are sensitive to the beginning and end of words, and that allows them to distinguish one word from another within a brief sentence. Researchers Golinkoff and Hirsh-Pasek emphasize just how remarkable word segmentation is. Using the analogy of water, they note that speech is like water in that it goes on and on in a continuous stream. We slur words together, and there are no commas or periods in our speech. Thus it is truly noteworthy that actual word segmentation is discerned by young infants and is more or less in place at seven months. Even more extraordinary is the next step. That is word recognition—hearing a word and figuring out what it means. Laboratory studies by Peter Jusczyk and others reveal how babies make the extraordinary leap of linking that segmented sound—a word—to a thing or a person or a feeling. Mostly, at first, the linkage occurs with nouns. In any event, we can state with good evidence that comprehension emerges—for a few words—between eight and ten months. Remember, of course, that these ages represent approximations.

There's another auditory perceptual-learning activity that grows this month, primarily because of babies' improving fine-motor abilities and their visual skills. Most seven-month-olds bang toys, they push toys along a smooth surface, and they bring two toys together. These acts reinforce the baby's knowledge that she can make different sounds occur as she plays with toys. She can also be selective about the toy she chooses to bang simply by looking at the toy and feeling it. In other words, the baby's perception of sound, her visual perceptions, and her motor actions are coming together as an integrated pattern of behavior that will lead to more knowledge.

Vocalizations and Language

Most seven-month-olds babble repeatedly when they are content and in familiar settings. In contrast, they are often very quiet when exposed to new situations. Silence indicates thinking: that is, an appreciation of an unfamiliar setting, uneasiness with it, and the ability to control one's own vocal output.

The vowel and consonant sounds that babies utter and their intonations continue to drift toward the patterns of the language spoken in their immediate surroundings. Babies of this age also tend to invent their own sounds for different occasions.

Cognition

The seven-month-old is keen to study things other than his own body. He might fling himself at his rattles and persist in trying to reach them if they are beyond his grasp. He constantly manipulates the toy he holds, sliding it this way and that, or rubbing, banging, or chewing it. His behavior is purposeful; his attention does not stray. All the while he is collecting information about the relations between his actions and objects. There is a mind at work here.

One of the most fascinating types of exploring at this age is dropping toys from a height. When a baby is sitting in his high chair, the tray is his favorite launching pad. This drop-the-toy activity helps develop a memory of the object, of the object in space, and of space in terms of up here and down there. Dropping toys also contributes to an understanding of an object's characteristics. A dropped rattle makes a different sound than a dropped rag doll. The baby's *dropping games*, though sometimes annoying to parents, help solidify active explicit memory.

Social Development

At this age babies reveal their genuine enjoyment in social interactions. Their bodies often quiver with excitement when greeting a familiar person. Arms are raised in a pick-me-up gesture. And if they feel that they are not receiving a sufficient amount of attention, they cough or make babbling sounds. At seven months, babies have learned to recognize the behaviors that make a favored caregiver laugh. Swaying to the sound of music is a common one.

This is also the age when babies are increasingly receptive to social games such as peekaboo and pat-a-cake. Although their facial expressions show that they are puzzled about the ins and outs of games, they enjoy this kind of social play. They even try to muster an appropriate hand response to pat-a-cake but are largely unsuccessful. By eight months, they will have become more adept and delighted partners.

Emotions

As I've described the behaviors and growing skills of six- and seven-month-olds, I've mentioned how a new skill foreshadows a momentous developmental transition that will occur in the next few months. Earlier, for example, I described how a baby's ability to segment a word from a string of words has enormous implications for word comprehension. Much the same happens with the baby's emotions at this age: there are behavioral signs that herald important changes that will occur in a matter of months. What is on the horizon? The baby's almost immediate interpretation of something amiss when confronted with an unusual toy or a stranger, which is followed by feelings of wariness or fear. On the positive-emotion side, shortly thereafter, babies begin to smile at their own successful achievements. Ever watch a newly walking twelve-month-old pull a rolling pop-up toy? He provides lots of wholesome laughter as he recognizes his great accomplishment.

Okay, so what can we observe at seven months or so? First, babies of this age laugh almost immediately at a happy event, such as his dad playing hide-and-seek with a cloth napkin. Second, there is the immediate display of negative emotions to certain kinds of events. A looming object arouses alarm, the sight of a needle at the doctor's office brings tears, and when it is time to put on an over-the-head shirt the baby tenses, knowing that his arms may be briefly confined. Facial expressions may resemble hurt feelings, where the lip quivers and eyes become downcast and teary, or there may be a wary expression that suggests puzzlement brought about by uncertainty.

Emotion researcher L. Alan Sroufe suggests the development of emotions is tightly linked to the baby's cognitive development. At three months, when babies often smile at others, for example, we can assume they recognize a pleasing stimulus. However, the important point is that the smile is directed to any kind of stimulus, not one that has particular emotional meaning for the baby. Still, the baby's smile, says Sroufe, reflects cognitive *engagement* with his surroundings.

At along about seven months, the baby's cognitive skills include refined perceptual abilities, a set of expectations, and memories for some events and people. Given these capabilities, babies can almost immediately discern events that are within the realm of everyday pleasant experiences and those that are out of the ordinary: thus the baby's immediate delighted greeting to a favorite person and his irritation at an annoying event, such as being bundled into heavy clothes that restrict his movement or being alone in the crib, when in fact he wants company.

Overall then, at this age babies process some kinds of information quickly and make a judgment about the specifics of an event. They will respond immediately to a smiling parent but delay a response to a smiling stranger.

Sense of Self

The baby's sense of self in relation to handling physical space reflects a mix of awareness and disregard. He knows he can make his hands move to play with objects, bring food and toys to his mouth, chew his feet, and move about on the floor, rarely colliding with walls and furniture.

It's surprising then to see how babies blithely ignore particular hazards they approach head on, and of course respond with howls when head and obstacle collide. A seven-month-old had been crawling for about two weeks. Encountering a low coffee table, the baby tried to crawl under it, only to hit his head and cry. His father rescued him. After being soothed, the baby struggled to get down onto the floor. He headed straight to the table and again hit his head. His father retrieved him. Comforted, the baby headed back to the table with the same result. No learning there! No sense of self-protection as yet! No more access to the table. Keep this brief example in mind when you allow your baby floor freedom.

✦ DEVELOPMENTAL CLOSE-UP

Attachment

The six-year-old was a thief. He was also aggressive, hurtful, unrepentant, and unresponsive to love and affection. John Bowlby, the father of attachment theory, described this boy and others like him as *affectionless*—unable to accept or receive love. The six-year-old was so young, and so very troubled. Why? Bowlby set out to find answers.

Although the boy's behavior was similar to a group of other children who also stole and who were referred to the child guidance clinic, Bowlby soon learned their backgrounds differed. Appallingly abusive and neglectful mothers had reared the other boys. In contrast, the six-year-old lived in a good home with kind parents. Puzzled, Bowlby soon found a likely clue. *There had been a protracted separation of child and family.* At eighteen months the boy contracted a serious childhood disease that could have been fatal. Hospitalized for close to a year, he never saw his parents because hospital policies at the time (1930s) forbade visits. Nowadays we understand toddlers' emotional vulnerabilities, but this knowledge is relatively recent. In any event, when the boy returned home, his psyche was bruised: he could not adapt. In his young mind, he might have thought he could be sent away again. His behavior worsened. Attempts at discipline had no effect. It was this troubled history that led the child to the guidance clinic.

Bowlby looked for evidence of separation among the other clinic children, particularly those who were chronic thieves. He found it for about a third. Why does a young child steal? From author Robert Karen: "A child who's been separated from his mother, Bowlby argued, not only craves her love but also the symbols of her love." In other words, *the symbols are found in the things the children steal in their attempts to replace mother love*. Bowlby went on to write extensively about the effects of maternal deprivation—that is, separation—in early life. During the 1940s and 1950s he studied and wrote about disruptions in the mother-and-child relationship, the nature of the young child's tie to her mother, and the foundation of *attachment*. He immersed himself in other theories and ideas. Then in 1969 he authored the first volume, *Attachment*, of the classic *Attachment and Loss*.

A baby's attachment is an emotional tie and is often the baby's first relationship. When baby and mother communicate on an emotional level, the baby begins to feel a sense of confidence in the relationship. The baby becomes attached, so to speak, to her mother, who is available and responsive. Bowlby wrote that human babies and their mothers are biologically endowed with behaviors that foster close interaction. The attachment process starts with the baby's attraction to the mother. Initially the baby's mother feeds and cares for the baby. At around six months or so, the baby begins to discriminate her mother from unfamiliar people. This is followed by the development of the baby's wariness toward strangers. The next step takes place when the baby seeks her mother because something new and strange is occurring. Around the end of the first year, this behavior occurs with some regularity. Bowlby used the term "proximity seeking" to describe the baby's desire to be close to her mother when something unsettling occurs.

Theories need research for corroboration or refutation. This was especially the case for attachment theory because it was often surrounded by controversy. Fortunately, Mary Ainsworth, a developmental psychologist who studied with Bowlby, was eager to apply his ideas to real babies. Whereas Bowlby had laid out the theory of attachment, Ainsworth wanted to measure it and find out how and why babies differ in attachment relationships. Ainsworth collected data from babies and mothers from a yearlong study in Uganda, and then again from a detailed study in the United States. Her research provided essential support for attachment theory in two crucial ways. First, she systematically documented babies' behaviors when they were briefly separated from their mothers, when they were reunited, and when they kept their mothers in sight and played nearby. Ainsworth recorded individual differences among the babies in their reunion scenes. This she linked to the ways mothers cared for their children. Thus Ainsworth's second contribution involved descriptions of mothering that she related to babies that seemed to have good attachment relationships and those that did not. Together, Bowlby and Ainsworth's research provided professionals with a new way to think about the parent-and-child relationship.

In time Ainsworth and her colleagues devised a series of systematic laboratory-based observations in order to measure attachment in year-old babies. The measure was named the Strange Situation (SS), which consists of a brief series of episodes that increase in stress for the baby. Note how Bowlby's *separation theme* is embedded in the SS. The SS starts with mother and baby, then a stranger joins mother and baby, and subsequently mother and stranger take turns *leaving the baby alone*, or with the other. The SS generally lasts about twenty minutes. However, *it is the baby's reactions to being reunited with its mother that are considered crucial and indicative of attachment.* The baby should show pleasure as once again he is with his mother. Doesn't this approach resonate with Bowlby's account of the young thief who came back from his hospital stay and who could not effectively reunite with his mother?

In order to be an effective research and clinical tool, the SS had to provide categories of babies' behaviors that reflected different levels of attachment. So Ainsworth and her colleagues devised a set of categories that were based on the kinds of behaviors displayed by babies when reunited— after separation—with their mothers. The categories were secure, avoidant, and resistant. Years later a fourth category, disorganized, was added. The researchers also determined the SS and its classifications are most appropriate for use with twelve- to eighteen-month-olds.

Using the SS, numerous studies have shown that most babies seek contact with their mothers and are classified as being securely attached. Some babies avoid their mothers, and others alternate between seeking and resisting their mothers. These babies are labeled insecurely attached. Depending on the study and locale, anywhere from 10 to 30 percent of babies in the United States are classified in the latter two groups. The figures vary for other countries.

Bowlby and Ainsworth and a host of researchers put attachment on the research map with many hundreds of studies. Many scientists and clinicians believe that the theory and its measurement provide invaluable insights about the baby's first relationships and the implications for later development. Yet from its earliest days, attachment has been controversial. However, much of the original furor about Bowlby's ideas disappeared relatively quickly. Bowlby moved away from the sole emphasis on mothers as attachment figures. Soon there was realization that babies often have multiple attachment figures. Thank goodness, said fathers and grandparents!

In contrast, debates continue about the use of the Strange Situation to measure attachment: whether the situation is more apt to reflect the baby's temperament rather than attachment, if the SS is appropriate to use in cultures that are non-Western, and if an attachment rating taken from observations that are only twenty minutes in length have implications for long-term development.

Some newer attachment studies have been using a modified Strange Situation: in this procedure mother and child are in a room that contains various kinds of toys and furniture. The mother leaves the room for two timed periods (three minutes, five minutes) and then returns to the child. The issues of importance include the child's rating of security and the child's ability to handle the stress of separation. An important difference between this measure and the original Strange Situation is the nonappearance of a stranger.

The contentious attachment issue that is most relevant for parents has to do with day care and babies. Again I note that the issue is fundamentally one of separation. Do mothers who work jeopardize their babies' attachment because they create a separation from their babies? Thus the question is whether babies who are placed in day-care settings are more likely to show nonsecure attachments. The original data were mixed, with some reports indicating attachment quality was influenced by the number of hours in the day or the age of entry into day care. More recent studies suggest the picture is far more complicated than suggested in the earlier studies; in general, infant day care and attachment quality are not tightly linked. But, read on.

Although disagreements continue to exist, now there's enough information so that parents and others can make reasoned decisions about parenting, parent substitutes, child care, and more. A brief summary of findings most relevant to parents suggests the following: .

+ Attachment is an important concept in that it does speak to the emotional and social side of the relationship between baby and parents. Attachment, though, is only a part of the relationship: there's physical care, stimulation for cognitive and language development, socialization, and more.
• Babies do differ in how they respond to separations and reunions, and part of the difference reflects a baby's temperament. If out-of-home day care leads to continuing emotional upheavals for your shy or fearful child, you might want to rethink your child-care approach.
+ With some exceptions, attachment ratings of year-old babies do not foretell future developmental well-being. Recognize, though, there is still considerable disagreement here. However, in a major review of the attachment literature, Ross Thompson made a valuable proposal. He suggested that a secure attachment is most helpful during the early years when young children are so dependent on their parents and so much is going on in young children's worlds. A specific

attachment rating given at twelve months may diminish in importance when children become more involved with peers, teachers, and other adults.

+ There is still considerable disagreement about use of the Strange Situation in non-Western cultures. And in my view, we still have scant research about the validity of the SS among different groups of babies. Our culture is especially diverse; still, a substantial amount of research on attachment in the United States includes samples that are primarily composed of Caucasian middle-class families or families that are considered at high risk because they are financially impoverished, have minimal support systems, or contain abusive individuals.

+ As to the issue of attachment and day care, the large, multisite national study of day-care effects and attachment has shown that day care in and of itself does not have adverse effects on attachment. Inadequate parenting and inadequate day care do have deleterious effects on the parent-and-child relationship. Recall that the emphasis on inadequate parenting was one of Bowlby's early observations. Since inadequate day care is a substitute for parents, it follows that an inferior substitute can have the same deleterious effects as deficient parenting. It also follows that poor day care has an adverse effect on children's skills.

+ There are suggestive findings that give pause. Placing babies in day-care settings early in the first year may be associated with nonoptimal attachment if other adverse factors are also present. These factors include poor quality of the day-care setting and numerous changes in child-care arrangements. And children's behaviors may suffer if they are in out-of-home day care for many, many hours each week. These findings do need to be confirmed in other studies.

The issue for parents to decide is whether nonparent care—think again of separation—somehow distorts the evolving attachment relationship with the baby who is in a formative period of relationship development. Bowlby had suggested that attachments were formed during the first nine months of life. This is the time when babies begin to create nascent mental models of the emotional and social relationships that are most crucial to their well-being.

So as you make your decisions about child care, keep in mind that whether in a home or day-care setting, a caring, educated, and sensitive parent substitute helps a baby learn and develop and emotionally develop a trust in others. Think about the conditions that researchers have described that ought to be present in a quality day-care setting: adequate safety precautions; access to age-appropriate toys; trained staff who are sensitive and responsive to individual baby needs; and organization of the baby's day. As a parent, ask questions. Is the surrogate caregiver intelligent, sensitive, and knowledgeable about babies? Is the setting for your baby safe? If a caregiver takes care of several children, how many children does he or she care for, and how many babies are involved? If your baby is enrolled in a specific day-care facility, is it licensed and what is the training of the director and the staff? Trust your intuitions as well. Do you feel right about your baby in the setting and with the people or do you have a vague sense of discomfort? If the latter is the case, start looking again.

DEVELOPMENTAL HINTS AND ALERTS:
FOUR TO SEVEN MONTHS

How to Be Helpful

+ Talk, talk, and talk some more to your baby.

+ When your baby babbles to you, listen and talk to him.

+ Play music for your baby.

+ Find simple, colorful toys that she can grasp. Introduce different shapes and textures in her toys.

+ Use crib toys that make sounds.

+ Never leave the baby alone on beds, couches, or chairs.

+ Minimize your baby's exposure to TV.

Check with Your Baby's Pediatrician

If your baby is seven months old and does not

+ smile

+ have a day-and-night schedule

+ localize sounds

+ vocalize at all

Also check with your pediatrician if your baby's arms or legs seem very floppy or very tight.

SHARPENING OUR FOCUS

THE BABY AS SCIENTIST, GENIUS, MATHEMATICIAN, AND MORE . . .

Almost every season, it seems, there's another astounding report of babies' remarkable skills. Newborns remember the passages read to them when they were still in the womb. Newborns prefer to look at their mother's faces rather than other faces. Two-month-olds share intersubjectivity with their mothers—that is, babies have some sense of their mothers' minds. Two-month-olds experience anger. Three-month-olds' memory processes are capable of recall. Five-month-olds understand numbers. Babies are akin to scientists: they produce theories, test hypotheses, and evaluate their results. Babies are geniuses. I find some of these ideas provocative and challenging, and some I can easily incorporate into my views about early development. Others are more difficult, and I await additional research.

Is there a disconnect between researchers who study babies and parents who struggle with the day-to-day incessant demands involved in caring for physically, cognitively, and emotionally immature babies? If babies are so smart, why does the two-month-old cry her heart out just when Mom has come home from a tiring day at work? Why does the three-month-old smile at anyone—parent or stranger—who smiles at him? Why does the five-month-old try to put everything in her mouth? *Why don't these babies think smart?*

There isn't a reality disconnect. Rather, the last decade has seen an extraordinary convergence of events that have relevance for understanding infancy. There have been technological advances that have allowed remarkable studies of infant behavior particularly in relation to perceptual functioning. Neuroscience research has grown immeasurably with countless new studies relating to infant brain functioning and behavior. Researchers who study the behaviors of nonhuman primates and mammals have provided intriguing perspectives on animal skills. There's also been much rethinking about early development. Using this and other information, developmental scientists provide interpretations of research on infant behavior. It is worth noting that developmental scientists frequently interpret research results using theories and principles they feel most comfortable with.

Not surprisingly, substantive disagreements about interpretations exist among developmentalists. Most of the time these disagreements do not reach the public via traditional media outlets. There are exceptions of course: there's been a great deal of public debate about stimulation and early brain development and about day care and its implications for babies' emotional and social development.

Returning to the issue of clever babies, how should parents translate data and ideas for themselves? Here are some perspectives that may be useful for you.

It is absolutely clear that human newborns and very young babies have visual and auditory perceptual skills that allow them to participate in a human environment. At the very least, these skills make sense from a survival vantage point. The vastly immature human infant is more likely to receive care and nurturance if she can show she is capable of interacting with others. So in a sense it is not surprising to learn that during the first weeks of life, babies are attentive to human faces and voices; they even imitate a few facial expressions; and they seem to have a sense of three dimensions and detect differences in size, which probably allow them to *see* humans distinct from objects. Within six to seven months, babies distinguish the difference between one versus two objects, they recognize different colors and show color preferences, they use depth as a cue, and more. All of these competencies permit efficient interactions with humans and with the objects that are part of their own human environment. Philip Kellman and Martha Arterberry remind us though to consider important distinctions between the skills of young infants and those of adults. Infant skills are often far less precise and organized than they will be during adulthood; the competencies of infants represent a subset of adult abilities; infants use small elements of information as the basis for a response whereas adults use varied sources of information. These authors also indicate that we know relatively little about how perceptual abilities change over time.

Gavin Bremner offers another view of the young baby's competencies. He suggests that up until six months or so, babies are not aware of the perceptual or motor skills they possess. Babies' knowledge starts out as *implicit*; it is knowledge that is not in the realm of conscious awareness. Bremner's characterization of implicit knowledge is very similar to the kinds of implicit memory that I talked about earlier. Bremner argues that implicit knowledge begins to become *explicit* as babies become more physically involved with the objects, people, and events in their surroundings. The baby's developing reach and grasp mean he can take hold of things; he begins to be aware that he is holding something that is round and red.

The more the baby actively uses his arms and legs to connect to his world physically, the more attentive and conscious he will become of the qualities of objects. The baby feels the surfaces under his feet: grass, dirt, carpet, tile, wood. Each feels different on the bottom of his feet, and he'll learn to select the surface that goes best with the toys that he plays with. Later on, he'll learn the actual words—*wood, carpet*—associated with floor surfaces. And still later, he'll announce, "I want to take my truck to the dirt hill!"

My point, added to that of Bremner's thesis about the path from implicit to explicit knowledge, is that development in the early years is an ongoing process that leads to richer and more complex behaviors so that children can increasingly deal with a rich and complex world.

Not long ago, Marshall Haith and Janette Benson authored a chapter for their colleagues about the current vogue among some developmentalists to ascribe extraordinary skills to babies. I believe their ideas are relevant to parents who want to understand their baby's abilities better. So drawing from Haith and Benson, you might want to think about the following the next time you read a media report about very young babies and their astonishing intellectual activity:

+ Consider the words that are being used to describe the baby's activity. Suppose, for example, the headline says, "Babies can do addition." Ask yourself if your definition of addition—the actual counting of objects—is the same as that of the researcher who did the study.
+ Ask yourself how the research was done. Is a study that uses babies as participants vastly different in terms of tasks and measurements of behavior from one that uses older children? Do you feel comfortable drawing conclusions from one study and not the other?
+ Consider whether very young babies actually knew what they were doing when they responded to a particular stimulus condition.
+ Consider too the possibility that even though outward signs of performance may seem similar between a baby and an older toddler, their performances are based on different levels of understanding and perhaps different cognitive processes.

Overall my suggestion to parents is to read reports of recent research on babies. There are descriptions in books, newspapers, and magazines. Keep an open mind and ask questions. Do the research and the conclusions make sense to you, as a parent of a baby? Does the research fit into the real, everyday world of you and your baby? Then judge how you want to interpret the research and the data.

THE EXTRAORDINARY WORLD OF BABIES AND LANGUAGE

Most of us speak with ease and are so comfortable with our own language, we don't think about the thousands of words we understand, the thousands of words that make up our own vocabularies, and what we accomplish with words. I rather like Steven Pinker's adage: "Language allows us to know how octopuses make love and how to remove cherry stains and why Tad was heartbroken, and whether the Red Sox will win the World Series without a good relief pitcher and how to build an atom bomb in your basement and. . . ."

We use words to

+ be social with others . . . *How are you? Nice to see you.*
+ ask questions . . . *What time do we eat?*
+ provide answers and solve problems . . . *Two plus two equals four.*
+ direct others . . . *It's dinner time.*
+ tell others how we feel . . . *I'm happy today.*
+ praise, to condemn . . . *You are terrific!*
+ lie . . . *You are the most beautiful person in the whole world.*
+ talk to ourselves . . . *Okay on that one, not so good there.*
+ plan for the future and evaluate the past . . . *Tomorrow is the day I'll visit her.*
+ make up new words to suit our needs . . . *the Internet, World Wide Web, cyberspace*

It's rather amazing that the five-month-old who babbles endlessly will produce sentences that contain many words in far less than five years. The origins of language occur early. In the first year of life, babies make sounds and use these sounds to *talk* to themselves and to others. Babies listen intently to sounds, they distinguish human from nonhuman sounds, they learn to differentiate happy sounds from sad ones, and they begin to recognize words they hear frequently. Babies also learn gestures and use them to communicate. By the end of the first year, most babies understand simple words and phrases, are able to communicate with a word or two, and have a sense of the reciprocity of language. You talk, then I talk, and so on. The second year sees the growth of vocabulary, the combination of words into short sentences, the use of personal pronouns, and the awareness of language as a tool in social interactions.

Children learn language because biology has provided the recipe for basic language abilities and because a shared language system is intrinsic to human social interactions. It is countless social exchanges that help babies approach the threshold of language, with babies increasingly shaping the sounds they produce to match the sounds they hear from others. Babies are unaware of this vocal matching, but the more they match, the more sensitive they are to the sounds that they themselves hear and produce. The content and structure of babies' language is linked to the language of their culture; or stated another way, babies learn the particular language they hear day after day.

When parents talk to babies, they tend to produce lots of vocal inflections and to use words that are short, relatively common in our language, and easily reproduced. "Come," "go," "bye," "mommy," "daddy," "kiss," and "doggy" are examples. And parents use the same words over and over again. After all, how many ways can a mother tell her baby that he has a dirty diaper, she loves him, they're going "bye," or he smells sweet? Lois Bloom tells us babies' initial vocabularies tend to be dominated by words that are frequent and short. Parents of language-learning babies and toddlers also facilitate the use of words by taking cues from the child. The child looks at a toy and then looks at his parent and back to the toy. The parent follows the baby's gaze and talks as she does so. This seemingly simple act facilitates language growth. Other influential parenting actions include using uncomplicated language to label the child's experiences, asking questions, talking about emotions, playing games, and more.

Babies also help themselves acquire language because they often *rehearse* speech. An eighteen-month-old in day care hit upon the word "yukkee," which she said most of the day for weeks on end. Then there is Emily, who at twenty-two months had a rich vocabulary and produced a crib monologue that went like this: ". . . the broke, car broke . . . Emmy can't go in car, go in green car, no, . . . broken, broken . . . ," and on and on.

Young children learn many new words; indeed many children learn hundreds in the second year. But language growth rarely moves forward with perfect precision and timing. Early words, says Bloom, are often fragile and imprecise. Somewhat later, there may be a language spurt. However, it's not unusual for word growth to move along relatively consistently and then slow down for a time. Instead of learning a few new words a week, a toddler might produce two words every few weeks or so. Sometimes a toddler's speech goes in fits and starts and even comes to a temporary halt. When this happens it may be that toddlers are immersed in learning something else—discovering the joys of walking, finding out how toys work, identifying shapes. Sometimes, the young language learner just does not have the mental energy that language learning requires. At the very least, the language learner has to stop and attend to an *event* of interest, make a connection between the event and the words being used, store the word in memory, and retrieve the word when needed. It is hardly surprising that babies' speech development often starts and stops. Steven Pinker's statement that "language imposes greater demands on the brain than any other problem the mind has to solve" makes a lot of sense. Despite the often fitful nature of early language development, overall the growth of understanding and speech are rather rapid and efficient processes. Someone once said if we tried to teach children to speak, we could not do as effective a job as they do on their own in the space of two years or so.

◆ LANGUAGES AND THEIR RULES

Languages differ in how vowels and consonants are used, patterns of intonation, and use of accents or emphases within words or sentences. The toddler of English-speaking parents might say to her mother, "Want cookie."

She would pronounce the *nt* in want and the hard *c* in cookie, and perhaps emphasize the *want* in "Want cookie." Her speech would reflect the intonation patterns of English. Nobody actually teaches a baby how to make sounds or which sounds to imitate or how to construct a sentence. But babies do learn to match their own speech to the speech of the people in their environs. This matching process involves producing the exact kinds of sounds that make up the words in a specific language: *hot dog* in English, *burrito* in Spanish with its *rr* emphasis, *wurst* in German with its *w* sounding like the English *v*, and *kung pao* in Chinese. Word meanings, sentence construction, and intonations all have *rules* associated with their use. And rules are part of every language. Children learn the rules of a language (sometimes referred to as the *grammar* of a language) because they live in social groups where people constantly use words in all kinds of situations. The rules of a language are relatively arbitrary; here are examples.

+ *Phonemic rules* refer to the *acceptable* sounds that are found in syllables and words. Phoneme distinction is an important precursor to learning word meanings. *Met* and *net* or *pet* and *bet* are words that differ by only one phoneme, yet have vastly different meanings.

  English has forty-four phonemes; amazingly, these forty-four sounds make up thousands and thousands of words in the English language. Acceptable phonemes in the English language include the combination of *k, a,* and *t* sounds that make up the word *cat.* Around the world, people who speak English pronounce "cat" in much the same way. Sensitivity to a language's specific phoneme patterns develops during infancy. That is why adult monolingual English speakers have difficulty when trying to pronounce combinations of phonemes from other languages.

+ *Morphemes* refer to the smallest units of sound that can be defined in a language. In English *ed* is a unit of sound that typically refers to the past tense of any number of verbs. She *walked* to the store. I *believed* him! Similarly, the ending *ing* typically refers to the present tense. We are liv*ing* in complex times. *And* is both a unit of sound and a complete word. Bill *and* Sally went to the beach. Much to the chagrin of young children and second language learners, English contains lots of exceptions to morphological rules: we do not say *doed*, we say *did*; and we do not say *gived*, we say *gave*. Toddlers seem more aware of morphemes after they begin to speak in sentences.

+ *Semantic rules* refer to acceptable meanings of a morpheme, word, or group of words. In English, we agree that the word *cat* stands for a furry little creature who has four legs, has whiskers, and says meow. The group of words *The cat has . . .* conveys a meaning about a characteristic of a cat. And most people would agree that a cat would not produce a barking sound or wag her tail. Semantic rules must agree with the ideas—cats do not bark—that are part of a culture.

Although every language has rules for word meanings, languages have flexibility. People who ride the big Caterpillar tractors on farms often refer to their machines as "cats," and farm folk know that a tractor used to plow a field is not a four-footed animal. Nor is it a bug. Semantic rules are also flexible enough to allow new words into language vocabularies. Someone once came up with the word *catwalk* to describe a narrow walkway along a bridge. The word became part of the English language. Studies have shown that by midpoint in the second year, toddlers begin to be aware of some of the categories of words. But word usage that is out of the ordinary, such as catwalk or cat burglar, will not be understood for quite a while.

◆ *Syntactic rules* refer to the arrangement of words in a phrase or a sentence that convey a meaning. The simplest sentences in English consist of a noun, verb, and object. *I played ball.*

Children learn to build on this word structure to express more complex ideas. An acceptable arrangement of an additional word is: *I played ball yesterday*, or, *Yesterday, I played ball.* An unacceptable arrangement is, *Ball, I played, yesterday*, although many listeners would be able to unravel the sentence. A phrase such as *I played* has a great deal of versatility, and can be used in any number of sentences. *I played tennis. I played hooky. I played all morning.* The syntactic rules of English allow all kinds of phrases to be inserted into all kinds of sentences, and still make sense to the listener. Syntactic rules are typical of young speakers when they begin to produce three-word sentences.

◆ *Pragmatic rule* refer to conversational dos and don'ts. A don't that is sometimes ignored has to do with interruptions. It is considered polite to wait until one person finishes stating his thoughts before another person starts talking. Linguists call this "conversational turntaking." Even babies engage in vocal exchanges!

◆ IN THE BEGINNING: FOUR COMPONENTS OF LANGUAGE DEVELOPMENT

The path to language has four interrelated parts—the *perception of sounds*, *vocal productions*, *comprehension of others' speech*, and the young child's own *production of words and sentences*. Each of these parts is intricately interconnected, and in order to effectively communicate with another person the young language speaker has to be aware of the sounds of words, to understand at some level what words mean, and to produce approximations of words. However, noted language researcher Lois Bloom suggests the individual parts, the *threads* of language development, actually start out as distinct entities and come together during the first year because of experiences and growth.

The Perception of Sounds

There are two parts here: one has to do with hearing, per se, and the other with discrimination of different sounds. Newborn babies hear sound. Results from studies indicate the auditory system is far enough developed toward the end of pregnancy for fetuses to hear sounds, or at least sound intonations, through the mother's abdomen.

The loudness (intensity) of sounds is one aspect of sound perception. Loudness is measured in terms of decibel levels (dB). Normal speech is about 40 to 60 dB, and loud talk is about 70 dB. Rock concerts produce sounds that are well over 100 + dB levels. Newborns hear best with sounds that are in the decibel range of a relatively loud speaking voice and seem unable to hear sounds that are considerably less than 70 dB. In contrast, they startle at speech sounds that are 85 dB or more. Babies' hearing abilities mature rapidly. By the end of two years, children's sensitivity to sounds' loudness or softness appears to be equivalent to adult levels.

In addition to intensity, sounds are made up of *frequencies*; these are variations in tone qualities. A pure tone (like some radio alert warnings) has only one frequency. Violins have a number of frequencies, which are higher than those made by drums. Bird chirps have far more high frequency tones than do the barks of a golden retriever. Human speech contains many frequencies, from very high to very low. Think of the musical scale, "do, re, mi, fa, sol, la, ti, do," which lots of people began to hum after hearing the words, "Doe a deer, a female deer, . . ." and on through the scale in the movie *Sound of Music*.

The variability in frequencies gives speech its rich sound qualities and thus we find it appealing to hear others talk. There is an interesting difference in male and female speech. Although both males and females speak with many intonations, the frequencies involved in female speech tend to be higher than male frequencies. These differences are so distinctive that they are discernible to even young babies. Human newborns seem particularly drawn to female voices.

The privileged role of sounds made by humans. Auditory perception is far more challenging than simply recognizing differences in sound intensities, frequencies, and where sounds are coming from (localization). Humans also have to learn to distinguish human from nonhuman sounds and to pay particular attention to the content of human sounds. Still, it is rather amazing that very young babies not only identify speech sounds from nonspeech sounds, but they definitely prefer speech sounds. It may be that babies distinguish and prefer speech sounds because the sounds that make up words and sentences vary in so many interesting ways. Words invariably contain a mix of vowel and consonant sounds—think of the words *banana* or *pineapples*. Vowel sounds are soft, gliding, and last considerably less than a second. Vowels are produced with a relatively open vocal tract. In contrast, many consonants have an abruptness to them—they are shorter than vowel sounds. The reason is that consonants are mostly produced with almost complete closure of the vocal tract. Look in a mirror as you say the letters *a* and *f*, noting the placement of your tongue and the opening of the vocal tract.

Sometimes humans slur vowels and consonants together, which makes for even more variety and interest. "I'mgonnago tathestore." Combine this diversity with differences in inflection—directing a command to an older child versus declaring love to a special person—and you can begin to understand the potential power of human voices for babies. Although the sounds and sound combinations of speech fascinate young babies, this does not mean they distinguish one language from another. This ability emerges later in the first year.

Distinguishing specific speech sounds. Researcher Richard Aslin suggests babies are born with the ability to perceive a limited set of speech categories. A baby's experiences with a particular language begin to influence the perception of categories, phoneme contrasts, and intonations. Sometime during the last six months of the first year babies begin to show decreasing amounts of perceptual awareness of sounds that are *not* part of their particular language. They act as if they no longer hear the distinctive qualities of these sounds. In a series of studies, Janet Werker and her colleagues tested English-learning babies on variations of the *t* sound in the Hindi language. At six to eight months, most babies could distinguish the subtle differences although English-speaking adults frequently could not. By ten to twelve months, babies failed to discriminate the contrasts. Werker suggests that what is happening is a reorganization, which allows a sensitizing to phoneme contrasts that are relevant to one's native language. Increasing sensitivity to the particular sounds of one's own language culture prepares babies to be receptive to specific phoneme combinations associated with specific words. Later on, this will lead to the beginnings of babies' comprehension of morphemes and words.

Vocalizations

All babies vocalize, sometimes with cries and sometimes with coos, grunts, babbles, and all kinds of funny noises. In some instances these sounds are remarkably similar from one baby to the next. A coo emitted by a three-month-old English, Peruvian, or Japanese baby is pretty much the same. Yet just a few months later, these babies will begin to show variations in some of the specific sounds they produce. These differences arise despite the fact that the development of vocal proficiency is similar for all babies. In large part this similarity is tied to the maturation of babies' vocal equipment—the windpipe (trachea), voice box (larynx), vocal cords, tongue, and palate—and that is why the progression of sounds is similar across the world's language cultures during the first year of babies' lives.

Coos and laughter, along with other vowel sounds and the emergence of consonants, provide babies with the means to produce vocalizations that have phoneme qualities. The maturing vocal-tract system also allows babies to produce sounds that have variations in pitch and intensity. With these skills babies enter a period (from three months to eight months) in which they produce vocalizations when and where they want. They repeat sounds that please them and explore sound variations. Kim Oller describes this period as one of *expansion*, because the baby produces new kinds of sounds. Approximately midpoint in this time frame, babies become capable of combining vowels and consonants into a sequence of babbling sounds. Although babbles are clearly different from a spoken word ("bababama-mama" versus "banana"), the sound qualities of a babble have some similarities to the sound qualities of words.

Canonical babbling represents the next phase in vocalizations. This period, between five and ten months, is when babies vocalize *mama*, *bababa*, and other well-formed syllables. Canonical babbling seems to have a powerful genetic component; babies raised in very different kinds of environments begin canonical babbling around the same age and show similar proportions of speechlike sounds in their vocalizations. Yet the phoneme and intonation qualities of these vocalizations increasingly reflect the baby's language surroundings. Babble sequences also become increasingly longer and can be composed of strings of vowel and consonant sounds along with clicks, trills, and marked changes in pitch.

This is the time when babies reared in English-speaking families might begin to produce a babble such as "dada" or "mama" which sounds like an acceptable English word with well-formed syllables. However, these babbles are not connected to anything the baby is doing and tend to be separated from context. What seems to be happening is that the baby has discovered a sound he can make; he retrieves that sound and practices it. A number of terms have been used to describe this kind of sound practice, including "nonspecific speech" and "protolanguage."

Babbling seems to provide a background of many sounds for the baby to select from for the production of new words, and many of these core sounds will be reproduced later on in the baby's first words. Increasingly, babies' sound productions influence their own and others' behaviors. At about seven months of age, babies use their babbles to *talk* to others. They babble when they want attention, desire a toy, or simply want to be picked up. The more babies vocalize, the more they become familiar with the experience of producing a sound on demand. *Sound productions* bring babies closer to real words.

Are vocalizations influenced by a culture's language? Yes, particularly vocal elements that make up consonant sounds in a language. Variations in consonants give languages their distinct features, such as the guttural sounds of Germanic languages and the nasal tones of French. Not surprisingly, culturally based sound variations begin to emerge by the last half of a baby's first year.

Comprehension of Others' Words

To comprehend is to understand, and to understand words means that one person's definition of a word matches the definition of another person in the same culture. Our agreement about word definitions allows us to cooperate, to compete, to negotiate, to play together, and in all ways to be members of a community. Popular word games such as charades require agreement about word definitions.

The number of words that an adult understands is huge, so that learning a few new words hardly makes a blip in the memory store. But a baby starts out with no word comprehension at all, and somehow has to find her way into the words of her culture. What a task! Some researchers think that a baby's initial word understanding comes out of simple learned associations. Mom says, "Here's your bottle," thousands of times during the course of a year as she hands the baby his bottle. "Have you finished your bottle?" she asks as she removes it from his hands. "Want a bottle?" she asks late in the day when he begins to get a little irritable. Over and over, the word *bottle* is said in relation to this oblong-shaped container. The word *bottle* is the constant, despite changes in scene or time. Later, perhaps many, many months later, the baby begins to understand that bottles are containers. A jar is also a container, but a bottle and jar differ. This kind of understanding marks the shift from learning by association to learning the defining characteristics of things (and people). Language comprehension takes a big leap forward when this happens, which typically occurs toward the end of the toddler period and into the preschool years.

The comprehension of eight-month-olds might include a dozen or more words. The actual range of comprehension is substantial, from no words to several hundred. In one study, babies understood more nouns at first, then later on they began to realize the meaning of verbs, and still later they understood adjectives. The ten most frequently understood words included *mommy*, *daddy*, *bye*, *no*, *peekaboo*, *bath*, *ball*, *bottle*, *hi*, and *all-gone*. Ninety-five percent of children in one study understood *mommy* whereas about seventy percent understood *dog*.

The development of comprehension typically moves forward more rapidly than does speech production. Hirsh-Pasek and Golinkoff explain this unevenness by noting that comprehension relies on information that comes packaged in phrases and sentences uttered by the person who is interacting with the child. Parents use the same words and phrases over and over again. Given redundant packages, all that is required of the child is that she recognize the material in the word package and take apart some or all of its component parts. In contrast, in order for the young child to talk to another person, he has to expend lots more mental energy. He has to recall words, then has to assemble his own word packages (phrases and sentences), and then produce the right words.

Learning to Produce Words, Learning Labels

Of all the language achievements of early development, none is as dramatic as a baby's first words. Words enable the baby to tell others what she wants. Words announce to all that *I* am a real person! There are three specific periods that mark the growth of early language: the emergence of first words, the vocabulary spurt, and the shift to sentence production (as opposed to using one or two words by themselves).

First words. First words often consist of word fragments or have barely recognizable pronunciation. One perceptive mother described her baby's first words as "ma-ma" for her mother (mama) and for milk; "da-da," which referred to her father; "da" for down; and "da-yee" for doll. It would be relatively easy to miss these words in the course of a baby's babbles and even harder to distinguish the meanings of "da-da," "da," and "da-yee." Overall, first words, even when incorrectly pronounced, such as the example "da-yee," have similarity to the syllable structure of a real word, in this case, *dolly*.

Several conditions precede the onset of words: the baby has to recognize the particular characteristics of certain objects or people in her surroundings; the baby's vocal apparatus has to be mature enough so that she can produce certain sounds; the baby must be able to distinguish one word from another, such that he hears—and knows—that the word *throw* differs from the word *ball*; the baby has to begin to make a perceptual match between his own sounds and the words of others; the baby has to make mental connections to something that stands out, and then to the word that people use for that something; and lastly the baby has to recognize that she can make a sound that approximates the word others use to refer to that something.

First words tend to be restricted to the baby's own experiences, and babies also use words in their own ways. Katherine Nelson described a young word speaker who produced the word *clock* (in his own brand of baby talk). This child used the word *clock* to refer to clocks, watches, dials, timers, a bracelet, and a buzzing radio, drawing upon certain features that each of these objects shared—according to the child's view. This kind of broad labeling is a characteristic of early language.

Nelson describes this early period of word learning as "children finding their way into the language system." This typically occurs during the last part of the first year and into the second year. Often babies' first words refer to names of objects, because they associate a word with a thing or an event. In addition to naming things and activities, first words convey different messages. The same word can be used to command, to state ownership, and to impart information. How the word is used depends on what the baby is doing. "Buk," says fifteen-month-old Benjie as he hands his mother a book for her to read to him. "Buk," he says clutching a book to his chest. "Buk," he yells in the store as he sees books on display shelves. It is up to adults to figure out what the baby is trying to say.

The word spurt. About midpoint in the second year, toddlers often begin to show a naming explosion or word spurt. Now new words are learned daily with the child's vocabulary doubling or tripling within a brief period of time. Several factors seem to be involved. Toddlers begin to understand that words go beyond specific objects and specific events. Instead of using the word *dog* to identify only the dogs owned by his parents and grandparents, our grandson at this age came to realize that the word *dog* applies to all dogs. In other words, he was able to de-contextualize words from specific items to a class of things (in this case, the class of dogs).

It is not surprising that as soon as children understand the generality of words, they tend to become intrigued with naming objects. Many a young child toddles around naming everything in sight. If they do not know a name, then they demand to be told. "Dis?" asked Andrew as he pointed to my new purse; "Dis?" as he looked at the pencil; "Dis?" as he picked up a potato in the store. Nelson describes the child as taking part in a word-learning game. This is a game where the child has a set learning agenda and expects others to follow along in the game.

Along with the word explosion, the language of young children begins to reveal word combinations. This is the beginning of sentence construction.

Early sentences are incomplete but most of the time include nouns and verbs. "Daddy go," "Read book." These sentences, often labeled "telegraphic," lack prepositions, conjunctives, and pronouns. Children get better at making fuller sentences by the time they are three years old. Even though children have knowledge of word meaning and can speak in sentences, it is sometimes hard for them to make the right connections. A mother in one study reported her own confusion when her toddler daughter woke up from a nap saying something like, "Wee-wee in the mouth." Later when the mother went to make the child's bed, she noticed her daughter had thrown up. This is what the little girl was trying to tell her mother.

Individual differences. Although the rules of language and the individual strands of language are found in every language culture, individual babies within each culture vary in language development. These variations are observed most obviously in terms of the age when a baby begins to speak definable words. The size of vocabularies also differs within a given age. And some children are more facile than others in using words. These earliest variations tend not to be developmentally significant if you, as parents, provide your young toddler with rich and emotionally satisfying language exchanges. You talk, you read, you play word games.

If, at any time, you become concerned about your young child's language development, seek professional assistance for your questions sooner rather than later.

Eight to Twelve Months

Preview

Eight Months

Nine Months

Ten Months

Eleven Months

Twelve Months

Developmental Hints and Alerts: Eight to Twelve Months

Sharpening Our Focus:
The Acquisition of Speech
Temperament

FROM A DEVELOPMENTAL STANDPOINT, this five-month period is full of significant developmental events. Before we look at them, I want to mention how development in this period differs from that of earlier months. First, while important changes in motor abilities continue, there are equally remarkable advances in other areas such as the baby's language, mental abilities, social skills, and emotion control. Second, improvements in mental, social, and emotional skills more often than not involve new combinations of increasingly complex behaviors. These changes in the content and nature of development mean that to picture what is happening developmentally, we need fuller descriptions of behaviors. From here on, at each age level, I spend less time describing the growth of a specific behavior and more time talking about patterns of behavior and their implications.

Let's take a look at some of the specific developments that take place during this five-month period. Two milestones occur in motor development. By the end of this period, the baby has both of the uniquely human motor skills—the ability to walk upright and the ability to pick up objects with a refined pincer grasp. From now on, you'll see increasing coordination of hand skills, such that babies become markedly proficient in manipulating playthings; they start to feel comfortable using eating utensils; they attempt to use something like crayons to make bold strokes on paper. Be on the lookout for wall drawings, though! With regard to walking, after the baby becomes steady on her feet, she'll soon be walking backwards, running, and trying to jump.

In earlier pages, I mentioned the dramatic developments that occur in language comprehension and speech production. Babies begin to understand a few words. Indeed, you'll suddenly find yourself thinking your year-old baby understands you. So without thinking, you'll ask her to "bring Daddy your shoes," and she's likely to bring a shoe because she does understand. As exciting as this is, nothing quite matches hearing the baby's first words. The average for twelve-month-olds is three words, but the range extends from zero to hundreds. The upper ranges are rare. In thirty years, I've encountered one twelve-month-old girl who had a vocabulary of five hundred single words, another with a two-hundred-word vocabulary, and two boys who each had one-hundred-word vocabularies. One of these little guys uttered half a dozen two-word sentences. However many words your twelve-month-old speaks, or will speak, hearing your child talk to you is indeed sweet.

During the next four months, babies march inexorably toward intelligence. This is hardly a new idea: Jean Piaget described this decades ago. However, now researchers are better able to capture this transition. Studies show that babies intentionally adapt to novel challenges; they explore; they plan in a nascent way; they concentrate. It seems by twelve months, babies introduce lots of conscious awareness of their own actions. These *new* skills build upon competencies that have been developing for a while and are the result of many, many experiences and increasing maturation of cortical pathways.

Here are some examples. Noticing Mom sitting on the couch aiming for a brief respite, one twelve-month-old brings a toy for her to look at. Another stands at the back of a plush chair discovering how bits of his cookie fall to the floor. He gets down and carefully looks for the piece of cookie that has gone astray. At another time, finding a stick in the garden, he uses it to poke at his trucks. He begins to make small groups of things that seem to go together.

When we examine the social skills that develop between eight and twelve months, we find that many have cognitive underpinnings. Michael Tomasello suggests that babies begin to understand that others have both "intentional and mental states...." In other words, an eleven-month-old discovers she can gesture for help with a toy, and Mom will come to her aid because of the gesture. The baby points to a car, looks toward it, looks back at Mom, and Mom looks too. These coordinated looking-and-gestural behaviors indicate *joint attention*. And joint attention, along with the onset of *intentional imitation* and the growth of *attachment relationships*, represents behaviors that are basic to many of our social interactions. You'll begin to notice differences in the ways your eight- to twelve-month-old interacts with you because joint attention, imitation, and attachment are increasingly visible behaviors during this age period.

In the emotion arena, twelve-month-olds recognize they have some control over bothersome events. Presented with an annoying toy, they may try to push it away, which is a behavior that stands in marked contrast to indignant crying, observed earlier.

Overall, then, in this period we begin to see the marvelous balance between the baby's accumulation of skills that will support greater independence in the second year (e.g., walking and exploring) and the acquisition of behaviors (e.g., social referencing) that help obtain the assistance needed for learning, and social and emotional supports. There will be glorious surges and a few bounces back as you and your baby rocket through this period of wondrous development.

Eight Months

- gets into a sit without help

- turns objects with hands and explores its characteristics

- mouthing of objects peaks

- babbling has speechlike intonations

- associates words with events

- shows wariness to unfamiliar people

- shows memory of a "hidden" toy

SNAPSHOT

This month, body gestures, vocalizations, and pleading looks communicate babies' strong desire to be social, saying, "Look at me!" "Talk to me!" "Pick me up!" "Play with me!" An eight-month-old might jam his body against the side of his crib, squeal "Aahrahaa," and stretch his arms toward his father. He's just as likely to tug at his mother's jeans and make babbling noises when he wants something. Another baby, seated in her high chair, might lean toward her brother's plate of food and fret until he puts small pieces of bread on the high-chair tray.

At this age, displays of affection and social bids often go together. So a baby cuddles to her mother while they sit on the couch, and then taking one of her mother's hands, she moves it toward the other, saying, "Uh, uh, uh." She's telling her mother she wants to play pat-a-cake. Being able to communicate clearly is an impressive achievement, but being able to communicate to someone you care about is even better.

Quite the opposite happens with the baby's responses to unfamiliar people. With increasingly better visual perception skills, babies visually compare somebody who is new to those they know well. Wariness to unfamiliar people is relatively frequent, so don't be surprised if your baby pulls back from strangers. The refinements in visual perception that contribute to the baby's skill in comparing faces also account for the remarkable fascination eight-month-olds have with their surroundings. They peer out of car windows as if studying other cars, people, trees, anything. They take hold of a toy and scrutinize it for minutes on end. Visual investigations are supplemented with auditory ones: babies listen intently to the sounds of household appliances and vehicles. They follow the intonations of songs and music. When able, babies vocally play with the sounds they hear.

At this age, the baby is active in his own acquisition of information. One eight-month-old sat on the floor with a pile of blocks. He picked one up and banged it on the floor. Then he slid the block along the floor, stretched his arm so that he held the block way out in front of him, inspected it from afar and brought it near his eyes, and turned it around in his hands and examined it closely. Next he stretched his arm out and intentionally let the block go. He giggled as the block made noise when it hit the floor. He picked up another block and dropped it as he did the first. He did this again, babbling as each block struck the floor. Play that is purposeful and systematic foreshadows the sustained and intricate exploration of toys that repeatedly occurs in the coming months. It's not hard to imagine all the activity that's going on in that little brain.

This month is also the age when many babies reach a peak in mouthing toys, which does become less frequent after about twelve months. Mouthing most likely increases because it is a way to soothe gums that are sore from teething. As they mouth, babies also discover the exquisite sensitivity of the lip and tongue as sources of information. Some parents object to mouthing because of fears about safety. Of course, small, unsanitary, or otherwise unsafe objects should be kept away from babies. Other parents find the behavior distasteful because of family or cultural beliefs. Here parents should follow their own inclinations; babies' development is not impeded if they don't mouth toys.

✦ IMAGES OF DEVELOPMENT

Motor Control

Improvements in sitting and crawling and the beginning of creeping and standing with assistance are big motor achievements this month. All of these gross motor movements require a sturdy trunk that can support the upper body. The trunk must also be limber enough to allow the baby to pivot into a side position when he is lying flat and then rotate up into a sitting position. Muscles are now strong enough for these movements to occur.

In addition, getting into a creeping posture demands that the muscles around critical joints lock in place. For example, as a baby moves into a creeping posture, his hip joints have to lock so that his legs do not collapse from under him. In order for the baby to maintain the all-fours position, his shoulders and hips must function as skeletal supports and his trunk must stay firm and straight. Think of a suspension bridge: the baby's arms and legs are the foundation supports, and the baby's trunk and back make up the bridge.

Later in this month babies pull themselves up to a standing position. They may make tentative stepping movements. As with the onset of crawling and creeping, standing upright delights the baby and is often accompanied with whoops and hollers. Don't be surprised if your baby cries for help because he does not know how to sit down from a standing position. Sometimes they let go and fall.

Babies of this age show differences in how they get to a seated position, although the end result is the same. Some babies sit by rolling onto their stomachs, then moving into a crawling position, and finally twisting their upper trunk sideways and up while simultaneously moving their legs out in front. Others roll on their side, brace their hands against the floor, and push their trunk upright, using outstretched arms as levers. However a baby reaches a sitting position, when upright, she may rest quietly for a few seconds, as if replenishing energy.

Differences are also apparent in the ways babies crawl and creep. One baby might move around the floor by pivoting on her belly and propelling herself on her elbows, occasionally showing a primitive form of creeping on all fours. Her creeping is not yet particularly effective in terms of speed or distance, but it pleases her enough to babble with glee. Another creeps with ease, moving efficiently everywhere there's open space. Crawling and creeping babies poke their fingers into anything that has an opening. They pull on everything that seems pullable at ground level and do not understand safe and unsafe. So, although it's marvelous to see babies move on their own, they can be a menace to themselves. You can redirect your baby's crawling target but don't be surprised if he tries to head back to the same locale. Parents soon learn that floor-level hazards have to be covered or removed and floor-level breakables protected from the eight-month-old's explorations.

A new variation in eye and hand collaboration is seen this month; babies turn a small toy around in their hands. This fine motor skill is called *examining*. The baby's actions resemble the hand movements a coin collector makes when he scrutinizes a brand new penny. Examining toys is not trivial from a developmental standpoint; it is an example of sustained attention to objects, which is important for learning. You'll see examples of sustained attention in the coming months when babies look at books and magazines, as they explore toys and other objects, and as they watch the toys they pull along.

All of the motor skills that make eight-month-olds far more independent than before also have other developmental ramifications. Babies engage in social play such as clap hands; they gesture more effectively; they crawl across a room to get to the toy held by a parent; they crawl while babbling all the while. Babies are growing up!

The baby's new vigorous motor activity may bring on a weight spurt. Exercise turns fatty tissue into muscle tissue, and muscle tissue weighs more than fatty tissue.

Perception

Vision. Laboratory studies show that, at about eight months, the baby's visual receptors are becoming more sensitive to relatively distant objects and events. Now she sees clearly whether objects are close up or farther away. The behavior of an eight-month-old who visited one of my classes illustrates this nicely. The classroom had five rows of chairs with each row having about six seats. The baby, ignoring students sitting in front of her, was especially fascinated with two students in the back row (perhaps twenty feet away) who had particularly animated facial expressions. They smiled broadly to the baby, while she studied their faces. She then smiled to them in return, obviously having seen and processed their smiles.

Auditory perception. Babies' improved visual discrimination is matched by increasing sensitivity to sounds. As others talk babies listen intently, as if studying different words, which may explain why babies of this age are able to distinguish between different speech intonations. For example, babies in English-speaking environments are able to distinguish the difference in melody and word accents between the question "Is Michael going home?" and the statement "Michael is going home."

The eight-month-old also loves songs and music. He may show preferences for some songs and playfully imitate the cadence of a favorite song, while also capturing its many sounds.

Vocalizations and Language

This month the baby definitely begins to associate a word with an event. "Bye-bye" and a wave go together; "pat-a-cake" and hand claps go together. The baby also begins to recognize that a particular gesture means the same thing to other people as it does to her. She signals she wants to be picked up by raising her arms, and she assumes that other people know what the gesture means.

Similarly, when the eight-month-old regularly produces a particular sound, such as "mamamama" for a familiar person or "buh" for a ball, she has learned an important function of speech: people repeatedly use a specific *sound* to refer to a specific thing. "Ball" is the sound people use for the round thing that rolls. "Milk" is the sound for the thing that goes into the bottle. This association of sound and object does not mean the baby actually understands words and their definitions. This understanding grows in bits and pieces, particularly in the second year.

The ability to associate a specific sound (a word as we understand it) and an action often manifests itself quite suddenly, but as with almost all aspects of development, this skill has been gradually evolving for some time. Months earlier, for example, the baby's learning involved the association of two events that occur close together. At five months a bib signaled that food was on the way; if an adult put on a coat, then the door would soon open. At seven months, associative learning took another step forward as the baby began to connect sound with an event. For example, a baby might stop playing when the phone rang, waiting for someone to pick up it up. Similarly, she might crawl toward the bathroom when she heard water running in the tub. At eight months, the fruits of these preparations are becoming apparent in the baby's use of a sound to refer to a specific object.

Some of the baby's babbles now sound almost like real words, another step in the progress toward actual speech. This advance is helped along by two phenomena. First, the baby increasingly plays with sounds. She might experiment for minutes at a time with making the *b* sound in "bye," as if attempting to reproduce the word itself. Second, she often imitates the mouth and jaw movements of her caregivers as they speak, and this helps her learn about the actions she has to take to produce words.

Cognition

This month a few behaviors emerge that foreshadow the extensive cognitive growth that takes place between now and a year of age. First, the baby displays some primitive problem-solving skills. If given a string that is attached to a toy, he fingers the string inquisitively, experiments tentatively with pulling it, and watches to see if anything happens to the toy. The eight-month-old seems to have a vague notion that the string and the toy are somehow causally related. Through repetitions of his explorations with the string, he soon learns that it can be used to make the toy move.

Second, there is a good amount of shaking, dangling, and banging of toys this month. A baby seems to be purposefully investigating what happens when he strikes his truck on the table. His behaviors suggest that he has already acquired an ability, albeit a limited one, to engage in a goal-directed activity.

Third, there is the wonderful collaboration of eye and hand, and thinking and memory. When a baby looks for a toy that has been hidden under a felt pad, his actions tell us he remembers the toy. In other words, the toy *exists* even though he does not see it. This spectacular achievement is called *object permanence* and was described by Piaget as a major advancement in the growth of cognition. Eight-month-olds' performance on object-permanence tasks can be shaky, but they succeed often enough.

Not surprisingly, babies rapidly become surer of themselves in object-permanence tasks that involve only one hiding pad. In a matter of months, they find a hidden toy under the correct pad when presented with two pads. And still later they solve the problem even though three pads have been used. Piaget described this progression in terms of six stages in the growth of object permanence.

As an aside, researchers have studied object permanence with assorted animals. As a rule, dogs easily master simple object permanence (a one-pad hiding place) but get befuddled when hiding gets more complicated and involves several displacements of the object that is hidden (for example, put into a cup and then moved under three felt pads before being hidden under one). Eighteen-month-old toddlers handle this challenge in a breeze.

Social Development

The eight-month-old tends to focus affection on one or two individuals, usually parents, although a sibling or other family member can be the primary recipient of cuddling. Whomever the baby chooses, the baby wriggles, crawls, creeps, and rolls in an attempt to get close. The baby doesn't exclude other people from affectionate displays; rather, he simply gives one or two people more attention than he gives others.

As the baby's preferences intensify, his wariness toward unfamiliar people increases correspondingly. Sober facial expressions appear when an unfamiliar person comes too close, and sometimes the baby clings to a caregiver to offset his fear. This increasing discomfort in strange situations comes about because of the baby's growing ability to compare and contrast new environmental features with familiar settings as well as new faces with faces of known persons.

Emotions

Not all eight-month-olds are wary of strangers. A baby's response to unfamiliarity is influenced by temperament and the extent of exposure to novel situations. A friendly, relaxed baby accustomed to the comings and goings of many family members might show wariness only for a brief period, if at all. After only a short time, she might even flirt with a stranger to get the newcomer's attention. On the other hand, a generally subdued baby reared in a small family might show intense wariness that verges on fretfulness. Differences in babies' responses to newness do not appear to have long-term developmental consequences. Mostly they merely reflect individual styles.

Other features of a baby's individuality and emotional style are increasingly evident. In eight-month-olds, differences in wanting cuddliness, tolerance for dirty fingers, patience, delight in manipulating toys, and the pleasure derived from social interactions are common indicators of this variability. Now parents may be more inclined to draw personality comparisons with another family member. "Laura is good-natured, just like my dad!" said a mother as she likened her own cute eight-month-old to the baby's grandfather.

Sense of Self

Babies of eight months are acutely aware of their various body parts and actively engage in exploration of and experimentation with their bodies.

They massage their arms, run their hands inquiringly over their tummies, squeeze the flesh on the back of their legs, and poke fingers into ears. Babies are investigating what their bodies can do and which actions make them feel good and which hurt. This awareness and investigation builds into the baby's emergent knowledge of the body side of our selfhood.

Sometimes babies get up on all fours and sway back and forth in a trance-like state. This behavior is part of learning about the body, and much to parents' relief, it eventually stops. Babies also get into a creeping position, hitch their rears up an inch or two, and peer out between their legs. This is rather cute.

✦ DEVELOPMENTAL CLOSE-UP

Social Play

At eight months babies' interest in social play such as pat-a-cake and clap hands increases, probably because they have a better sense of their own role in social play. Of course, the baby's ability to coordinate arm movements helps as well.

Social play is not only fun, it provides the eight-month-old with important learning opportunities because of its unique characteristics. First, in social play there is a designated role for each participant and the roles of the various players need to be coordinated in order for the game to proceed. Thus a baby introduced to pat-a-cake soon learns that she is expected to respond in a certain way. She also learns that her response elicits another round of play, whereas a nonresponse leads to the conclusion of the game.

A second feature of social games involves content. A game of pat-a-cake requires hand clapping, but it does not include waving good-bye. The baby learns that disruptions in content (a good-bye wave inserted in pat-a-cake) stop the smooth flow of the game. The third characteristic of social play is that it contains repetitive sequences that are woven into a repetitive chain. In other words, the game of pat-a-cake does not consist of a single episode; rather, there might be four or five or more. Repetitions are valuable because they provide the baby with opportunities to work on receiving and responding to cues.

In a very real sense, social play is like a routine: both contain a sequence of events, an organization of the sequence, and a goal (making the game happen). The sequence, its organization, and its set goal constrain the baby's attention so he fully concentrates on the activity. Routines offer effective, and relatively effortless, ways to learn!

There are three general types of games that parents play with their babies. One type, that most resembles directed teaching, is where parents playfully make sounds and encourage the baby to reproduce these sounds. The baby's participation is relatively easy to sustain.

A second kind of game incorporates movement and requires the baby's visual and auditory attention. Examples include pat-a-cake and peekaboo, the most popular games of this age. Each of these games has its own rhyme, specific physical movements, and rules for the adult and the baby. These games are initially difficult for babies, because they have to pay attention while simultaneously coordinating what they see with what they hear, and produce appropriate arm movements.

The third group of games is largely physical. It includes a declaration of "I'm gonna getcha" at the same time the parent approaches the baby and rubs or hugs her. Here the baby learns to anticipate the physical tickling, hugging, or rocking that accompanies a verbal cue. Then there's the "horsey" game in which the baby rides on the adult's knee.

Studies of babies' game participation skills show that at eight months the baby is a novice who is just learning the rules. By nine months, babies are more involved in games, and in succeeding months they get better at being a fully involved partner.

Social Bids

Social bids take many forms: a wave; "come sit by me"; an embrace; "see you tonight?" Whatever their form, the bid provides an overt signal of wanting to share another's company. For months now, the baby has shown enjoyment when around others. By seven or eight months, babies make particular social bids. Increasingly they recognize the people they want to be with, and that they have the motor skills (gestures) to communicate their desires.

According to researchers, babies offer three kinds of social bids to other people. The first kind is a social-interaction bid. Here the baby's goal is to draw *attention* to himself by using eye contact, sounds, or hand gestures to attract notice, to solicit comfort, or to request participating in a social game. Sometimes the baby will issue an appeal for help with a brief hand movement. These are intentional acts in which the baby communicates awareness of another person's capabilities.

A particular subset of an attention bid involves teasing. This behavior is most often observed in toddlers about thirteen to fourteen months of age. In teasing, the child clearly wants an adult to look at what he is doing; teasing may also be an attempt to find out if a behavior is acceptable. In any event, teasing frequently involves activities that have already been prohibited. If the baby has heard "Don't touch the phone!" often enough, he will just as often seek eye contact with a parent before moving toward a phone. In my view, teasing represents a cognitive breakthrough for young children in that they recognize they have some control over another person's actions and emotions. Teasing at this age is not malicious.

The second type of social bid involves attempts to gain *joint attention* in which the goal is to direct another person's visual attention to a particular object that interests the baby. A behavioral sequence in a joint-attention bid may go like this. The baby looks at a toy and then at his father's face while pointing to the toy. If his father fails to respond to his actions, the baby will repeat them again because he perceives there is something amiss in his father's lack of response. These overtures may be a bit vague at first, so even an attentive parent may not see or register the bid; and even when the baby repeats it, it may not be understood. Attempts to obtain joint attention often begin in earnest at about nine months. Michael Tomasello considers joint attention a significant developmental achievement, in that the baby is now aware that he is an intentional being. Stated another way, the baby knows he can make things happen.

The third category of social bids involves the baby's attempt to share or give things to another person. This action again represents the baby's awareness of others. My colleagues and I saw a great deal of this type of activity when we were studying the play of one-year-olds. The babies were seated on the floor with their mothers nearby. A small basket of toys was set down beside them. The most common behavior was that the baby picked up a toy, looked at it, perhaps played with it briefly, and then took the toy to his mother for her to see. Notably, the baby merely held the toy out to his mother; he did not actually try to get her to take hold of the toy. As soon as his mother looked at the toy, the baby crept or walked back to the basket and sat down to play alone with the toy.

When parents respond to social bids, they empower their babies! They contribute to the baby's sense of mastery and motivation to be with others and to participate in their activities. Paraphrasing Tomasello, it is these kinds of activities that open the possibility for babies to learn a great deal, including the nature and activities of their human culture.

Nine Months

- *shows signs of intelligent behavior*
- *makes speechlike vocalizations*
- *recognizes simple cause-and-effect relationships*
- *tries to influence social interactions*
- *frowns when displeased*
- *feeds self finger foods*

At nine months, again there are obvious changes in the baby's motor and language abilities. He stands without assistance and begins to create word sounds, "mabama," "badaba," that have no meaning but are precursors to real words.

These behavioral changes are so distinctive that it is easy to overlook the less obvious but dramatic surge in cognitive capabilities that also occurs this month. The nine-month-old is far more mentally competent than he was just a month ago. All along, the baby has been building his fund of information—how people and objects look, how people treat him, how people use objects, how a room looks, how sounds come from some things and not from others. Now, at nine months, the baby begins to devise new ways of dealing with the world using his store of knowledge. He is acting intelligently.

What does intelligence mean? Well, intelligence among older children and adults is defined in terms of the ability to solve problems, particularly those that arise in novel situations; make decisions; and engage in planned behavior. There's awareness that you don't have a ready answer but that something needs to be done. In short, intelligent acts are effective adaptive behaviors. Babies' first displays of intelligence involve intentional attempts to do something about events that are not to their liking; they begin to act adaptively.

What is intelligence for a nine-month-old? The baby is sitting in a corner of the living room playing with her doll. Her brother and a friend enter the room and go behind a couch to play. The baby sees only the tops of their heads from where she sits, but she hears their whispers clearly. She wants to join them; she starts crawling toward the sounds made by the two boys but soon encounters the couch. Here is the problem: How can she get to the boys with this obstacle in her way? Two months ago she might have simply stopped and cried when her path was blocked. Now she assesses the situation. She uses information she already has: the sound of her brother's voice; the presumed location of the boys, based on her ability to see their heads; the location of the couch in relation to her own location; and the space around the couch. She also knows she can move on her own. With this knowledge, she figures out a way to circumvent the obstacle that prevents her from reaching her goal. Her solution is to crawl around the couch.

It's not at all clear why intelligence emerges at nine months. We do know that interconnections between the frontal lobes and the rest of the cortex expand in the last part of the first year. This is also true about the interconnections of the language centers of the brain. Obviously, there must be more. Neuroscientist William Calvin gives prime consideration to the unique roles of human language and our efficient human hands in distinguishing human from nonhuman primate intelligence. Taking Calvin's idea one step further, perhaps human babies' growing awareness of language as a communication system and their growing awareness of what they can do with their hands provide the necessary boost for the baby's innovative actions that we label *intelligent*.

Other interesting behaviors observed this month include babies' fascination with objects that produce sounds, such as telephones and audio sets. Nine-month-olds are also intrigued with photographs of other babies and children as if recognizing likeness with themselves. They poke at holes or openings in food, cups, shoes, and buttonholes, and put small objects into open containers as if discovering that an opening means something can go inside. The nine-month-old capitalizes on his newfound ability to point— he can now separate his index finger from the rest of his fingers—and his curiosity about inside spaces (the inside of a bowl) and holes. He can probe these with his index finger.

This month cognitive development also involves improvement in the baby's capacity to distribute her attention effectively and engage in multiple tasks. In other words, she does not become distracted when many different events are happening. A baby can sit in her stroller, eat from the spoon her mother touches to her lips, finger her doll tenderly, and keep an eye on the dog at her feet. Periodically she might babble to herself. Not very long ago this baby needed to focus all of her attention on just one task in order to do it well.

Attention is helped by the baby's newly developed wariness. Instead of grabbing at something new that catches his eye, he pauses and looks carefully before he touches. What is this thing? What can I do with it? This reflective behavior promotes learning.

These cognitive advances are reflected in social behaviors. The six-month-old baby barely touched a parent's hand to send a message. At nine months the baby has a touch that is firm; in one instance the touch was clearly directed to his mother to share the piece of bread she was eating. This kind of behavior is another example of babies' recognition that they are a part of a physical and social world.

The growth of babies' capabilities in this and ensuing months has profound effects upon parents, who view their baby as increasingly capable. Parents now begin to teach their babies in informal ways about toys and other things. They extend their sentences and use complex words and phrases to describe how such a toy as a jack-in-the-box operates. Parents also gradually begin to direct the baby's attention to what is safe, nice, dirty, and so on, and even begin to issue directives ("No!" when the baby crawls to an electric outlet). These changes in parents' behaviors, which now reflect some direct attempts to teach the baby, go along with views that suggest that a considerable amount of parenting of young children involves guided or assistive learning.

For all the wonderful changes, there are times when you absolutely know your nine-month-old is still a baby. Irritability and sleep upsets often reappear this month. According to some studies, about a third of babies who have been good nighttime sleepers now wake up at night and cry. Several reasons have been put forth as explanations, such as teething, physiological growth, and the onset of dreaming. However, scientists are not really sure why sleep disruptions happen. These upsets can produce some sleepless nights as parents try to comfort a distraught, overtired baby; often most upsets disappear just as inexplicably as they made their appearance.

✦ IMAGES OF DEVELOPMENT

Motor Control

Overall, nine-month-olds have good control of their bodies; their gross-motor movements are mobile, efficient, and quick. In addition, their grasp is purposeful and largely coordinated; their fingers adapt to objects of different size, shape, and weight.

Sitting is balanced and steady, and the baby can maintain a seated position for many minutes. Babies of this age can lean forward to pick up a toy and then easily re-erect to a well-balanced sit. Last month they might have struggled to get into a sit from a lying-down position, but this month they move adeptly from lying down to sitting and back.

Nine-month-olds spend a lot of time pulling themselves to a standing position and standing, with their legs easily supporting their weight. Holding onto a crib rail is necessary in order to maintain balance while standing. Standing gives babies a new perspective on the world, so it's not surprising they pull on anything at all to get into a standing position. They do this even though they have difficulty sitting down; indeed at this age they mostly flop down.

Reach and grasp show more refinements. The baby easily picks up a small block by neatly folding her hand around the object. She uses her thumb with her first and second fingers to execute this maneuver. Her fingers are also becoming more independent of one another. The baby can now use her index finger by itself to poke.

All along, as the baby's grasp has become more refined, she has not been able to release objects when and where she wants. When she has lost interest in a toy, she has just let it go. At nine months, the last major component of grasp, the voluntary release of objects, begins to take shape. As with most motor skills, this new ability is at first crude and clumsy, and the released toy may not land where the baby intends. But now the baby tries to release a toy by extending her fingers just a bit rather than flinging the toy, and her ability improves quickly. Voluntary grasp and release move the baby farther along in her quest for knowledge: in a few months she will stack blocks more or less precisely and she'll be able to put pieces in puzzles where they should go.

Perception

Vision. Now the baby is likely to notice a small object, such as a small piece of cracker that is lying next to a whole cracker, and he processes this information relatively quickly. In fact, the nine-month-old often finds tiny objects irresistible. A nine-month-old visiting my class ignored his father's efforts to entice him with a doll to creep a short distance. He had spied a small piece of paper lying about three feet away from his father and crept swiftly to it, picked it up, and put it in his mouth.

Vocalizations and Language

At nine months, babies are clearly moving nearer to producing spoken language. The baby has been combining vowels and consonants in babble for several months now. The mixture of sounds and the length of vocalizations make some babbles sound almost like sentences. "Gaga dah dahdah mmmm ummm" can almost be mistaken for a chant in a foreign language. Some nine-month-olds also produce sounds that closely approximate real words: *mamama, dadada, baba.*

Many of the wordlike sounds that babies produce are not directed to a specific object or event, so they are really precursors to words. However, a few babies produce specific sounds for particular items much as an adult would use a word to refer to an object. A baby may use one sound to call a parent (*mmm*) and another for the puppy (*gaga*). Some nine-month-old babies can actually produce an approximation of a real word or two. In these instances, the baby does not know the adult meaning of the word he produces. He has learned an association of the sound of the word with an object. *Bah* stands for bottle, the word he associates with his bottle.

Most nine-month-olds gleefully imitate sounds produced by others. They are also more skilled at reading gestures, and they try to imitate some of them, as well.

Cognition

In addition to changes in the baby's problem-solving skills, recall memory, and attention control, there are other developments this month. For one, the baby displays more curiosity; she peers and pokes at anything and everything. She also seems to be more aware that her own actions can make something happen. She creeps to her basket of toys and pulls out a push-pull toy with a long handle. She sits on the floor and uses the handle to push the toy away from her, listening intently to the sounds the bell in the toy makes. When she pulls the toy toward her, the bell rings again. She stops moving the toy, and the bell stops. Next she drops the handle and extends her arm. She looks at her arm, but the bell does not ring. The baby has just learned that it is the effect of her arm on the toy that makes the bell in the toy ring.

Other behaviors attest to a primitive awareness of cause-and-effect relationships. I watched in awe while a baby tried to drink from her bottle while clamping the nipple tightly in her teeth and elevating the bottle slightly with an open palm. A problem arose! The milk could not flow through the clenched nipple, and, the milk could not reach the nipple unless the bottle was angled higher. With barely a pause, the baby tipped the bottle upward and relaxed her tooth grip. The baby had some understanding of cause-and-effect linkages.

Knowledge of cause and effect is also directly linked to the baby's increasing understanding of goals. In particular this month she begins to recognize that there can be more than one way to achieve a desired endpoint. I demonstrate this in class by placing a nine-month-old's favorite toy inside a ring and attaching a string to the ring. I set the ring with the toy inside of it a few feet from the baby; I then extend the string toward her so that it is just within her reach. The baby has three ways to get the toy: she can crawl directly to it, she can pull on the string to bring the toy to her, or she can tug on her mother's hand to bring the toy closer. Most nine-month-olds use all three approaches if I repeatedly put the toy in the ring. In effect, babies tell us they now realize that several options are open to them. In addition, if they correctly solve the ring and string problem, they also show recognition of a means (string) to an end (toy). These problem-solving behaviors are important precursors of more complex reasoning skills.

Social Development

The baby is intent this month on exercising control over his social interactions. When he wants to get a parent or his sister to play with him, he can move toward them on his own. He may try to direct a parent's gaze to something of interest by looking back and forth from object to parent, and he occasionally insists on eating the same food as his parents at dinner. Controlling a social situation sometimes involves exclusion rather than inclusion. When a nine-month-old's mother reprimands him, he sometimes turns his head away as if he doesn't want to hear.

This month babies show increasing affection for specific individuals. They may purse their lips when a favorite person approaches, a precursor to throwing a kiss. Some nine-month-olds become subdued when a favored person leaves and cry even if left with a familiar baby-sitter.

Emotions

The baby's increased interest in *control* occasionally produces difficult moments for parents. Suddenly the baby protests against lying down for diapering. Wriggles turn into frets that lead to wails and uncooperative thrashing about.

The nine-month-old is developing a real frown, which he displays when he is unhappy about something. Because nine-month-olds remember schedules with greater ease, they frown and cry when everyday routines do not go as expected. Other events elicit frowns. A nine-month-old had a cold and a bad cough, and the family doctor prescribed a mild cough syrup. The baby took it the first time, making a face that indicated he did not like the medicine. He even accepted the medicine the second time his mother gave it to him. Not so the third time. As he saw his mother approaching with the spoon, he frowned, turned away, and clamped his lips tightly.

Babies of nine months strive to exert some independence, but their efforts occasionally remind us that they are after all babies. When they get tired or bored, they seek comfort by insisting that a mother or father holds their bottle even though they can easily hold it themselves. Sometimes when fatigue overwhelms them, they just want to be held.

Sense of Self

The baby feeds herself finger foods, indicating a rudimentary sense of independence. Also, increased control over body movements, in combination with improved recall memory skills, means that she has more knowledge of her own body. She doesn't actually have to move or to feel a body part to know it exists. Researchers suggest that at nine months she is able to recognize herself and her mother in a mirror and that she responds slightly differently to her own image. In addition, placing a hand on her father's hand to get him to give her a toy, or frowning to indicate displeasure, are early manifestations of the psychological self.

Recall Memories

For many years my mother and I lived on opposite coasts. Sometime after her eightieth birthday—when she began to show signs of Alzheimer's—I increased my yearly visits. The visits soon became emotionally exhausting. One of the ways I coped was to prompt her consciously to talk about memories of her large family. Each succeeding visit revealed fewer and fewer spoken remembrances of husband, parents, siblings, and other relatives, and then there were none. She seemed to have lost the ability to recall. Hoping to keep alive her memories of her own self-identity, I gathered photographs that dated from her teen years into her eighth decade and made a small album. I had hopes that the photographs would cue her recognition memory. I don't know if they did, but from reports, I know my mother looked at the album almost every day for the next year or so. Then she showed no interest, perhaps losing memories of who she was. Soon too, except for rare, brief moments, there was scant acknowledgment of nearby family or caregivers. My mother's final memory progression was simply this: recall to no recall, recognition memory to virtually no recognition memory. She had lost her memory for words, for key episodes in her life, for scripted actions, and for herself.

I think of my mother's memory loss and its downward spiral from time to time as I try to understand what babies know and what they remember. We know from research that the growth of babies' memories mostly moves from recognition memory to recall memory.

Yet there are major disagreements about how to evaluate babies' recall memories—what memory researcher Jean Mandler defines as "bringing past events to awareness"—and the meaning of research findings. While it is clear that babies can access early memories that rely on conditioning and visual-recognition memory, how shall we evaluate babies' recall in the absence of verbal reports?

Two techniques, object permanence and deferred imitation, are frequently used to define recall memory. Object permanence, described in the chapter on eight months, refers to presenting a baby with an object that is then covered with a cloth. If the baby removes the cloth, shows no interest in it, and immediately reaches for the toy, then we infer recall of the object. One problem with interpreting the task as pure recall is that the pad that covered the toy could serve as a recognition cue for the baby.

Piaget first described *deferred imitation* as indicative of recall memory. In an episode recounted in numerous textbooks, when Piaget's daughter was about sixteen months old, a slightly older child visited the family. The daughter was in her playpen when the visiting child had a full-blown temper tantrum. The next day, while in her playpen, the daughter mimicked the tantrum (she had not had tantrums before). Although the playpen might have provided a clue for recalling the memory tantrum, clearly the girl brought a past event into awareness. Recent studies by Patricia Bauer and Andrew Meltzoff show that relatively uncomplicated instances of deferred imitation can be elicited toward the end of the first year, and more complex ones during the second year. Thus, at the very least, we can say that there are some changes in the baby's memory system occurring in the nine- to twelve-month transition. As parents, you're likely to see instances of deferred imitation.

Beyond those, I want to suggest you look for other evidence of your baby's memory processes. First, let's look at how we use our memories and then use this information as a point of departure for ideas you might consider in relation to your baby's everyday memories. I'll primarily focus on babies between eight and fourteen months of age.

Ulric Neisser, a noted cognitive researcher, has long been interested in how people use memory in their everyday lives. He's the scientist who suggested that one way to think about memory is to consider how we use it. Here's a summary of his list:

We use memories to

+ *define ourselves* in terms of our previous and present activities and consider the future. Some of our defining memories are blurred, whereas others are explicit. We have, however, memories of families, accomplishments, feelings, friends, and more.
+ *evaluate our past activities*, perhaps thinking about ways we might have done things differently. To use Neisser's words, we remember "in search of some sort of self-improvement."
+ *learn* by way of capitalizing on the experiences of others we know or read about. Did somebody act in a certain way that resonates with who you are and your goals?
+ *carry out* the myriad kinds of family and work activities that are part of our everyday lives. These activities range from remembering tonight's dinner guests to working through strategies for handling an on-the-job issue.
+ *engage in intellectual endeavors.*

Most of these memory uses rely on words and ideas, which your baby is temporarily "deficient in" except in a primitive form. But your baby does have the capability to sharpen his memory in terms of Neisser's *defining himself*. And you can help. Consider this. From about eight months on or so, babies love to look at themselves in mirrors. In a matter of weeks, they also stare with fascination at picture books, particularly those with illustrations of people; and toward the end of the first year they are intrigued with photographs. My guess is that the baby's attention to human figures, and hearing you talk about people and what they look like (keep it simple, though), reinforces the baby's *body memory*. In effect, by providing access to mirrors, books, and photographs, you would be using recognition memory to facilitate the baby's image of the self and other humans.

Our hands and their activities also define selfhood because hands speak to some of our physical accomplishments. Babies become increasingly aware of their own hands in relation to toys and objects at about six months. By twelve months, they often laugh with great zeal when they do something with a toy or blocks. This pleasure with self-creation has been called *mastery motivation*. Providing babies with interesting, age-appropriate playthings (e.g., simple nesting toys, puzzles, small toys that have wheels) also facilitates the baby's recognition of the self as *doer*. This may be the reason that babies of this age are endlessly fascinated by all kinds of objects. As parents you have a role in your baby's play: *provide playthings that invite your baby to invite you to participate*. Let her take the lead, however. Joint play activities help solidify your relationship. But don't be surprised in about a year, when your toddler insists "me do" or "I do." These words reflect a sense of accomplishment and your child's memory of her self as a doer.

Admittedly my thoughts about babies' activities and the development of recall have not been validated with research. Yet applied judiciously by parents, the ideas may foster everyday memory for the self before language becomes available as a tool for accessing memories.

Ten Months

+ creeps, stands alone

+ holds toys, implements by handles

+ begins to group similar objects visually

+ looks at parent for visual cues

+ experiments with vocal sounds

Last month the baby showed new skills in dealing with everyday difficulties in her physical world. This month she displays a similar resourcefulness in her dealings with the social world; her social intelligence is emerging. She figures out better ways of picking up information from her parents, and she gets better at communicating her wants. These growing social competencies have an effect on others. Her parents increasingly view her as a social partner as opposed to a social rookie. Parents often reduce their use of baby talk, playfully ask for specific kinds of responses ("Wave bye-bye to Grandma"), and sometimes consciously hold back assistance, watching to see what the baby can do on her own.

Let's look at an example of the ten-month-old's social intelligence. It's a warm spring day, and a baby's mother opens the back door to let in air. The baby follows her, crawling to the threshold. "Should I go farther?" she seems to ask as she turns and looks at her mother's face. Her mother frowns and says, "No, my love!" The baby's eyes never leave her mother's face. She sees the frown, registers it, pauses, and then crawls back into the kitchen. Another day, the baby's brother brings her a new bright green rubber turtle. Her eyes open wide, acknowledging her fascination with this strange new thing. Something holds her back; she's not sure what she should do. She turns to her mother who is standing nearby and looks at her face. Her mother smiles, and the baby reaches for the turtle. The baby is engaging in *social referencing*, looking at someone's face for information.

Whether the baby accidentally finds a cue in another person's facial expression and acts on it or purposefully turns to another person's face to find a cue, the behaviors show flexibility and awareness of the intrinsic value of another person. What a milestone this is! And do be aware of all the baby skills that have fed into social referencing. The baby has the realization that faces contain valuable information; she has the ability to differentiate one facial expression from another; she recognizes that faces belong to people who can provide help; she realizes that she can act on the information contained in a face.

Indirectly, the baby's ability to engage in social referencing will aid socialization. As babies increasingly learn the value of others, they will also try, at least some of the time, to go along with parents' wishes.

Babies, just like adults, do not want to lose the support of people who can help them.

A baby's discovery of her mother's and father's facial expressions as a source of information also goes along with her discovery of details she has not appreciated until now. She is absorbed by the small design on a piece of cloth, the tiny wheels on a miniature toy train, the texture of her applesauce, the lines on an animal cracker, and the mole on her father's face. The ten-month-old stares, touches, and pokes, all the while seeming to ask, "What is this?" Babies peer intently at pictures in an alphabet book as if studying the different shapes and colors of the letters. Although their interest in each page might be relatively short-lived, their overall attention indicates they differentiate one picture from another. Babies at this age are also beginning to show interest in simple puzzles. They move a round block toward a puzzle that contains a circular cutout; babies are aware the circle and its cutout go together.

Let's look at the ten-month-old's efforts to communicate her needs and wants. She turns her head to and fro to indicate "no," "maybe," "yes." Then she occasionally uses a languid finger point, not fully developed as yet, to call attention to something she wants her parents to look at. Recall that last month the baby began to use index-finger probes. Well, this month she is able to combine the acts of extending her index finger and extending her arm, which result in a point. As she gets better control of the point and recognizes its social and communicative value, she'll use it more forcefully and more often.

At ten months babies are also learning that certain sounds—that is, words—go with specific people, objects, and happenings; and now they repeatedly use sounds to identify similar kinds of objects. One ten-month-old created a sound that stood for her toys. One day she said "yass" to a toy in her hand. Several days later she handed a toy to a boy in her play group and said "yass." A week later she said "yass" while watching the mobile in her crib spin around.

Elementary vocal classification includes events as well as objects. One ten-month-old used to mutter "ghhghh" when her play was suspended for a diaper change. She made the same sound when her mother temporarily stopped feeding her to wipe her chin or when her mother pulled her away from an electrical outlet. These three events have the common theme of interruption of a pleasurable event.

The ten-month-old's efforts to make herself clear to others are helped along by her parents' emotional displays. Their smiles, verbal encouragements, and waves greet each success. On the other hand, even the most loving parents emit groans, frowns, or issue sharply worded commands to tell the baby that some activities are taboo.

This month the baby is less likely to put toys and other things into her mouth than she was a month or two ago, although parental vigilance is still necessary. If she does mouth her toys, she's likely to look at them first as if checking them out.

✦ IMAGES OF DEVELOPMENT

Motor Control

Down on the floor on all fours, the ten-month-old demonstrates his expertise in the science of creeping. He has become a brilliant technician in finding out-of-the-way places to explore. Fortunately, this month he is more inclined to stop, at least momentarily, at a sharply worded "No!"

Standing in his crib holding onto the rail, the baby loves being able to stand and babbles cheerfully as he peers around. While he stands, he often practices lifting one foot and then the other, although sometimes he just stands in place and perches precariously on his toes. He also cruises, that is, he walks around his crib or playpen holding onto the rail. Toward the end of the month he might gingerly let go of the rail and briefly, albeit unsteadily, stand alone. Overall, for many babies the pace of gross-motor development seems to slow down this month, as if the baby were getting ready for the big leap to walking.

At around ten months, fine-motor enhancements involve tuning the precision of grasp and extending the ways the grasp can be used with everyday implements. A ten-month-old picks up a spoon, scrutinizes it, and purposefully bangs it against the side of a bowl. Although his movements with objects are not terribly effective, the baby is learning to use hands as instruments for doing specific tasks.

This month, another kind of fine-tuning occurs that has to do with how the baby picks up objects that have a handle. At six months the baby picked up a small bell by wrapping his hand around the base of the handle. When he was eight months old, his hold on the bell was unchanged, but he investigated the bell's clapper and purposefully shook the bell to make it ring. This month the baby's sharpened perceptual skills let him see the bell anew. He now understands that a handle makes it much easier to hold and ring the bell, provided the handle is grasped at the top. With this in mind, he intentionally grasps the top of the handle, rings the bell, and babbles contentedly at his own cleverness.

By this age, some babies begin to show a preference for using either the left or the right hand in their bell-ringing play. In the months ahead, hand preferences become more pronounced, but it will be some time before babies opt exclusively for one hand over the other.

Perception

Vision. Discrimination abilities are continuing to develop. If presented with a very small, clear plastic bottle that contains a small piece of food (perhaps a cooked green pea), the ten-month-old will point at the pea through the bottle's sides. She may also try to reach the pea by poking or shaking the bottle. Her actions indicate that she is aware that the pea is separate and distinct from the bottle itself.

Laboratory studies show that if a ten-month-old is shown a picture that contains sketches of birds that have slightly different features along with a drawing of a rabbit, she ignores the rabbit. She also looks at each of the birds as if she is visually grouping them, demonstrating that she is now able to ignore irrelevant details (for example, different-shaped beaks) when making a classification. Because this ability is so new, babies make perceptual groupings of this kind only after previous, repeated exposures to each of the objects displayed in the stimulus. Why do we care about these early forms of classification skills? The ability to classify represents an efficient way to store a lot of information with a minimal amount of effort.

Babies who effectively make comparisons between two objects are necessarily proficient at managing visual attention, and at ten months, babies show that they are adept at shifting attention from one object to another. When a baby looks at a toy, looks at her dad, glances again at the toy, and then stares at her father's hand, we infer that attention control is quite effective. Each of the baby's actions is well-defined, and she moves comfortably from visual signal to visual signal.

Vocalizations and Language

Along with development of finer sound discriminations, babies are adding to the associations that they can make between words and actions. Some babies recognize that the phrase "Clap hands" means "Bring hands together." Many babies also discover that "Give it to me!" means "Let go of what you're holding or somebody will take it from your hand."

Vocal acts are now a regular part of the baby's everyday behavior, with strings of vocalizations coming forth when playing alone or with others. At this age babies imitate new sounds, such as trills, and experiment with "cuh" for cookie and "bah" for bye. The baby vocalizes new word sounds fairly regularly, and most of them comprise syllables in the language the baby regularly hears.

Cognition

This month, everyday play is often composed of similar types of actions as it was last month—for example, touching, shaking, dangling, throwing, biting, and rubbing toys—but now the baby expands her applications of these techniques. One new type of exploration is demonstrated when the baby rubs her fingers around the inner surfaces of cups; the notion of inside and outside is a fascinating new discovery.

A noticeable new play behavior is the baby's use of specific sequences of actions over and over again. These repetitions of sequences illustrate her ability to organize her behaviors to meet a goal (for example, learning about a specific toy) and to remember the action plan she has developed. A baby might pick up a tinkly soft ball, bring it to her lips briefly, turn it in her hands, shake it vigorously, and then set it down. Then she picks up a hard block and repeats exactly the same sequence of actions. She then tries out the sequence with a doll, and then goes back to her ball. This systematic exploration of toys helps sharpen her knowledge of shape, texture, and sound. There is another benefit as well: the repetition of hand movements helps refine her fine-motor skills.

Social Development

The ten-month-old clearly recognizes that he needs to communicate to others, and he effectively uses gestures to overcome his inability to produce comprehensible language. One of my former colleagues shared the observations she had made of the gestures of her young son, David. The baby's behaviors graphically illustrate sociability, emotional range, and the ongoing mastery of social communication.

Before David was ten months old, he had already learned several gestures. He waved at "hi" and "bye" on request and played pat-a-cake with his sister. Around the time he was ten months old, he started to shake his head from side to side as an adult does, to indicate "no." (Shaking the head to indicate "no" is one of the earliest gestures babies make.) As far as his mother knew, he discovered head shaking all by himself.

David's head shaking was done so regularly and deliberately at ten months that it was possible to identify its three distinct meanings. First, he shook his head from side to side as a sign of displeasure. This was the scene. At ten months he was an extremely messy eater and invariably deposited food on his chin, chest, and elbows as he ate. After each meal his mother went to the sink, picked up a damp washcloth, and walked toward David to begin the cleanup routine. One day he actively shook his head as his mother approached, as if to say, "No! Get that thing away from me!"

Thereafter, he would shake his head as soon as he saw the washcloth in his mother's hand.

David also used head shaking as a cue to himself to control his own behavior. Like most ten-month-olds, he loved to play with telephones. The one that appealed to him most was the phone on his mother's bedside table. Whenever he headed for this phone, his mother would call sharply to him. As soon as she had his attention, she would say, "Not for David." One day as he crept toward the phone, his mother called out, "No, David." He stopped, looked at her solemnly, shook his head, and briefly suspended his movement toward the phone. His mother was convinced that David was dimly aware that he was not to touch the phone.

David's third use of head shaking was in a game he invented. While sitting in his high chair, he would look at one of his parents or his older sister until he established eye contact. Then he would rapidly shake his head back and forth, laughing all the while. The game was best with his older sister; if she shook her head, he repeated his head shaking and laughed with glee. At the time, David's mother wrote, "I can't think of any other give-and-take game that he plays with such obvious pleasure, although he does smile and occasionally chortle with pat-a-cake."

Emotions

The ten-month-old can be an intensely emotional baby. Our grandson Andrew began to greet his grandfather with loud shouts of glee when we visited in our red truck. He seemed to adore truck and grandfather equally. Andrew's negative emotions could be comparably as strong. He would actively turn away from people visiting our home who were unfamiliar to him. When one friend tried to approach him with outstretched arms Andrew did not move, but cried bitterly in protest.

Sense of Self

Being able to stand alone evokes a series of adjustments in the baby's image of his own body and its relation to his surroundings. His whole perspective on the world begins to change, as he no longer has to look up to almost everything. Now he's on an even level with more of the world, and he can even look down on the family cat. What an ego boost!

The ten-month-old loves to imitate body actions. His father covers his ear with his hand; the baby tries to do the same. Stretch a leg; the baby imitates.

Babies of ten months seem to understand increasingly their own mirror reflections. A baby looks into a mirror and sees a toy close by; still looking at the mirror, he picks up the toy and plays with it. In my view, the baby is making some kind of connection with his own actions and the reflection he observes in the mirror. The net result is his growing awareness of the physical side of his selfhood.

◆ DEVELOPMENTAL CLOSE-UP

Social Referencing

Early in the child's second year of life, parents begin to issue firm dos and don'ts, usually with the goal of protecting their child from injury. Dos and don'ts are part of socialization lessons that parents direct toward their children. Socialization practices come out of parents' beliefs about what children must do to protect themselves from harm, to meet family norms, and to live with, and adopt, values from the family's sociocultural group.

Socialization is rarely easy, because most very young children don't have the cognitive resources to reconcile and balance their own needs with the needs and values of others. However, several precursor behaviors help the socialization process. These precursors reflect the very young child's growing awareness of the intrinsic value of *good* parents and other caregivers. Among other things, good parents provide emotional warmth, soothing, and assistance. Social referencing, looking to another person for guidance in an unclear situation, is a precursor behavior. By the end of the first year, babies are becoming ever more sensitive to other people's facial expressions as a form of assistance when they need information.

Social referencing is a universal behavior. We invariably require information quickly about something or other (for example, the social niceties one is expected to observe at a formal reception given by a foreign diplomat). We feel awkward admitting our ignorance so instead we look around and observe the social protocols at this event. Our information-gathering behavior isn't too different from that of a ten-year-old who sneaks a quick look at the face of a trusted buddy rather than admit that she doesn't know what to do next in a board game. And our behavior and that of the ten-year-old are quite similar to that of the ten-month-old looks who looks at his mother's face when he receives a new toy and isn't sure if he wants to explore it.

Joe Campos and his colleagues first described social referencing behaviors among ten- to twelve-month-olds. They used a variation of the visual cliff experiment, which had been used to study depth perception. In the variation, babies saw what seemed to be a shallow surface that led to a steep drop, but in reality it was all an optical illusion. For the study, babies were placed at the illusionary shallow end of a very large box, with their mothers encouraging them to crawl across the seeming drop. Sometimes mothers smiled; other times they frowned. Babies tended to cross when their mothers smiled. Based on these and other studies, it was assumed that babies looked to their mothers (or others) for a facial clue that, in effect, said, "this is the way to act." An ancillary interpretation was that babies were clued in to their parents' feelings or intentions about the object or event that was bothering the baby. Stated another way, the baby responds because he is a mind reader. (Some qualification is in order here: often our facial expressions reflect our feelings, but not always. Astute adults can make the distinction, but babies cannot.)

In any event, additional research using different eliciting conditions for social referencing suggests the following: We can better understand how and when babies seek information if we take into account the varied situations that elicit social referencing. Although babies clearly use others' emotional expressions as a guide for their own behaviors, something else can be happening. Consider this scenario. Mom has just bought a sleek, colorful vacuum cleaner and is smiling while she explains its features to her older son. Baby Jane crawls close because her beloved older brother is nearby, yet she is fearful of the vacuum's sound and looks at the vacuum and at Mom for reassurance. Mom offhandedly smiles at Jane, thinking more about the vacuum and not the baby's visual inquiry. The baby crawls toward the vacuum. Maybe she registered Mom's smile, but her older brother might have inadvertently influenced her behavior as he lay on the floor examining the vacuum's nifty wheels. The distinction between behavior that comes about because of intentional information seeking and behavior that is prompted by incidental pickup of cues may seem trivial. However, at its core is how we interpret a baby's behavior and whether we are inclined to provide babies with more knowledge, intentions, and capabilities than they have.

Despite these qualifications, we know the enormous value of social referencing for babies. Ross Thompson, for example, proposes that social referencing reflects babies' increasing ability to obtain emotional meaning from activities they share with others. Beyond infancy, Thompson suggests, social referencing allows young children to compare their own assessments of a situation with those of another individual. In so doing, the child begins to see where his ideas match or differ from those of others, including peers. In my view, this kind of matching is a critical piece of socialization.

Some other points about social referencing are worth noting. Social referencing does allow us to make inferences about the kinds of knowledge the baby brings to the situation. First, there is recognition that facial expressions and gestures convey meanings. Second, there is knowledge about the meanings of certain expressions (a smile says, "All is well"; a frown says, "I don't like . . ."). Third, the baby is able to decontextualize the message. In other words, the baby effectively interprets the other person's facial expression whether it occurs at home, in a store, or in a park. Given this complexity of interpretive demands, the fact that ten-month-olds engage in social referencing is additional testimony to their burgeoning mental activity.

In another vein, Mary Gauvain suggests that social referencing is a form of *cultural apprenticeship*. The baby, as an active learner, uses social referencing to seek information from more experienced individuals whose behaviors often indicate the social and cultural norms of the baby's and its family's community. She also reminds us that parents can inadvertently pass along their own biases, via their facial expressions, to their babies.

Lastly, here's an idea for an amusing parenting pastime. The next time you engage in social referencing, think back to your baby's or toddler's social referencing. Surely, it will be entertaining to compare the situations that prompt your behavior and the situations that prompt those of your child!

Eleven Months

- ✦ *walks while holding on*

- ✦ *releases objects voluntarily*

- ✦ *temperament style more pronounced*

- ✦ *recognizes alternative means to an end*

- ✦ *directs word-sounds to specific objects and people*

◆ SNAPSHOT

Many eleven-month-olds are often preoccupied and at times downright obsessed with learning to walk. They practice standing and walking while holding on to some kind of support: their crib, along a couch, and down one side of their parents' bed and up the other. Insistent about standing and cruising, they're often unwilling to sit or lie down. Much to the chagrin of their parents, they struggle to stand while in a high chair. And just in case you don't get the message about this extraordinary developmental transition, eleven-month-olds stand in their cribs calling out word sounds long after they're supposed to be asleep! Life is suddenly a little more trying for parents.

The eleven-month-old's determination to walk fuels his desire to exercise his independence and motivates him to try new ways of doing things. He experiments with taking big steps and small steps and holding onto the crib rail with either his right hand or the left one. He understands that there is more than one way to do things. With new and different experiences, his actions become more planned. An eleven-month-old, while cruising in his crib, bumps into his teddy bear, which is resting against the crib rails and blocks his path. Without a moment's pause the baby drops down, creeps around the bear, grabs hold of the rail, pulls himself up to a standing position, and resumes cruising around the crib. Neat behavior.

The baby's interest in walking seems to make him more tuned to different kinds of movements and their effects. He deliberately jiggles a bell's clapper as if wondering how the sound comes about; surely he senses a link between moving the clapper and sound. He sits on the floor and rolls his ball repeatedly, studying its easy motion as it rolls here and there. His eyes are riveted on the movements of his father's keys as he dangles and shakes them. He even accents his favorite forms of communication with motion; he vigorously nods when he laughs and shakes his head when he says, "No!"

Although gross-motor activities are dominant this month, fine-motor skills show changes as well. Most important, babies are better able to release toys easily and accurately. Although this development may not seem profound, a coordinated release is a momentous precursor to more sophisticated forms of play. Without it, the baby would find it difficult to build with blocks, fit puzzle pieces into a puzzle, or put pegs into a pegboard. A coordinated release is also useful for putting a spoon back into the soup bowl or putting the toothbrush into its holder.

There are also modest though important gains in language skills this month. Babies seem to understand a few of the words that are directed to them, and they associate a person or an object with a word. Mama, Dada, and teddy bear now seem to have meaning. The baby also produces more sounds that are like real words and some sounds that are actual words.

Overall, eleven months is an age at which important achievements occur, even though some may not be particularly dramatic. A variety of developments are happening, including maturation of skills (the ability to release a toy voluntarily), integration of skills (maintaining balance when upright), and consolidation of skills in preparation for new abilities (cruising prior to walking).

✦ IMAGES OF DEVELOPMENT

Motor Control

Don't be surprised if your eleven-month-old cruises around the edge of her crib until she literally collapses from exhaustion. A brief rest, and she's raring to go again.

Cruising helps babies attain better control of their body when standing in an upright position. It also helps clarify their sense of where their upright body is in space. Remember that babies are used to navigating by creeping on the floor, so their view of near and far space, room arrangements, and even people changes as they move about standing up. Cribs and playpens are great practice areas for babies because they offer confined, safe spaces that still allow lots of walking time and opportunities to study surroundings from the perspective of an independent, upright walker.

At this age you're likely to observe differences in babies' movement styles. In contrast to one baby's intense, almost passionate need to cruise, another is more easygoing, methodical, and tactical. He might look like a participant in a spontaneous, old-fashioned hoedown, and she might appear to be readying herself for a carefully choreographed dance.

Babies who are particularly adept at gross-motor movements tend to approach activities as if they have a plan in mind: it's a nice coordination of problem solving and motor skills. An eleven-month-old who was in one of our studies did the following in the lab room, which contained several sturdy wooden chairs of different sizes. The baby knelt and placed both hands palm down on the seat of one of the chairs. Then she raised one knee so she could set her foot firmly on the floor. Next she pushed off with that foot and her hands so that she rose slowly into a stooped-over position. Then she slid one hand toward the back and side of the chair seat and pulled up with this hand against the seat while simultaneously pushing down on the seat with her other hand. She stood up. After standing for a few seconds, she then pushed the chair in front of her body, which she proceeded to use as an effective mobile support for cruising around the room.

Babies of this age are simply blissful about their own physical activities. They reach for this and that, try to climb on anything that seems climbable, practice raising and lowering one foot and then the other, and pick up one toy after another. Another eleven-month-old in our lab stood before a toy basket and stretched herself as tall as she could get trying to reach the toys in the basket. There was a doll on the bottom of the basket that she wanted, but it was just out of her reach. As she tried to climb over the side of the basket to get the doll, it tipped over. There she was, sitting under the basket with the doll now lying next to her. No cries for help. She managed to crawl out from under the basket, picked up the doll, and played happily.

In terms of fine-motor skills, babies like to place objects (small blocks) into small containers such as a cup. This action takes quite a bit of control. You'll also see examples of control during mealtimes. Babies will use the thumb-forefinger grasp to pick up and feed themselves large and small pieces of a cookie. In addition, they'll more or less carefully put pieces of food—a cookie—down on the high-chair tray. A month ago, efforts to "let go" might have resulted in the cookie bouncing off the tray and onto the floor.

Language

Comprehension. In the last few months babies have learned to figure out some of their parents' gestures, facial expressions, and intonations. Some clever researchers have shown there is a definite increase in the number of words the baby comprehends at twelve months versus nine months. It is most likely that eleven-month-olds do make associations between a few words and objects or people. In fact, numerous parents have reported that at eleven months the baby is more responsive to a phrase such as "Give it to me!" or the word "No!" or his own name than he was last month. Sometimes, though, it is difficult to tell if the eleven-month-old actually understands that a specific word names a specific thing (person, object) or if his response is based on his recognition of his parents' gestures, body language, and speech intonations.

Overall, though, comprehension seems to be relatively limited at this age. So don't be disappointed if your baby doesn't always respond as if she understands. One study that involved slightly older babies showed they understood fewer than 25 percent of the simple nouns and verbs their mothers used while playing with them. Another researcher showed that babies and toddlers use a lot of guesswork in their efforts to understand words and phrases.

Production. Determining the growth of the baby's speech is far easier than trying to find out what he understands. In casual observation, it's clear that eleven-month-olds tend to direct more of their word sounds at specific objects, people, or events (*da* for "daddy," *buh* with a wave for "bye-bye"). They sometimes combine these sounds with appropriate affective expressions; for instance, *buh* may be accompanied by a facial expression of expectation and a gaze at the door. Babies of this age also work on learning to speak by closely watching the mouths of others and moving their own mouths in imitation of their speech.

Even during this early period of speech acquisition, differences appear in the number of words babies produce. Some babies say six words, while others do not produce any. A baby might say only one word, "Uh," which he mostly utters softly. But then when he points to his spilled juice, he yells, "Uh, uh, uh!" No matter how many words the baby speaks, he invariably says fewer words than he understands. His word comprehension will continue to exceed his word production for the next year or so of language development.

One word that some eleven-month-olds have in their vocabularies is "no," which they accompany with headshakes. Sometimes they even nod their heads and say "no" when they want to communicate agreement rather than dissent. They do this because they don't have a "yes" word. First, the word "yes" is too hard for them to pronounce. Second, the eleven-month-old usually has no understanding of "yes" because it's a word not commonly used by parents when talking to their babies. To express encouragement, parents rarely say "Yes" to their baby; they are more likely to say "Good baby," or a similar phrase. So it is not too surprising that an eleven-month-old says "No!" to a cookie even though he loves cookies and dearly wants one. This "No" is the all-purpose action verb. This is the word the baby associates with making things happen.

The "No" of eleven-month-old babies is quite unlike the "No" of eighteen- or twenty-four-month-old toddlers. That "No!" tends to signal self-assertion and resistance to a parent's request. Sometimes the need for self-assertion is so strong that a two-year-old also says "No!" when he really means "Yes." Although the child can say "Yes" and knows what it means, he may be so determined to declare his independence he does not say what he really means.

Cognition

This month babies appear to catch on to the notion that there is more than one way to be entertained; they are likely to try another tactic when a first choice is not available. For example, a baby has been playing with her father's keys. Now he needs them. Unlike earlier months, she is easily mollified when Dad replaces the keys with a magazine. She busies herself right away with turning pages and making word sounds at some of the pictures.

The eleven-month-old is also moving toward a greater appreciation of the characteristics of objects. If given a set of nesting objects like the old-fashioned Russian dolls that fit inside each other, the baby will attempt to nest them. At this age she sometimes correctly fits one object into another, but she is usually unsuccessful at fitting the whole set together. When given a narrow rod six to eight inches long, she uses the rod as a pointer and taps a nearby toy. With this simple action, the baby shows she recognizes a functional use for the rod.

Social Development

This month also increasingly reveals differences in toy play of boys and girls. Boys begin to move around more actively than girls, whereas girl babies engage in more intricate toy examinations. Many girl babies prefer soft, cuddly toys, while boy babies often display a preference for "action" toys. These differences arise even though parents might try to rear their babies in gender-neutral environments.

But, of course, rearing environments contain any number of gender-specific clues in terms of clothing, hair styles, grooming aids, and the like. However, a number of scientists believe that some biological influence is at work here. Studies of spontaneous play of nonhuman primates reveal strong preferences for rough-and-tumble play among young males. Whatever biology's role, and despite often observed gender predispositions, it helps when parents remember that many normally developing girl babies enjoy playing with action toys and many normally developing boy babies favor cuddly toys.

Another interesting social development occurs this month: the baby begins to respond warmly to a greater number of people. Her various interests support affectionate attachments to people who play various roles in her life. It is not uncommon for the eleven-month-old to form special relationships with her father, a friendly next-door teenager, a grandfather, and so on. She knows that each one acts and reacts to her in different ways, and she obviously enjoys these differences. This increase in the baby's social network, so to speak, has implications for emotion supports. During upset times, the baby understands there can be different sources of comfort. This helps when parents and baby are briefly separated.

In addition to changes in social responsiveness, babies of this age tend to be increasingly exposed to other babies. We know from government statistics that in our culture more mothers of infants work outside the home than ever before, and often this transition to work takes place toward the end of the baby's first year. Nowadays, many babies receive daily care in various kinds of group-care settings. In addition, at-home moms often attend local Mommy & Me programs, which include groups of babies and toddlers. And, of course, many mothers plan their daily schedules around gyms that provide workout time for themselves and child care for their young children. Invariably parents ask questions about the social effects of being with other babies.

Research suggests that babies' social skills are given a slight boost by exposure to other babies. The eleven-month-old doesn't show prolonged interest in other babies, but she does creep toward another baby, sit close to him, and sometimes even hold out a toy to him. Some researchers also suggest that early peer exposure paves the way for easier preschool peer relations. Only more research will tell; right now there is not enough data to support this suggestion conclusively.

Don't be concerned if your eleven-month-old isn't too interested in other babies. At this age, there's so much to learn about the world that most eleven-month-olds simply go about exploring toys and entertaining themselves with toy play.

Emotions

The eleven-month-old has his emotional ups and downs, but on balance his mood is buoyed by increased independence and the thrill of moving about in an upright position. Despite his generally positive disposition, there can be some rough moments. Anger appears every so often, as babies seem to become easily frustrated at this age. Babies' ways of "handling" frustrations differ greatly. Some express these emotions with physical acts, like the son of the great scientist Darwin, who beat a toy he didn't want! Others might react to an unwanted toy by crying, forcing a parent to intervene.

Some babies are cautious now about venturing into new space, while others forge ahead into unknown areas. Some are generally serious and quiet when they play alone, whereas others grin and babble incessantly. Some show their desire to be near a sibling, whereas others ignore them. Some no longer accept a bit of cracker to eat, insisting on the whole thing. Others are content to eat whatever is offered. Some fret when a favorite person leaves, while others play merrily. All in all, around this age each baby is beginning to show individuality; the baby's personality is emerging.

Sense of Self

Moving about in an upright position strengthens the baby's sense of the independence of her physical self. She is becoming more aware that her body is under her control and she can move wherever she wants. With so much attention focused on her body and movement, it is not surprising that babies quickly learn the names of body parts. When parents ask, "Where is . . . ?" babies are likely to point correctly to nose, tummy, and toes. Mirror watching is greatly enjoyed, particularly if babies are able to greet and wave to the mirror image.

This month the baby's improved ability to carry out a role in more social games reinforces a sense of mastery. She can be quite insistent this month about feeding herself; she doesn't mind that clumsiness with spoons and cups leads to a mess.

✦ DEVELOPMENTAL CLOSE-UP

Parenting: Culture and Development

Every so often I'm reminded of the vast cultural changes that have taken place in our country in the recent past. At a local plant nursery, a middle-aged black man cuddled his gorgeous toddler son while his younger Chinese wife paid for plants. At a wedding, white, black, and Latino couples mingled with white and black, white and Latino, and white and Asian couples. It was fun to watch their young children romp on the lawn and try to figure out who was related to whom.

Professional groups concerned with parenting and children's development are trying to understand this rich cultural diversity and to determine if and how parenting changes because of it. The reason for this interest is clear: a sizable amount of our knowledge about effective parenting and young children's development comes from studies of Caucasian children of primarily Euro-American ancestry. This pattern is gradually changing in the United States, as researchers are involved with studies that include black, Hispanic, and Asian children.

Historically, there were a few classic developmental studies that included samples from around the world and detailed studies of parenting of young children in cultures other than that of mainland United States. A careful examination of cross-cultural studies reveals more similarities than differences overall in early development, suggesting that effective parenting probably encompasses a wide range of approaches at least for the early years. Studies of parents and babies from other cultures have tended to emphasize differences, some of which have provoked debates about traditional American ways of child rearing with respect to feeding schedules, soothing, and sleep arrangements. There's also renewed discussion about the ways we interpret patterns of parenting: Ruth Chao's research, focused on parenting influenced by Chinese cultural patterns, reminds us that sound knowledge of a culture likely provides more accurate interpretations of parenting.

Now I step back and briefly describe how parenting advice evolved in the United States. It's not hard to make a connection and envision how research on parenting and child development also evolved. Then I end this close-up by saying there is still much that we do not know about diversity and culture and children's development. However, I also include a mini-model that you can use to think about your own parenting style, whatever your cultural background.

During the early part of the 1800s printing in the United States became increasingly mechanized, and our young republic was soon blessed with countless magazines and books. Education for young girls grew dramatically because of the enticing things to read, including fashion magazines from Europe! This was the era when a significant number of parenting-advice books began to appear for the general public, and the first pediatrics book was published (which also contained child-rearing advice). Major disagreements soon surfaced about how best to rear children: Physicians disagreed with mothers; church folk such as the Calvinists disagreed with the Transcendentalists (for example, Ralph Waldo Emerson); self-anointed child-rearing experts disagreed with both physicians and mothers. There was no disagreement though on one point, albeit it was largely unspoken. The books' audiences were white middle-class families, whose backgrounds were largely Dutch or English. Many parents from these families could read, and many aimed to secure their status as upstanding members of the rising middle-class community.

Despite sporadic attempts to enlarge the audience for child-rearing books by appealing to other groups of parents, it took another 150 or so years for this to occur. Slowly, there was recognition of cultural and ethnic diversity among parents who not only wanted advice but also wanted to maintain a sense of cultural and ethnic identity in their parenting approaches. The study of young children's development has also increasingly recognized that parenting and cultural beliefs go hand in hand. Each parent brings lots of family and cultural history to child rearing, even with babies and toddlers. The point is not to deny these histories, but to recognize strengths in individual cultures and ethnic memberships, and at the same time recognize the universal physical and psychological needs of very young children. Given the diversity in our culture and differences within cultural and ethnic groups, developmental scientists have yet to determine when and if a culturally based parenting mode is especially enhancing, particularly detrimental, or inconsequential in terms of babies and toddlers' overall developmental well-being. Note, I am not saying that culture is unimportant. Of course, it is. The point is to understand culturally encouraged practices in relation to babies. Does it matter in the first two years of life if a cultural norm proscribes use of pacifiers or encourages siblings (including toddlers) to sleep in the same bed or discourages toddlers from autonomy seeking or encourages fathers to play with their babies? Increasingly, researchers are attempting to find answers.

As a parent, you may be interested in Ross Parke and Ray Buriel's tripartite scheme of parenting. I have used this approach with students as a way for them to think about how they plan to parent their young children. I've adapted Parke and Buriel's model should you want to do the same with reference to you and your baby/toddler. The arrows from one box to another suggest patterns of influences. Yes, a baby's behavior can influence parent behavior! The pluses and minuses within each box are cues: Do you do a lot

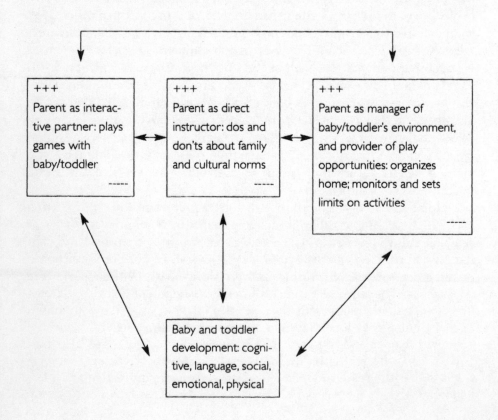

or a little of each kind of activity? What factors influence how you respond to your baby? Nobody is scoring your answers. You might consider your style and those of mothers from other cultures. Where do you think there's lots of agreement, or differences? Don't be surprised if you learn that researchers ask similar questions.

Twelve Months

- walks alone

- combines two toys in play

- speaks a few words

- holds toy out to parent

- forms attachments

- shows nascent emotion control

The twelve-month-old straddles a developmental threshold: she is no longer a dependent baby, but she is not yet a full-fledged toddler; she requires a few more months to develop the complex social and language capabilities and sense of self that we associate with toddlerhood. Overall, though, this is a wonderful time for the tyro toddler. She is inquisitive and has a wide-eyed appreciation of her surroundings that speaks to an ever growing intelligence. Her pleasure in her locomotive independence seems to know few bounds. The one-year-old enjoys herself and her parents enjoy her, even though they may not be sure if they are dealing with a baby or a child.

The first birthday is a major milestone: increasingly, developmentalists recognize the age as an important landmark for cognitive, emotional, and social growth. Twelve months ago there was a helpless fretting newborn. Six months ago, though chirpy and happy, the baby couldn't get around on her own and sometimes had difficulty showing people what she wanted. Now she walks a bit, understands numerous words and phrases, says a few words, uses her hands to communicate to others and to play with toys, controls her attention when she wants to explore an object fully, and to some extent can control a fearful emotion. These are impressive accomplishments and will serve as vital building blocks for development during the second year.

The birthday girl is hard at work. For one thing, she eagerly continues to practice her walking skills. Unassisted walking is a source of amusement for her, and even a brief stroll broadens her field of exploration and increases opportunities for learning. In addition, walking frees her arms and hands whenever she moves; before, they had to be used in crawling and creeping. So now she uses her hands for moving toys from place to place, another big step in the transition from babyhood to childhood.

Walking is a developmental event that parents of the one-year-old view with mixed feelings. It signals the end of needing to attend to her every wish, but it also marks the beginning of a long period when parents will have to monitor the baby's wanderings. As soon as children begin to walk easily, they no longer like to spend time cooped up in playpens. They would much rather be walking in the kitchen, living room, and other places where there are enticing things to get into. Vigilance is essential.

Although walking is the big event this month, there are other important changes as well. For the first time the baby is able to exquisitely coordinate her attention control, her problem-solving skills, and her ability to use her hands as tools. All three came into view as a twelve-month-old sat on her mother's lap in my classroom. I placed a cardboard tube about five inches long on the table and draped a chain made of a dozen or so paper clips across the tube. The baby looked intently at the tube and chain; her hands were still. Then she made a move, using her hands as she worked through solutions to solve the *problem* of putting the chain inside the tube. It's a great example of an "Aha!" moment. The baby rolled the tube on the table and stood it on end. Next she picked up the chain with one hand and tried to insert it into the end of the tube, which she held more or less steady with the other hand. She saw the connection between tube and chain, tried to make it happen, but did not have the coordination for success. After repeated attempts the baby looked at me, as if knowing I could help her. Her mother also glanced at me. I nodded. The mother showed her daughter how to solve the problem. They grinned at each other.

You'll probably notice new forms of play around this age, which often reflect other kinds of improved cognitive and perceptual skills. The baby might make a collection of a ball and colored rings, presumably because all of them are round. She'll put all her yellow blocks into her toy basket, leaving out all blocks of other colors. In addition, her play includes multiple examinations of a toy. She pokes, fingers, inspects, scratches, mouths, and rolls a toy. She repeats these maneuvers repeatedly until satisfied. These repetitions are not stereotyped; she deliberately introduces variations into her routines. What happens if I push the truck? What if I pull the truck? What happens if I push the truck on the carpet rather than on the wood floor? One-year-olds demonstrate sharpened visual-perception skills as they fit covers onto jars, remove a round puzzle piece from its circular hole, and attempt to insert different-sized toys into a plastic jar. They soon discover that some fit and some do not.

Although the one-year-old seems to relish playing in her own way with her own toys, she is also eager to bring others into her play. Sometimes all she wants is acknowledgment of a toy. She takes a preferred pull toy to her mother as if inviting her mother's participation; she pulls the toy away as soon as her mother reaches for it. The message is "Tell me you see me and my toy." She drags a favored doll to her older sister when she comes home from school. A twelve-month-old who has been reared in a family that emphasizes reading often tows a picture book around, hoping somebody will read to her or at least point out pictures.

Bear in mind that children of this age communicate with gestures, eye contact, and vocalizations as they seek parents' recognition, participation in exploring activities, and assistance when they need help. Parental sharing means a lot to the year-old's emotional well-being and, invariably, helps with his burgeoning thinking and speech skills.

Yet, also, there are many little ways that year-old children show they are beginning to develop assertiveness and possessiveness. These new behaviors are due partly to the pleasure they gain from being in control and doing things on their own. Shrugging away assistance, they devote many minutes to removing a shoe. They persevere at feeding themselves, although eating without help means that food may be splattered, and the best part of a cookie falls to the floor. There is insistence on walking by one's self although falls are frequent. Walking, playing, and talking are endless sources of satisfaction, which will help as toddlers develop their own self-identities.

Children of this age are fun, but they do present challenges. Yes, they need lots of positive support for their explorations, learning, and speech. They also need monitoring for safety. Sometimes, too, they collapse with fatigue, and at the end of the day they need structure and attention. They also need special attention when the family or day-care scene gets busy. Although children of this age love to be with others, their tolerance for other children, family friends, and visiting relatives can be measured in minutes rather than hours.

In all, the first birthday closes out a year of acquiring many basic skills. It also opens the door to a period when these foundation behaviors are used to develop more complex skills and to establish independence. From now on, more and more childlike behaviors will be evident.

◆ IMAGES OF DEVELOPMENT

Motor Control

At around a year of age young toddlers stand on their own and walk independently. The characteristic gait of toddlerhood is wide based; that is, the feet are spread apart. This posture lowers the body's center of gravity and increases stability, which is just what the beginning walker needs. In fact, the designation "toddler" comes from the word *toddle*, which literally means to move unsteadily. Whether he has been walking for a week or for a month, the one-year-old is still unsteady on his feet. Walking demands a great deal of his attention; he checks where his feet are and where his body is in relation to a room and its furniture.

Because balance is initially very precarious, the young walker often combines walking while holding onto a support with both hands, holding on with one hand, and walking without assistance. With practice, holding on becomes less frequent. The pace of growth in self-locomotion skills picks up rapidly after the child consistently walks without holding on. In the next few months young toddlers learn to walk backwards, run, and jump.

Just six months from now, parents will be admonishing, "No running in the house!"

At this age fine-motor skills are fairly well developed. The year-old child adeptly holds a string of beads, and his fingers move methodically over each bead. While performing this deliberate investigation, he intermittently points to the dog. He easily goes back and forth between bending his fingers to inspect the beads and straightening his fingers to point at the dog. He never once looks directly at his hands. Hands are coordinated enough for stacking small objects and placing very simple puzzle pieces.

Reach, grasp, and release are easily accomplished with either hand. The important achievement is that one hand is used to hold a toy and the other to perform some action on it: he holds his pegboard with his left hand and tries to insert the pegs into the board with the right hand.

Perception

Visual attention. Every once in a while I like to remind parents of the more subtle ways that babies change in the first year. One of these ways involves the baby's control of attention, which I've mentioned periodically. I again want to highlight the baby's controlled attention (also called sustained, or higher-level), which occurs when the baby is about ten to twelve months old. At this age, babies turn to an object of interest, look at it for a long period, and turn away when they've lost interest for the moment. Research by Michael Posner and Mary Rothbart has linked this behavioral change to new linkages formed in neuronal pathways. Perhaps the most important long-term developmental consequence of sustained attention will be the child's increasing ability to give undivided concentration to learning. More specifically, Holly Ruff and Mary Rothbart have noted the tasks that require higher levels of attention, which include planning, decision making, troubleshooting a problem or dealing with those that are technically difficult, and resisting the temptation to do something that might elicit difficulties.

Why do I refer to sustained attention in terms of a subtle developmental transformation? My answer is simply that sustained attention can be masked by the baby's seemingly insatiable fascination with standing and walking—if the baby is just beginning to walk. In a series of studies, we have found that nonwalkers at twelve months were better able than new walkers to control their attention, and walkers with a month or more of experience showed different forms of sustained attention. The more experienced walkers could sustain attention to a book and equally well sustain attention to a rolling toy. This is another example of the interrelatedness of behaviors that is increasingly prominent toward the latter part of the first year and thereafter.

Hearing. Sometimes development involves losing an ability so that a new, more mature form can take its place. Toward the end of the first year, babies are less able to discriminate sounds that are not in the language of their primary caregivers. One study showed that year-old babies reared in the United States had difficulty discriminating various *t* sounds common to Hindi. What this means is that babies are becoming more sensitive to sounds and words of their own culture.

Language

Comprehension. At twelve or thirteen months the baby experiences a dramatic upswing in understanding word sounds. Just a month or two ago the baby seemed to comprehend only one or two words. Now the young toddler generally responds appropriately to twenty to fifty words. She nods her head, points, and runs to carry out commands such as "Show me . . . ," "Get the . . . ," and "Where is . . . ?" The first words that are usually recognized refer to the people, toys, objects, animals, or activities a twelve-month-old regularly comes in contact with. Words she initially understands usually include *sleep, kiss, look, come, get, dolly, bear, ball, car, shoe, bottle, no,* and *doggy* (or the dog's name).

There is, however, a substantial amount of variability in comprehension skills at this age; some twelve-month-olds understand as few as three words and others more than a hundred. Family makeup may be a factor. For example, babies who have older siblings are exposed to far more spoken and gestural language than are only children. Research also suggests that at this age girls understand more words than boys. This gender difference may be due to slightly faster biological maturation; however, studies show that little girls tend to be talked to somewhat more than little boys and this increased experience may account for the differences.

When I describe comprehension at this age, I do not mean to imply that the young toddler fully understands the definition and concept of words such as *shoe, ball,* and *teddy bear.* Whereas to his older sister a shoe represents a piece of apparel made of certain materials that has a specific style and a conventional use (you wouldn't be likely to wear party pumps to play softball), to the year-old child a shoe, whether it is a shoe, slipper, or boot, is simply something that is put on a foot. Similarly, in the world of the one-year-old, anything that moves on four legs and is furry is likely to be thought of as a dog, whether it is a dog, a cat, or a tiger at the zoo.

Occasionally twelve-month-olds inadvertently fool their parents about the words they understand. Sometimes they produce a proper response to a request because they really do understand. Other times they guess right because they pay attention to a look or a gesture that accompanied the request.

Production. The twelve-month-old routinely says fewer than a dozen words, and it is not uncommon for a total vocabulary to consist of only two or three words. As with comprehension, there is considerable variability in the language production of year-old children. I have seen a few year-old children with more than a hundred words in their vocabulary, but these children are rare. Scientists are not sure why there is such developmental variation in language production. Familial inheritance, the presence of siblings and other relatives, the nature of caregiving, and patterns of parent conversations with the baby are all factors that researchers are continuing to study.

Words that include *m*, *b*, *d*, and *w* sounds seem to be easiest to say at this age. That's why *mama*, *baba* (for bottle), *da-da*, *buh* (ball), and *wah* (water) are often among the first spoken words. Besides their own real words, young toddlers often mimic the speech of others. Put a toy telephone receiver in their hands and they jabber away, mimicking the sounds of conversation. Baby Michael uses *sh* to refer to something that goes on his foot and *baba* to denote anything to drink. He talks all the time, even though he does not have many real words. His speech is a combination of real words and nonsense sounds, technically called jargon. "Mmabahgon," he said one day, which sounded a lot like "Ma, my bottle is gone." It's not certain that that was what he meant, but his intonation was just right.

Cognition

Increasing activation of the frontal lobes of the brain occurs around this age. Studies of babies and nonhuman primates using Piaget-type tasks tell us that behavioral inhibition—that is, not immediately reaching for an object but studying it first—is essential for success on certain cognitive tasks. Twelve-month-olds tend to be successful inhibitors whereas younger infants are not.

Cognitive achievements linked to this age period include the beginnings of functional play, the onset of imitation of everyday actions demonstrated by others, the use of multiple strategies to aid memory (staring, pointing), the use of multiple approaches when babies are confronted with unusual tasks such as figuring out how to go down a steep ramp, the use of various problem-solving approaches to try to solve Piaget-type or similar tasks, improved recall memory in terms of retrieving imitative acts, and the clear distinction made by babies between those individuals who can offer social and emotional support and those who do not. We'll look at some of these achievements.

Imitative learning is common at this age and helps generate new forms of play. A baby bangs a spoon on a bowl, imitating her sister eating ice cream. Another holds his toy hammer by the handle and pounds away just like his father. Imitative learning has defined links to functional play, which is play where babies use toy-sized replicas of our culture's tools and implements. In functional play, the baby uses the toy on himself (a comb) or on another person or a doll. In our culture, babies might have access to toy brushes, combs, dishes, brooms, eating utensils, and more.

Play this month also includes a great deal of trial-and-error exploration including shaking, tapping, biting, rolling, and throwing toys. Then, there's inserting toys into containers, putting one toy on top of another, and using one toy to touch another. Mostly, these activities reflect the baby's desire to see what he can do with objects, to learn about their characteristics, and to better understand spatial awareness related to things (or people) being up, down, on top of, under, and inside. A note of caution: explorations can include stove knobs, VCRs, plants, harmful agents, and more. You'll want to encourage your baby's desire to explore but also protect him. Also be mindful of your possessions that won't withstand constant intrusions by little hands.

Memory skills again improve this month. Whereas the nine-month-old solves object permanence tasks that involve one hiding place, the twelve-month-old manages to remember when the hiding task is more complex. For example, in the laboratory I take a small car, put it into a small box, remove the car, and then place it under a piece of cloth. The task not only involves multiple stimuli, it also demands spatial awareness as the object is moved about. The year-old baby generally finds the car without difficulty.

Studies show that year-old children have what is called cross-modal recognition memory. This complicated term means that a child can hold an object in his hands and, without seeing the object, correctly select a drawing that matches the object. Everyday crib behavior illustrates this capability. A baby likes to look at and cuddle his soft toy rabbit before going to sleep. During the night he wakes up and gropes for the rabbit in the dark room. He immediately recognizes it when he touches it.

At twelve months, the toddler is just beginning to arrange objects by size. He repeatedly attempts, in a process of trial and error, to arrange the rings of his stacking cone and the pieces of his nesting toy in order. Success will come in a couple of months as the toddler figures out spatial configurations, sizes, and sequences.

Social Development

The one-year-old dearly loves toys, but this love is matched by his affection for people. He is particularly affectionate toward a few people. He runs to his father and kisses him when he gets home. When his father sees a helicopter in the sky and points to it, he looks up. He recognizes at some level that his father wants him to share this experience with him. These examples remind us that this is the age when babies communicate to others through joint attention, gestures, showing and sharing toys, and noticing the facial cues of parents and others.

Changes in social behaviors also include the development of more attachments. The baby forms multiple attachments because different people offer him various kinds of enjoyable experiences. His older brother plays rough-and-tumble games with him, an older sister adopts him as her toy soldier, and his grandfather gives him rides on a bright red truck. Multiple attachments also increase the twelve-month-old's willingness to explore; he has any number of people to turn to for comfort and reassurance.

Also at this age, children assume greater control in social games. During object-permanence studies I was involved with, many a one-year-old viewed the tasks as a game. They began to assign new roles to my colleagues and me. They would take the toy that was being hidden, hide it under one of the felt pads, and look expectantly for a response from us. Of course, we played along with much glee and laughter, acknowledging a nice example of the interrelationship of cognitive and social skills.

This month parents often introduce a few simple rules to help keep the child safe and the family's possessions intact. Sometimes the one-year-old responds to a "No!" or "Don't touch!" But don't expect too much because the baby just does not understand: this is where a parent's gentle assertiveness, monitoring, and consistency will help.

Emotions

The year-old child is emotionally aroused by others' distress and may cry if she hears someone crying. She doesn't make any attempt to offer help or comfort; she simply acknowledges the other's misery with her own cries. The young toddler also cries when something happens that is not to her liking, such as being refused more ice cream or being exposed to a situation that was fearful to her at another time (the doctor's office). The twelve-month-old also laughs a lot this month, at her own cleverness, at her own jokes, and in play. She even acts as if she's beginning to develop a sense of humor.

In some children signs of jealousy appear at this age. Jealousy is an interesting emotion developmentally because scientists are not sure about its origins, why it appears when the baby is about a year old, and why not every twelve-month-old displays it. In some cases, jealousy is most apparent when siblings are present who demand/need parent time, but it can even surface with pets. Baby Ann's family just brought home a puppy. Ann clearly loves this new family member, and she's often down on the floor petting the puppy and stroking its fur. However, Ann frowns and frets when her father pets the puppy, and she tries to insert herself between her father and the dog. She doesn't yet understand that her father's affection for the puppy in no way lessens her father's love for her.

Sense of Self

One psychoanalyst described this month as a time when the toddler begins "a love affair with the world." Walking and the ability to use words to express thoughts and feelings contribute to the love affair; they are also the cornerstones of what will be the toddler's sense of personal identity. The world is hers to master and to conquer. Every once in a while she stops to peer at herself in a mirror as if to say, "This is me!"

Also, the one-year-old's increased efforts to include others in her experiences and her imitation of others may signal that changes are taking place in her awareness of self. At some level she seems to recognize that "belonging" has something to do with knowing about others, knowing about her own separation and her own existence, and recognizing that it is others who often make us feel good and occasionally make us feel sad.

◆ DEVELOPMENTAL CLOSE-UP

Emotion Control

Sometimes our emotions make trouble! We yell in anger, later regretting the outburst. We become paralyzed by a fear, later regretting inaction. Sometimes we blame ourselves, sometimes others, and occasionally resolve to do better. Anger and fear are the emotions most of us try to control. There are times we consciously avoid people who make "our blood boil," and we avoid situations that send "shivers down our spine." Paraphrasing James Gross, we learn that effective emotion control means trying to make appropriate matches between our emotions and the situations we encounter. We control our emotions by using personal resources—thinking and evaluating, for example—to maintain social contacts that are important for us and to achieve goals we set for ourselves. Emotion control can also limit physiological stresses.

Humans dislike persistent and continuing high states of arousal, albeit individual tolerance levels vary. This aversion probably explains why even young babies suck their thumbs to try to calm themselves or older babies reduce rising arousal levels by distracting themselves with play. The fact is that consistent high arousal in babies reduces their ability to learn, may interfere with their physiological health, and often adversely affects their interactions with other people. Much the same can be said for older children, as well.

Parents start teaching babies emotion control from the newborn period on. In the early weeks, crying occurs because of physiological discomforts. Even at this age, soothing by parents helps babies recognize the contrast between the unpleasantness of distress and the more enjoyable state of non-distress. Later on, babies begin to experience the psychological states of pleasure, happiness, boredom, fear, and anger. Parental soothing again has a role in reinforcing the distinction between unpleasant arousal and calmness.

Babies learn some forms of emotion control during the first two years, and their emotion-control abilities reflect development in other domains of behavior. Cognitive and language development are especially important, as you can see in the following table that lists common causes for upsets, and how and why children respond.

Research tells us that emotion control is somewhat easier for babies who are not especially irritable and for toddlers who talk earlier rather than later. Continuing support from parent helps too. Even babies who tend to be irritable can learn more effective emotion-control strategies with supportive and sensitive parenting.

Overall, research also suggests that young children are more likely to develop effective emotion control when parents are responsive to their babies' and toddlers' upsets, help their children find ways to control their emotions, and talk about emotions and emotion control in a nonthreatening way.

Recent research also provides compelling information about the role of

Age	Examples of situations that lead to upset	Examples of emotion responses	Developmental limitations
5 months	Body restraint: diaper change	Fusses, cries	Doesn't understand *offending* action
12 to 15 months	Restrictions: can't play in toilet, garbage pail	Cries; attempts to push parent away	Can't *control* situation or talk about wants
18 to 24 months	Boundaries: asked to follow mealtime routines; can't touch others' possessions	Cries; yells; tantrums; hits/bites	Sees *threat* to self; can't figure out parent wishes, and can't describe self-goals

language in emotion control. Emotion researchers such as Suzanne Denham, Judy Dunn, and Carolyn Saarni have reported how children's abilities to talk about emotions is essential for their later emotional and social competence.

What exactly do young children talk about in their emotion-focused conversations? Judy Dunn found that toddlers often mentioned their own feelings in disputes they had with their mothers. More recently, Kristen Lagattuta and Henry Wellman reported that the parent and young children's emotion conversations tend to involve issues around negative emotions (e.g., being sad, angry, fearful) rather than positive ones (e.g., liking someone), probably because negative emotions are troublesome to the people who are involved. These researchers also found that parents and their children actively engaged each other in emotion conversations, although parents often guided the direction of the conversation; discussions about negative emotions often referred to past events rather than ongoing or future events; conversations about negative emotions tended to focus on the cause of a negative emotion (e.g., "Why did you cry?"). Conversations about emotions seem to enhance young children's abilities to understand their negative emotions, and to generate effective coping strategies to manage their negative emotions increasingly effectively.

The essential message: Talk to your toddler about his or her emotions. It's the conversation that matters.

DEVELOPMENTAL HINTS AND ALERTS:

EIGHT TO TWELVE MONTHS

Hints

+ Play social games with the baby such as baby gone, pat-a-cake, and how big

+ Provide simple puzzles of one or two pieces, with simple shapes (a circle)

+ Hang a play box on the side of the crib

+ Read to your baby. Use uncomplicated picture books, as well as books that have a few words accompanied by simple drawings

+ Let your child hear nursery songs

+ Provide blocks and plastic jars with large openings for dropping objects in and taking them out

Safety Issues

+ Make safe places for crawling and walking

+ Cover all electrical outlets

+ Remove lamp cords, and other touchable objects that can cause things to tip over

+ Put safety closures on low cabinets

Alerts

Seek advice at the end of twelve months if your baby does not

+ grasp toys

+ sit by herself

+ differentiate among people

+ show interest in social games or smile or laugh

+ make vowel or consonant sounds

SHARPENING OUR FOCUS

The Acquisition of Speech

The baby's first words are an extraordinary accomplishment of early development. The transition from no speech to words is sudden and dramatic, although, of course, the baby has been learning language from birth onward. He has been listening, sorting through sounds, associating sounds with objects and people, and acquiring information about his everyday world. One week the baby makes sounds that have no meaning to us, and then suddenly he says a word that is comprehensible. "Puppy," Andrew declared at thirteen months when he looked at Natasha, his family's short-haired Doberman. "Puppy," Andrew said two weeks later when he saw Charlie, our small, shaggy cocker-poodle. Actually, neither dog was a puppy, but that did not matter: Andrew was speaking; he was saying words.

Why did Andrew select *puppy* as one of his first words? Lois Bloom, a noted researcher of babies' and toddlers' language, says that children's first words refer to things they know best and that are interesting. That is why words such as *mama, dada, doggie, bye,* and *gone* are common first words. Natasha played a major role in Andrew's family life, and she was also a big dog. Interestingly, Andrew's father occasionally called Natasha Puppy, although more often he called her Natty or Natasha. Somehow Andrew sorted out these words and realized that puppy applied to both his dog and our dog. I never heard Andrew refer to Natasha as Charlie or vice versa.

How speech develops and grows is a tantalizing question. Several ideas have been proposed. Bloom suggests that speech comes after babies develop an understanding of people, events, and situations. Recall that between nine and twelve months, babies begin to remember objects and people even when they are out of sight. Also around this age babies detect commonalities in characteristics, such as *birdness* or *dogness*. Babies also distinguish between familiar and new faces. They are building a storehouse of knowledge that Bloom believes is a prerequisite to language development.

The list that follows is one that I summarized from Golinkoff and Hirsh-Pasek's book, *How Babies Talk.* It suggests the kinds of knowledge that lead into first words. The examples are mine. As you'll see, dogs, particularly small ones, are invariably appealing to toddlers. And they love to talk about them.

+ FIRST WORDS

  + The spoken word goes with a particular object. Andrew's use of *Puppy* labeled the family's pet dog, and our dog.
  + The word is used intentionally and purposefully, but not necessarily

correctly, according to adult standards. Just recently, a thirteen-month-old looked at our Yorkshire Terrier and said, "Baby!" Here the toddler used his knowledge of size (very small, as a baby is) to label the dog.

+ The word takes in the whole of the object; Andrew used the word *Puppy* to apply to the whole dog, not just some of its parts.

+ The word is used to define or label objects that have similar features: Andrew said *Puppy* when he saw the big Doberman and our small cocker-poodle. In a matter of days, he said *Puppy* when he saw a dog in one of his picture books.

+ The baby utilizes an active memory system to retrieve the word that has been learned, and what it represents to him. Sometime after Andrew used *Puppy* for Natasha and Charlie, he came up with the word *a'mal* to label all other animals. Then later in his second year, he learned words such as *cow*, *pig*, and *lamb* and used these words to correctly identify animal pictures. Interestingly, when he was two he first saw a live cow close up in a stall at a county fair. As far as he was concerned this was not a cow. Andrew was terribly frightened by the size of the cow and also unable to match his picture-book knowledge of cows with the real thing.

It's an interesting bit of history to recollect how scientists ignored the knowledge babies bring to word learning: many believed that babies learned language solely by imitating the speech of others. Fortunately, this idea began to be rejected when language researchers like Bloom recorded sentences that were true baby creations. Imitation could not be a reasonable explanation for toddlers' phrases such as "Mommy sock" or "No dirty soap."

After imitation was dethroned, *biology* became an explanation for language. Noam Chomsky argued that the principles of speech for all languages are innate: a genetic blueprint lets a toddler reared in an English-speaking household innately derive information about English grammar, in which nouns typically precede verbs in a sentence. Chomsky viewed environmental influences as switches that set universal principles in motion; otherwise, he did not think they had much of a role in language acquisition. Today only diehards reject the importance of the language that a child hears in his everyday experiences, and the knowledge children gain before they speak.

The most popular current view of speech acquisition is a modified biological-environmental one. Yes, the premise goes, there is some kind of biological basis for language because children learn words without being taught. Indeed, Steven Pinker's book *The Language Instinct* offers a good read about biology's role in language. Yet virtually everyone recognizes two critical features of language: children use words to label things that they *already know* from their own experiences, and other people who are in the child's social milieu have vital roles in facilitating the child's language growth. It is a fact that young children who are reared in meager language environments do not have robust language and cognitive skills.

From a developmental standpoint, it's interesting to observe the wide range of individual differences in speech among children of similar age. At fifteen months, some children still do not speak any discernible words, others say half a dozen words, and a few have a vocabulary of fifty or more words. This variability is typical. Of course parents do become concerned if their 2½- or 3-year-old does not speak. Yes, seek advice if you're worried; you want to make sure there's no hearing problem or any other difficulty. However, it pays to remember that several immensely gifted children, including Einstein, did not speak until past two years of age.

While most of us tend to think of language development in terms of the number of words a toddler utters at one or another age, scientists who study the growth of speech also consider other issues. For example, they ask whether the words that are produced are single words, two-word sentences, or sentences of three or more words. Typically, single words characterize the speech of children who are between twelve and twenty-four months, whereas two- to three-word sentences are often used by many two-year-olds ("Mommy tummy hurt").

Language researchers are also concerned with word meaning. When do children use words that are consistently appropriate to an event? Even novice speakers do so surprisingly often. "Up!" "Down!" "More!" are examples. When does word imitation occur? It seems that children echo words they are in the process of learning, not the words they know well. "Feeway," two-year-old Andrew would say when I announced that we were going to drive on the freeway. After a few weeks, Andrew stopped imitating "feeway."

New words, Bloom says, cost the child cognitive effort. Here's an example one of my colleagues related about her toddler daughter. When Giuliana was sixteen months old, she pooped in her diaper while she and her mother were in a department store. My colleague rushed to the ladies' room, only to find it closed for cleaning. Repeatedly, she knocked on the door, loudly calling "Miss! Miss! Miss!" When the cleaning woman opened the door, my colleague thanked her profusely. Shortly thereafter Giuliana was given a new doll, which she promptly named Miss. The department store episode had obviously made a big impression on her. Fast forward to Giuliana at twenty-one months. Every evening when she came home from day care, her mother would greet her with "I missed you!" One night Giuliana picked up her doll and said, "Miss, I missed you!" No sooner had she uttered the words than she turned to her mother with a stricken expression on her face as if to say, "I don't understand what I'm saying." Her mother comforted her and explained as well as she could why a word could be a name and also refer to a feeling of loss.

Sometimes, too, a stressful situation brings on a struggle with words. If the "cognitive effort" is disproportionately high, the child reverts to a stock of ready-made phrases that cost little psychological energy. The mother of three-year-old Sam and five-year-old Bruce has reminded them about inside and outside toys. While playing outside, Bruce mounts Sam's tricycle. Enraged, Sam can only manage to pull a familiar phrase from memory. "That's not an outside toy," he yells. Bruce gets the message even though the words are not quite right.

Language researchers also consider speech in terms of its grammatical construction. Children show marked variability in the elements they use in a sentence and in sentence construction. Differences include the use of prepositions, tenses, singular and plural forms, negations, and contractions. The question for the researcher is what kind of sentence can children produce when they are two or three or four years old?

Another researcher and her colleagues recorded and analyzed the crib monologues of Emily, a remarkably precocious two-year-old. Emily's sentences were long, contained complex clauses, and were replete with adjectives. Yet Emily's monologues rarely contained *ing* endings, possessives, articles, or the third-person singular. At twenty-one months, Emily said, "So my daddy went in the meeting in the car." This is a complex sentence for a two-year-old to produce. Two months later she produced this very awkward sentence: "On Saturday go Childworld buy diaper for Emily." This sentence tells us that mature forms of speech can be interspersed with immature speech forms during the course of language development. Young children can get tongue-tied just like grown-ups!

Speech for the child is fundamentally a tool for communication. Children use words to tell others about who they are—their activities and their feelings, desires, knowledge, and caring. Here are some examples.

COMMANDS TO OTHERS:

Eighteen months: "No!" when asked to put toys away; "Mine!!!" when asked to return another child's doll.

Twenty-four months: "I do it!" to a laboratory assistant who started to open a box of cookies.

Twenty-four months: Ann to her father while sitting at the table: "Daddy eat."

Twenty-four months: Andrew greeting his grandmother with a football: "Grandma, tackle me!"

UNDERSTANDING PAST TENSE:

Twenty-seven months: Andrew to his mother after she gives him a cold drink: "I was thirsty."

PLEASURE AT ACHIEVEMENT:

Seventeen months: Sarah to me: "I found it!" after retrieving a toy hidden under one of two felt pads.

Thirty months: Michael to his grandfather after he had erected a tower of blocks: "I did it!"

ATTEMPTS TO UNDERSTAND:

Thirty months: Allie to her mother while raking leaves: "Why don't leaves turn blue or purple in the fall?"

Thirty-three months: Neal to his mother while in the park: "Why can't you pick up a hole?"

TEMPERAMENT

Almost everyone knows someone who is easygoing, who doesn't get upset about day-to-day hassles, is generally calm and happy, and likes being with others. Then there are other kinds of people, some of whom tend to be jumpy, irritable when the unexpected arises, moody, and demanding. Irritable people can be tough to deal with; fortunately some also have sought-after qualities. Consider my maternal grandmother: she created emotional firestorms and havoc until she "got her way." She was demanding and critical, particularly with selected children and grandchildren. Yet at times she was generous and supportive, and her unbridled energy and curiosity were windfalls for many of us. My grandmother was full of *temperament!*

If my grandmother had been a participant in temperament-related research, she would have been interviewed, tested, and asked to fill out questionnaires, with a goal of comparing her behaviors to the behaviors of others on characteristics such as adaptability; emotionality, including irritability; intensity of responses; impulsivity; and more. The question of interest might have been: is this woman's typical mode of behavior unusual when compared with women of similar age and background?

As you probably realize by now, the study of temperament is an analysis of individual differences in behavioral styles. The issue for scientists and clinicians is to understand if, when, and how a temperament style leads to behavioral and social problems. There is now sound and consistent evidence, for example, that young children who have very difficult temperaments are especially vulnerable to poor parenting and thus more prone to serious social and emotional disorders later in life.

Is one's temperament the same as one's personality? Some temperament researchers such as Mary Rothbart and Jack Bates think not. Personality tends to include our cognitively influenced view of our self, how we deal with others socially, the nature of our individual skills and how we perceive these skills, the particular values that tend to guide our actions, our view of the world as benign or unfriendly—and our temperament. Said differently, personality represents *much* of who we are. In contrast, temperament represents *part* of what we are, primarily with reference to our emotionality, adaptability, and sociability. Given that babies are simply too immature to have views and values, some researchers suggest that personality and temperament are indistinguishable during the early years.

The study of children and their temperament styles began in earnest during the 1950s and 1960s when psychiatrists Stella Chess and Alexander Thomas asked if children's temperaments influenced how they developed. Some children seemed so easy to parent, whereas others were incredibly difficult. Chess and Thomas described three kinds of children: The *easy* child shows positive mood, is adaptable, and is mild to moderate in intensity of response; the *difficult* child has up-and-down moods, withdraws from new experiences, has low adaptability, and shows high negative affect; the *slow-to-warm-up* child is inactive and uncomfortable in new situations and tends to withdraw from them. Parent and child communication was most apt to suffer when children had difficult temperaments and parent and child could not adapt to one another.

Chess and Thomas also defined temperament according to dimensions such as activity, rhythmicity, adaptability, threshold, intensity, mood, approach, and persistence. Questions soon arose about their classification system and their definitions. Shortly, new questions arose about definitions of temperament, how best to measure it, whether stress influenced temperament, if temperament was inherited, if one's temperament style could change, and more. The study of temperament took hold, and has led to thought-provoking research. Some of the most interesting, I think, concerns babies and their temperament styles.

I'll briefly highlight five topics that might interest you as parents of young children. These are definitions of temperament, measurement of temperament with babies and young children, questions about temperament and heritability, the links between temperament and attachment, and the stability of temperament from early life to later. But do keep in mind, all of these topics are associated with some disagreements and controversy.

Definitions. Current definitions of temperament, with specific reference to babies' behaviors, include dimensions related to fearfulness, irritability and fussiness, a generally happy state that includes smiling and cooperativeness, activity level, attention span and persistence, sociability, and rhythmicity (regularity of functioning such as sleep). This list, partly derived from temperament researchers Mary Rothbart and Jack Bates, has similarities to temperament defined for older children. For the older age group, temperament is considered to include irritability and uncooperativeness, persistence, sociability, rhythmicity, emotionality, self-regulation or inhibitory control, and attentional focusing. Variations in definitions are partly a function of the way temperament is measured.

Measurement of temperament. Three popular ways of collecting information about babies' temperaments include use of parent questionnaires, laboratory-based observations of babies or toddlers with structured conditions, and observations of parents interacting with their children. Sometimes only one of these approaches is used, and at other times all three are. The questionnaires and structured laboratory observations came out of many years of thinking about temperament and many years of working through the content of temperament measures. Mary Rothbart's temperament questionnaire contains questions for parents about their baby and is quite popular with researchers. It is comprehensive, which is in line with her definition of temperament that broadly addresses babies' differential levels of reactivity and regulation. Jack Bates's temperament questionnaire is quite brief. He has suggested that temperament is manifested largely in social interactions, and thus the short form has been effective in defining troubled parent and baby interactions due to high levels of baby irritability. Hill Goldsmith's laboratory measures rely on observations and have been used in a number of studies. The measures are particularly useful when researchers want to achieve precision in presentation of stimuli that are likely to prompt differential-temperament responses.

Temperament and heritability. This issue is somewhat complicated, so let's start with some background ideas. You and your dad are low-key, easygoing individuals. Now you could be easygoing because you and your dad have had a warm and close relationship or you and your dad could have similar temperament styles because you and he are biological relatives who share certain kinds of particular genetic material. However, you and your dad can't be genetic mirror images of each other because half of your genetic background came from your mother. At most, you and each of your parents are 50 percent genetically similar. Yet, even this amount of shared genetic material might account for some degree of temperament similarity between you and your dad.

The extent of genetic influence within a population of individuals is labeled "heritability." How does one go about studying heritability? Typically, approaches involve the study of identical and fraternal twins, or adoptees along with analyses of their adoptive and biological parents, along with careful analyses of the kinds of environments that are similar or different among children in a family. Use of sophisticated modeling and statistical techniques are essential for data analyses.

Researchers have identified genetic influences for certain forms of intellectual skills, for forms of mental illness such as schizophrenia and bipolar depression, and for temperament. Depending on the population group that is studied, heritability estimates tend to be higher for intellectual functioning than for mental illness and for temperament. Irrespective of heritability levels, there is evidence for a link between temperament and mental illness (such as bipolar depression), but at this point there isn't enough evidence for a link between temperament style and level of intelligence.

It's important to always keep in mind that even if an aspect of our behavior is heritable, environmental influences substantially influence our behaviors. However, environmental influences are not equal among siblings: environmental influences often vary greatly within a family because of parenting and other childhood experiences.

Heritability and babies. Although we tend to think that a baby's behavior is just like that of Uncle Joe or big sister Sue, babies' temperaments are actually a work in progress. Analyses of heritability of temperament with toddler-aged children show higher heritability values than studies of babies.

In one twin study with toddlers, Hill Goldsmith and his colleagues found evidence for heritability of activity level. This is interesting because there were minimal environmental effects on activity levels. In other words, if parents in the population group that was studied tend to be active and have high energy levels, it is more likely than not that their child will have similar energy-related characteristics. The researchers found both genetic and environmental effects for pleasure (e.g., a generally happy state) and effortful control (a complex behavior that includes controlled attention and behavioral inhibition). Here family genetic background and parental rearing patterns are both important for a positive outlook and for the ability to concentrate and to pay attention. However, research findings were unclear about the temperament styles related to fearfulness or proneness to anger. Yet in another study, researchers reported that negative emotion was the primary aspect of heritability. At this point we need to acknowledge mixed results; however, it seems that heritability is highest for irritability and activity level.

Attachment and temperament. One of the big questions about attachment is whether attachment style is more or less equivalent to a baby's temperament style. That is, are securely attached babies essentially easygoing babies, and insecurely attached babies simply irritable babies? Another question is whether the attachment relationship is undermined if babies tend to be irritable month after month (in the absence of any physical problems). Does irritability cause parents to be less responsive to their babies?

I'm partial to the approach taken by Brian Vaughn and Kelly Bost in their analysis of research focused on temperament and attachment. They analyzed data from forty-seven studies where one or more aspects of temperament were studied in relation to attachment (mostly measured with the Strange Situation). I'll highlight their review of studies of babies' irritability because this topic is probably most interesting to parents.

First, Vaughn and Bost evaluated the claim that attachment and temperament were actually two sides of a single coin, namely the coin that represents the interactions of parent and child. After their in-depth scrutiny of studies, they concluded that "there is more to temperament than can be explained by individual differences in parent-child relationships." In other words, temperament and attachment are not just different words for the same idea. They are different aspects of individual differences. This conclusion makes sense if we think about the diverse aspects of temperament style (for example, persistence) that probably have limited effects on how a young child manages to deal with separation from a parent.

A second point is that parents' reports of baby irritability or difficulty often do not go along with ratings of secure or insecure attachment that are made by observers who record child behaviors during the Strange Situation. Here again I have to point out that these findings are contradicted when other attachment measures are used in home-type settings. In these situations, babies and young children who are reported to be difficult or irritable are also less likely to turn to their parents when upset. However, even here the magnitude of the statistical relation varies considerably across studies. Sometimes the statistical result is strong, sometimes weak. So the finding is not a certainty. In my view, this is important and reassuring information for parents who are attempting to deal responsively with a difficult baby and who worry about their relationship with the baby.

However, Vaughn and Bost do emphasize the conditions that lead to risky relationships. If a baby shows marked irritability during the earliest weeks of life and if the baby's parents have minimal social or economic resources, there is increased vulnerability for negative parent-baby interactions and later insecure attachments. On a positive note, research has shown that when quality interventions are provided to high-risk mothers, the quality of attachment often improves.

So, if you're a parent of a baby who is irritable and temperamentally difficult, try to obtain some time off now and then. Even a brief time away from an irritable baby reduces stress. Also, try to obtain professional advice about ways you can tailor your parenting to the baby's needs. Overall the goal is to help your baby adapt more successfully to his surroundings and to keep your relationship on a good path. Temperament is not destiny, and good experiences make a difference.

Temperament and stability. When psychologists use the term *stability* they generally mean that relative rankings of individuals at time 1 are fairly similar to relative rankings at time 2. Thus, a high score at time 1 and a similarly high score at time 2 reflect high stability, as does a low score at time 1 and a low score at time 2. Low stability occurs when there is a high score at time 1 and a low score at time 2, or vice versa. Stability is frequently used to study individual differences in intellectual abilities, temperament, aptitudes, and achievement.

Suppose we ask one hundred parents of eighteen-month-old toddlers to rate their child's irritability on a scale of 1 to 10, and we rank ratings from high to low. It turns out we obtain a good distribution: there are a few toddlers at the high end of irritability, some at the low end, and most in the middle. Two years later we again ask parents to rate their child on irritability levels. If the toddlers who were rated high on irritability are still rated high as preschoolers, and the lows are still rated relatively low, and the middle group is more or less the same, then we conclude irritability is a stable temperament dimension. Alternatively, if there has been a fair amount of shift in parents' ratings, then we conclude instability.

In terms of actual research, Chess and Thomas indicated the strongest stability they found in their long-term study of temperament was intensity of response. In contrast, Rothbart and Bates's review of temperament studies indicates some degree of stability for measures of proneness to distress (irritability) and for approach (sociability) versus shyness. Findings for activity level are mixed. However, it is possible that stability ratings are influenced by who does the ratings and where children are observed. Kenneth Rubin and his colleagues observed children for stability of shyness (or inhibited style) across a three-month period. They found stability only for those two-year-olds who were consistently observed as being inhibited across different situations.

There's yet another study of stability of temperament that raises interesting issues. The data came from a large longitudinal Australian study that included temperament measured in infancy and several additional times through eight years of age. Not all temperament variables were stable. The strongest stability was found for approach (shyness, sociability) and rhythmicity (such as sleep patterns) from infancy through age eight. In contrast, stability for irritability was found only for the age period from early infancy to age three. Also interesting is the fact that the temperament attribute of persistence was stable only from midpoint in the toddler period to age eight. This result likely reflects how well the young toddler manages attention. Recall that sustained or controlled attention begins to appear at about twelve months or so. And persistence becomes a key factor by the end of the preschool period in terms of school readiness.

∿

SO, AS A PARENT think about your child's temperament and your own. Try to make reasonable adjustments, so that your parenting and her temperament more or less match. In other words, don't be supercritical of your child-care skills but do try to be sensitive to the temperament style of your baby or toddler. Be flexible. Seek advice if you and your child seem to be on vastly different temperament "wavelengths."

Think about the fact that aspects of temperament are likely to be stable, and other aspects change. Consider the temperament qualities you might want to promote.

The Second Year: Toddler Times

Preview

Fifteen Months

Eighteen Months

Twenty-One Months

Twenty-Four Months

Developmental Alerts: Eighteen Months, Twenty-Four Months

Sharpening Our Focus:
Parenting and Stresses
The Child and the Chimp

✦ PREVIEW

DO YOU LIKE MUSIC? I hope you said yes because my next bit of advice concerns music for your well-being. The toddler years invariably bring parents lots of emotional highs and more than a few emotional lows. Get hold of some CDs that can increase your pleasure gradient when your toddler charms you, and some that will bring you out of the doldrums when your toddler brings you to despair. You'll come out of this, just as parents have done for aeons. Just remember, though, your toddler truly needs your love and support for healthy development.

The terrible twos! Myth or reality? In jest, but with more than a grain of truth, years ago psychologists Joseph Stone and Joseph Church described toddlerhood as the first adolescence. At both ages, mood swings and emotional outbursts appear unpredictably. Unreasonableness, self-centered behaviors, and stubbornness are common. Yes, but both ages also represent growth: there are new ways of thinking about the world, renewed commitments to others who have emotional significance, increasing understanding about the self, and a desire for knowledge and challenges. All of this and more imply major developmental transitions, which are rarely easy for anybody. Church commented that times of major change are often accompanied by "disruption and turbulence." Many developmental scientists, myself included, agree.

Unlike the adolescent, the toddler does not have a large core of knowledge about people, events, and objects. His language is as yet insufficient to explain the depth of his desires and goals. He does not yet have peers and friends that can serve as support systems. It is not surprising that toddlers are easily threatened by perceived psychological or physical intrusions, including those that force a choice between increasing social demands to conform and the desire to enhance their own sense of independence. Undeniably, toddler-related developmental bumps occur. If you can mostly maintain a sense of humor and go the extra distance with patience, sensitivity, and supportiveness, you and your toddler should be fine.

So much dramatic and far-reaching development takes place during the second year that I find it useful to use six descriptive benchmarks to describe growth: thinking using ideas that can be retrieved and communicated to others, play that involves increasing amounts of pretense, exercising autonomy in the service of self-identity and goals, ever increasing skill in verbal communication, showing concern for others who are distressed, and growing control over emotion displays. The interplay of all of these domains—cognition, emotion, social skills, selfhood—comes together in rich ways in the second year. Many times the result, especially as your toddler reaches two years, is a level of thinking and social skill that will surprise you.

It's also true that toddler turbulences often arise because of differing rates of growth, particularly related to cognition, language, and selfhood. The toddler has an appreciable amount of information about himself, his family, individual roles, acceptable behaviors, and how to act, but all too often he doesn't have the words to tell others all that is on his mind. It's no wonder that frustrations take hold now and then and result in tears and physical pummeling (kicking, pushing, biting, hitting). Try to keep a lid on these kinds of outbursts, and when things quiet down, remind your toddler about dos and don'ts.

During the second year toddlers do become increasingly adept in thinking and remembering words and ideas. Emotion words include *mad, sad*, and *happy*; self-related words such as *I, me, my*, and *mine* reflect toddlers' knowledge of their own identity and selfhood; and words such as want as in "want my blankie" reflect the ability to communicate needs. Interestingly, toddlers' ideas also find expression in words that take on unconventional meanings. Remember the child who used "baby" to refer to a small dog?

There's also data that suggest toddlers begin to have a sense that their own desires may differ from those held by others. We're not sure just how extensive this knowledge is at this age. Later on, during the third year, many children begin to bargain and negotiate in earnest. At that point, we're quite sure children know what they want and are aware their parents may disagree!

In terms of pretense, pretend play is an activity where the toddler uses props that simulate real things. A wooden block becomes a toy truck. A large leaf becomes a blanket for a small doll. Pretense means that the child has an *idea in her head*, a mental image, of the real thing. She understands she can make believe: one object substitutes for another if the real one is not available. Pretend play is tightly linked to thinking in terms of ideas or things.

Autonomy and independence are also high in the toddler's world scheme. And the development of her selfhood depends on exercising some autonomy. However, problems arise with parents because toddlers do not yet understand they are members of social groups and they are to abide by family and social norms. Thus the limits that parents often place on the toddler, which prevent them from doing things on their own terms, are a source of frustration.

Another source of frustration arises from the toddler's occasional inability to make the world of objects do his bidding. If the tower he is building falls down, he perceives it as a defeat, and he cries. Fortunately, by the end of the second year most toddlers understand that some problems are beyond their skills. So before frustration sets in, they seek help.

Emotional displays are a distinctive feature of this age, but not all emotional developments in this period are disruptive. For example, the toddler is definitely more concerned about others' feelings and seeks to help others feel better. His ideas about comfort seeking may not match ours, but the thought does count. Also during the second year, a nascent form of guilt emerges. This feeling of doing something wrong, then apologizing for the act and thereby reducing a parent's annoyance, does help socialization.

Toddlers also show frequent displays of their humor and they play jokes that take the form of playful teasing. Here's a wonderful play on words offered by two-year-old Lilly. She and her grandfather are discussing frogs, when she tells her grandfather a frog is sitting on her. Uncertain about her words, the grandfather asks for an explanation. Lilly replies, "The frog is sitting on the lily pad!"

Lastly, the second year sees evidence of increasingly effective, self-generated forms of emotion control. I've already mentioned turning to another for assistance. However, emotion control is also represented by the toddler's use of blankets, bits of cloth, and soft and cuddly dolls. These items are used by toddlers to allay fears of one or another kind.

＊

THAT'S A PANORAMIC VIEW of development in the second year. What about some age-specific behavior characteristics? Well, the fifteen-month-old climbs and explores, is fascinated with toys and their characteristics, teases and tests parents, and seeks help for others who are in distress. The eighteen-month-old is more self-absorbed because of his growing self-awareness. His vocabulary may have grown to fifty or even one hundred words, but his cognitive and memory skills have outstripped his spoken language, and the gap between his comprehension and speech production actually widens this month. For these reasons and others that we don't fully understand, many eighteen-month-olds are restless, irritable, and stubborn from time to time.

At twenty-one months the toddler is emotionally calmer but more exacting. He has begun to develop a sense of how things "should be," and his requests can be incredibly specific: he wants to wear this shirt, not the other. Fortunately, he is beginning to use two- and three-word sentences, so he can make more of his thoughts known. He also often tries to use the ideas he has acquired. His play reveals that he remembers elaborate sequences of events.

By the end of the second year, the toddler easily entertains himself and in turn is easily entertained by his surroundings. He has an increased interest in age-mates, his pretend play is more complex, he shows that he understands family members' roles, and his language skills are less of an impediment now and cause less frustration. However, he has developed a more structured idea of the world, and he can be contrary when he is unable to impose his viewpoint on others. When he doesn't get his way, tantrums may result. Change is upsetting at this age, and for parents it can be especially trying to move, to find new babysitters, or to take the child on a long trip.

Learning to be your own person isn't easy. Balancing self-desires with social demands can be challenging. I don't make excuses for toddlers; they can try your patience. Indeed, I sometimes contemplated returning my grandson to his parents not long after they dropped him off for a weekend. He was a handful—difficult to please, uninterested in toys, irritable—between eighteen and twenty-one months, but he came out of this mode soon after.

I suggest you focus on the times when things are going smoothly and keep those in mind when difficulties set in. Invariably, they too will pass; just try to maintain your emotional equilibrium and patience. Overall, you will find the second year a wonderful period in your child's development.

Fifteen Months

+ *climbs*

+ *loves to explore*

+ *engages in functional play with toys*

+ *teases others*

+ *tries to help*

◆ SNAPSHOT

The fifteen-month-old is a toddler on the move, poking into things as if his curiosity knows no bounds. Let him explore, as long as it's safe for him, and your possessions are protected from prying fingers. But do know that in your home, everything the toddler encounters is fair game: drawers, the laundry basket, cupboards, closets, books, the vacuum cleaner, and the water in the toilet bowl.

You may see some persistent and repetitive behaviors as your toddler sets about learning about an object and how he can control the learning situation. I had been studying Tim's cognitive development for a number of months. When he was about fifteen months old, I presented him with some familiar cognitive-play tasks. One task involved figuring out how to get a cookie placed on the far side of a lazy-Susan turntable. Unlike previous visits, this time Tim discovered he could turn the lazy Susan on his own to get the cookie. Suddenly he gave the Susan a spin, and then he spun it again and spun it again. He slowed the Susan down and turned it slowly and then speeded it up again. His eyes grew big, his cheeks became flushed, and he breathed heavily. In his eagerness Tim forgot all about the cookie. The lazy Susan, which had been the means to reach a goal, had become his all-consuming passion.

Another fifteen-month-old, Noah, showed a similar preoccupation with repeated explorations, although the circumstances were quite different. Noah's mother was teaching him how to put big plastic keys into a toy-key box. As they sat on the floor together, Noah watched his mother intently for several minutes. Then he suddenly stood up and, swiftly taking a green key, ran to the door of the playroom. He touched the toy key to the key-hole. Then he dashed from room to room in his large, rambling house, at each room touching the key to a doorknob. His mother and I trailed behind him, but he never saw us; indeed, he never glanced at anything other than the key and the doors. What a sense of power he must have felt as he put toy key to door after door.

Obviously Noah had learned about keys and their relation to doors from his parents. And taking a cue from the toy key, he imitated the action he had observed many times previously. I like to think that Noah knew that his play was not the *real thing*, but the imitated activity itself provided him with pleasure. Noah was showing that he wanted to be in sync with other members of his family. Joseph Church's book *Three Babies* also provides a fine description of a fifteen-month-old's imitative acts, all of which relate to cleanliness and orderliness. The mother dusts furniture; her toddler daughter dusts as well. Sometimes the act is spontaneous but mirrors the child's earlier observations: She attempts to straighten her crib's bedclothes and systematically places her dolls in position; she tries to clean the bathtub; she puts her toys and books where they belong.

Michael Tomasello makes the point that this form of imitation suggests the child is affirming his place with others: "we" use this tool. The child is learning family and culturally based activities. The learning involves two critically important pieces: First, the child's attempt to reproduce the goal of the adult—to dust a piece of furniture to make it clean—and, second, the way the adult used an object (a piece of cloth) to achieve the goal.

Although you want to encourage imitative learning and make the most of your toddler's thirst for knowledge, keep in mind his judgment about safe and unsafe is still quite immature. You do need to be concerned about protecting your child from harm and keeping family possessions intact. You may find yourself increasing your dos and don'ts. "The TV is a no-no, don't touch." "Hold my hand as we go up the stairs!" Just keep them to a reasonable level, and toddler proof all you can. At this age, your toddler may blithely go on his way after a reminder. But he may also tease.

Toddler teasing is not malicious; rather it seems to be a way of checking whether parents really mean what they say. Dad says don't touch the VCR. What will happen if I do? If I shake my head no when Mom offers me a spoonful of my favorite fruit, will she let me eat it anyway? The cat sits on the coffee table and Mom doesn't say anything. Can I sit on the coffee table?

Does he understand that he is being ornery? No. Is he a challenge? Yes. Just remember all the cognitive activity that's going on in that little head.

Along with fifteen-month-olds' delight in imitation, there's a new dimension to their emotional ties with others that often takes the form of wanting to be with parents. This can take the form of bringing a book to be read from, dragging a doll for dressing and undressing, or gesturing for you to play music so he can dance for you. Church describes a toddler who lined up her dolls in preparation for her father's return home from work. This strengthening of emotional ties goes along with the toddler's response to the physical or psychological pain (sadness) expressed by a parent. Their faces show genuine concern. Even though the toddler may not be able to verbalize her feelings, she is again showing an increasing understanding of the affectional ties that bind people together.

Despite all of the cognitive and social activities of fifteen-month-olds, they still find time for lots of physical activity. At times, they seem to be operating a perpetual-motion machine. Climb the bottom step, go down, climb up, down, and on and on. Drag the footstool, climb it, roll off it, climb it again. Enjoy watching your fifteen-month-old walk, climb, sway, dance, and otherwise move about. Again, just keep her safe, and don't be surprised if she bristles with indignation when you restrain her unsafe exuberance.

Clearly, toddler behavior is increasingly complex and rich at fifteen months, but the highlights mentioned here are general trends. There is much variation among children of this age with respect to temperament styles, their need to explore, their language skills, and their tolerance for frustration.

◆ IMAGES OF DEVELOPMENT

Motor Control

Children of fifteen months still keep their feet spread apart in the characteristic gait of toddlerhood. Every so often they fall, but they ignore these interruptions and go on. And they hardly ever creep.

This month's primary new motor activity is climbing. Trying to climb out of the crib is relatively common, and chairs, tables, stepladders, patio benches, and couches are also particularly irresistible lures. Climbing up is accomplished fairly handily, but getting down unassisted is another story. At this age most toddlers do not have the balance to retrace their movements and get safely off the couch or table. For this reason, parents and toddler often have a standoff or two about where climbing is allowed.

An occasional clumsiness at this age is a reminder that some motor skills are still recent accomplishments. Rising from a sit to a stand is an example. Because balance is still imperfect and legs are not strong enough to maintain a squatting position, toddlers get up by rolling from a sit into a creeping position, raising their bottoms, and then using hands to push up into a stand. They may teeter a bit when upright. Yet some aspects of balance improve almost daily. By the end of the month most toddlers can stand briefly on one leg.

At this age there is increasing precision in grasp, and toddlers are fairly proficient in using cups, spoons, and crayons. They usually hold a spoon with a full-palm overhand grasp, they easily build a tower of two or three small blocks, and they turn pages of picture books and magazines.

Perception

At ten months babies seemed to recognize some of the similarities among groups of animals; that is, they could distinguish drawings of two different kinds of birds from the drawing of another animal. Now at fifteen months toddlers are even more adept at distinguishing the ways objects can be grouped.

Laboratory studies show that when toddlers of this age are given a set of objects—for example, toy milk bottles that differ slightly from one another and six toy dogs that also differ slightly—they sequentially touch the objects that go together. Fifteen-month-olds also discern that a plastic-toy Dalmatian dog and a wooden-toy dachshund have fundamental similarities. Recognizing similarities is a form of chunking information. In this instance, the toddler is chunking common qualities of dogness perhaps even before he has a word for dog. In his everyday world, the young toddler chunks information about many things: shoes, tables, chairs, and so on. Stated another way, the child is engaging in a more complex form of perceptual classification. The importance of classification is that it frees the toddler from having to devote cognitive energy to reanalyzing dogness every time he sees a dog; he now recognizes that a dog is a dog is a dog!

Language

Comprehension. At fifteen months children understand many more words than they did three months ago. Exact numbers are difficult to come by because it is very painstaking to evaluate comprehension at this age. However, mothers' reports suggest that comprehended words may run into the hundreds. Toddlers of fifteen months demonstrate they understand names for a wide range of toys, household objects, and clothing; the verbs used in everyday social interactions (*come, go, kiss*); and names of people and pets.

A toddler in one of my studies demonstrated the occasional difficulties in judging comprehension. The child's mother asked her to pick up her toys. The toddler continued to play. Did she understand the request? The answer to this question became crystal clear when her mother tried another tactic. After a few minutes of fruitless pleading, she asked, "Do you want your dinner? If you do, then pick up your toys and you can eat." In a flash, the fifteen-month-old picked up the toys.

Production. This month is another period when the pace of language development is uneven. The fifteen-month-old is not totally at a loss in communicating. On the contrary, he has a set of gestures that often serve him well—pointing, tugging, and pulling; facial expressions of delight and displeasure—and he has a small vocabulary of words to convey some specific meanings plus a number of recognizable grunts and sounds that he uses regularly as a stand-in for words. Of the ten, fifteen, or forty words he may have, many are for labeling everyday objects and people.

However, there are times when the fifteen-month-old wants to talk about himself clearly and directly—I am tired; I am hungry; I want to go outside; I want you to change my shirt—but most of these words are not yet in his vocabulary. Moreover, the fifteen-month-old is not yet able to use sentences of more than one word. Even if he knows a specific word that is appropriate to his wants, it may be difficult to convey his wants with just a single word. Compounding these difficulties is the fact that language skills at this age degrade when the toddler is fatigued, hungry, or upset, yet these are the times he most wants to talk.

Despite these limitations, toddlers use their vocabularies ingeniously. One sixteen-month-old had an eight-word spoken vocabulary. One of his favorite words was "dirtee," which he used to refer to soil, pebbles, and dirt on his clothes. For a while "dirtee" was the most frequent word he said, and he seemed uninterested in saying other words.

Toddlers who have larger vocabularies also tend to use words that show their recognition of similarities among certain things. One child used "moon" as a classifying word for the moon in the sky, oranges, and a ball. Another used "po-po" to indicate red berries, red earrings, and a red toy truck. A noted researcher described how a 14½-month-old used the word "ah" to tell an adult that he wanted a particular toy. He used "ah" several ways and several times (along with pointing and eye contact) to indicate that the toys the adult picked out of a toy box were not the ones he wanted. When the adult finally picked up the right toy, the child opened his hand to receive it.

Cognition

Researchers often use play activities to demonstrate cognitive growth at this age. The behaviors of Tim and Noah described in the snapshot represent play that is a form of trial-and-error learning. What happens if I do this or that? Trial-and-error learning is especially easy to observe with playthings such as blocks, sticks, and play dough. Carefully and methodically, a fifteen-month-old takes a toy rake and uses it to tap a rectangular-shaped block. She then pushes the rake, stands it on the prong end, and brings it back to the rectangular block again. She takes the rake to the play dough, indents the dough slightly, and peers at the change in the shape. This kind of learning has several benefits: the toddler increases her knowledge of what she can do; she learns that a hard object can have an effect on something soft; she learns that the shape of a hard object means that it can stand alone or can be stacked. As with Tim and Noah, trial-and-error activities may not have a well-defined goal, and even if they do include a goal, the toddler doesn't need to reach the goal to have a productive learning experience.

Play also reflects the fifteen-month-old's increasing awareness of the function of objects. Functional play is the term researchers use for children's attempt to use a toy brush to comb their own hair or use a rag to wipe a piece of furniture. Functional play can come about only when the child identifies a real object and associates the object with an action.

An advanced form of functional play is occasionally seen in the fifteen-month-old's play with dolls. Here the toddler takes small-scale versions of real objects and applies them to a doll. She feeds the doll with a toy bottle or puts it to bed in a toy crib. In this kind of play, toddlers also transfer to the doll the kinds of care they have received. In effect they see the doll as a stand-in for themselves and themselves as a stand-in for a parent. When the toddler engages in a parent role using a doll as a child, she is engaging in an early form of role reversal that increases her understanding of the activities of parents as opposed to the activities of young children.

One final comment about functional play: it is a transitional form of play. It is more advanced than the play of the twelve-month-old who is just beginning to combine two objects with or without regard to the objects' characteristics, but it is less advanced than the pretend play that is often observed at about eighteen months. In pretend play, the child makes believe: she combs her hair with an imaginary comb. She does not need to have the real object in her hand; an image of the object in her mind is enough.

This month the toddler's play often shows an increase in learning about cause and effect. One of the most favored toys in my laboratory is a jack-in-the-box. With a great deal of assistance from his mother, a fifteen-month-old turns the handle so that the jack pops up. He laughs merrily, and shrugging away his mother's assistance, he begins pounding on the box in an attempt to close it. He then bangs the box on the floor and tries turning the handle. He hasn't yet figured out that he has to push the jack into the box, but for the very first time he is indicating that he knows the jack has to go back into the box before he pops up again. The boy sees a cause-and-effect relation.

This kind of play shows not only causal awareness but the beginnings of a systematic plan to operate the jack-in-the-box on his own. What the fifteen-month-old lacks is knowledge of the final piece of the causal sequence. His mother (or father or big brother) can play a vital role here by showing him how the jack goes into the box in the context of a joint-play activity.

Social Development

The fifteen-month-old is especially interested in including others in his experiences. One toddler who saw a bird in a cage pulled his mother to the cage, pointed at the bird, and then pointed upwards as if telling his mother that birds fly in the sky. Another pointed to the family dog and said, "Grrr."

As mentioned previously, a social behavior that develops around this age is comforting, sharing, and helping others. Researchers call these prosocial behaviors. Being able to respond prosocially involves a link between the child's developing cognitions, his ability to feel and interpret emotions, and his socialization experiences in which he has been cared for by others. Knowing when and how to comfort and help requires that the toddler distinguish among facial expressions, have had some exposure to other individuals' different responses to his own and another's distress, recognize that the distress one feels occurs because someone else is feeling distress, and sense how to respond.

The toddler months are the first age at which children have developed enough cognitive, social, and emotional prerequisites for prosocial acts. Children younger than fifteen or sixteen months are not unaffected by someone else's hurt, but their cognitive immaturity makes them uncertain about the source of their own distress and how to respond to another person's distress. Precursor behaviors are observed in babies, particularly toward the end of the first year. For example, one developmental scientist described how a twelve-month-old handled his own distress by sucking his thumb and pulling on his ear. Upon seeing his father's sad face, he looked sad, sucked his thumb, and pulled on his father's ear. A thirteen-month-old responded to an adult look of distress by offering his doll.

There is some disagreement about the origins of prosocial acts. Some developmental researchers suggest that caring is a part of being human and therefore the toddler's caring is simply a function of a maturing biological predisposition. Others disagree, proposing instead that prosocial behaviors are learned from close and affectionate relationships with others. I tend to agree with this view. Children learn from parents who are themselves openly caring and who offer explanations about hurts experienced by others.

Toddlers' prosocial behaviors are not directed indiscriminately. Those who have siblings may be less inclined to share and to offer comfort to them than they are to a parent. (In fact, one researcher has documented numerous instances of teasing and fighting among toddlers and siblings.) The point is that a child's history of experiences (including emotional experiences) with siblings and peers is brought to bear on prosocial acts. Thus, the seemingly simple act of showing caring rests on intricate social interactions.

Emotions

In my own studies, we found rapid mood swings at this age: the fifteen-month-old can be gleeful one minute, fretting the next, and laughing a minute or two later. Toddlers are often delighted with themselves, but they do have a low tolerance for some frustrations. If they are involved with peers, disagreements may arise about possessions. Some toddlers might get upset while waiting to get dressed when they're anxious to go outside. Although crying is fairly common, there are few instances of real tantrums.

This month the toddler's love of physical activity causes her to demonstrate attachments in several new ways. She will move over and sit close to another toddler, even though she doesn't actually play with her peer. When she is across the room from her brother, she periodically establishes eye contact to maintain her feelings of inclusion. While she is more inclined to wander about, she regularly looks back to see that a favorite person is still somewhere in sight. Mothers in one of my studies reported that toddlers engaged in more clinging at this age.

Sense of Self

Many of the behaviors that characterize this age illustrate the toddler's evolving sense of self. Trial-and-error activities and particularly persistent repetitions of behaviors demonstrate interest in mastery (competence). Preoccupation and annoyance with having dirty hands or being particular about what she wears indicate an increasing awareness of the appearance of the physical self. Frequent displays of clinging and empathic behaviors suggest that the sense of belonging is becoming a more conscious element of self. The rise in actions imitative of parents and siblings answers the toddler's awakening sense of the self within the context of the family.

◆ DEVELOPMENTAL CLOSE-UP

Socializing Children to Everyday Standards of Behavior

Some of my research focuses on when parents begin to communicate dos and don'ts to their young children and how children respond to these requests and commands. Why do rules matter? Simply stated, families and societies continue and grow by socializing the young to accept values, conventions, and norms. Research repeatedly shows that effective socialization does not rely on harsh directives on the part of parents or slavish obedience on the part of children. Firm, fair, emotionally warm, and age appropriate are the characteristics typically associated with parents who successfully impart values to toddlers. Sister's room is off limits, as is Mom's computer and Dad's desk. You have to wear clothes. Biting is a no-no.

Parents often start socialization lessons when babies begin to walk and talk. Parents implicitly reason that a newly walking child is a potential menace, and they also assume that a talking child is able to reason.

During the past decades, my colleagues and I have seen hundreds of children between the ages of one and seven years. We now have a good idea of what middle-class, educated parents ask for in the way of everyday rules, how their young children respond, what children understand about rules, and some of the factors that enable children to improve at going along with rules. It is clear that the road to socialization to rules has bumps and pot-holes for almost all parents and children.

One of the ways we learned about parents' dos and don'ts was to ask them. Specifically, we asked about the behaviors they tried to prohibit and the behaviors they tried to encourage. At fifteen months, most of the prohibitions were directed at safety: no climbing without supervision, no running in the street, no touching a light socket, or no playing near a hot stove. Although safety prohibitions continue to be a high priority for parents well into the preschool years, the content of the prohibitions changes. Older children are asked to hold an adult's hand while on an escalator or in a parking lot, not to go outdoors and ride a tricycle alone, and not to talk to strangers.

Increasingly, as children grow older, parents' prohibitions become more customized; that is, they reflect a family's unique routines and values. At twenty-four months, some specific ones are not pulling the dog's tail, not banging toys on baby brother's head, not putting small things in the mouth, not using a pacifier during the day. At forty-two months, prohibitions include not drawing on the living room walls, not removing clothes when company is visiting, not trying to hang up the phone when someone is using it, and not fighting with children in school. And at forty-eight months, numerous prohibitions are directed toward making the child a citizen of the community: not screaming in public, not playing with guns, not going to the neighbor's house too early in the morning, not using bathroom words, and not fighting with others.

Parents in our studies were as concerned about encouraging behaviors as they were about issuing prohibitions. This concern was generally quite modest when children were thirteen to twenty-one months old. By twenty-four to thirty months, mothers reported their interest in fostering independence. They encouraged their children to play on their own, try new foods, pick up after themselves after toy play, cooperate in dressing, and walk instead of being carried. At age four or so, as with prohibitions, the theme of being a good citizen appeared. Children were encouraged to play nicely, develop table manners, dress themselves, observe family religious practices, read on their own, learn physical skills such as swimming, engage in family routines such as clearing the table and taking out the garbage, and be polite to tradespeople.

Although parents introduced prohibitions and restrictions relatively early, the children's compliance evolved slowly. Parents' reports were corroborated by the child behaviors we observed in homes and in the laboratory. Overall, children learned safety rules, prohibitions about others' possessions, and rules about being nice to others earlier and more successfully than other rules. Children had the hardest time learning to wait: to wait until a parent got off the phone, to wait for mealtimes, and to wait to open birthday presents. In another study of preschoolers, mothers also reported that learning to wait (until Mom gets off the telephone) was the most difficult challenge for their children.

It is intriguing to observe the ways young children find to resist their parents' wishes. Early in the second year, they ignore and tease, even on safety issues. Beth, at fourteen months, took her teddy bear outside to the driveway. Her parents watched surreptitiously while she walked over to a berry bush that they had repeatedly warned her not to touch. Beth picked a berry and showed it to her bear, all the while saying "No!" Turning suddenly, she spied her parents. Beth flung the bear aside, put the berry in her mouth, and ran. Yes, her behavior was illogical from an adult perspective, but it was obvious that she was issuing a dare to her parents: What will you do to me for breaking a rule? Her parents lectured her, and later reported they never again saw Beth approach the berry bush.

Throughout the second year, we found that crying was a relatively common way to resist a parent's request; at about thirty months, crying was observed far less. Outright refusals ("No!"s) began to appear at around two years. During the third year children began to engage in a primitive form of negotiation with their parents; by this, I mean the child's willingness to continue a dialogue with parents even while negating a request. Sometimes negotiation involved an attempt to avoid the requested action: "I have to go potty." "Read me a story first." As children reached four years, many negotiated by indicating they would obey but on their own terms. One child, when asked to put away toys, said he would, but first insisted on putting away only the trucks. Another asked which fast-food place he and his mother would go to when he finished putting his toys away.

Although parents do get weary of arguments from their children, child-initiated negotiation is a wonderful behavior. It allows children to gain a sense of importance. But more important, successful negotiation shows children that talking is a reasonable way to work out disagreements. And learning to negotiate with parents helps later on, as children have disputes with their peers. This said, I advise parents to set clear limits on when they allow negotiation. It's not acceptable for safety rules, likely not for bedtimes, and probably acceptable for occasions such as choosing the clothes to wear on weekends.

What about the bumps and potholes that I briefly mentioned earlier? Well, socialization invariably moves slowly. It's hard for toddlers and young children to accept restrictions placed on their own preferences when they're also learning the pleasures of self-awareness and autonomy. Sometimes, too, a toddler easily responds to parents' dos and don'ts and then, after a while, becomes largely noncompliant. Mostly, this is a temporary, albeit difficult, situation. Don't give up on the dos and don'ts that are essential for the child's safety and the family's well-being. Be flexibly firm on others. Be patient. This too should pass. Alternatively, if your child is constantly and consistently noncompliant after the age of two, seek advice.

Eighteen Months

+ *thinks using ideas*

+ *pays attention longer*

+ *engages in pretend play*

+ *has larger but still constrained vocabulary*

+ *seeks others' help*

+ *is occasionally restless, irritable, and stubborn*

+ *shows caring behaviors when others are upset*

The eighteen-month-old, a picture of conflicting behavioral maturity and immaturity, straddles a developmental fence. Sometimes she acts "grown up," playing contentedly with her toys; holding "conversations" with her parents, dolls, and herself; and more or less following her parents' requests. She is delightful to be with because her play is imaginative and she pays attention for longer periods of time. She clearly loves to be with others, showing great pleasure with children or adults. Other times, though, she reverts to babylike behaviors. She is fretful and clinging, unable or unwilling to play, listless with her food, and whiny when asked to do just about anything. "No" is a frequent word whether she means it or not. Restlessness is also an issue, and public excursions (restaurants, church/synagogue) can be nightmares for parents. What is happening?

Let's look first at behavioral maturity. The famous psychologist Jean Piaget viewed this age as one that ushers in six months of momentous cognitive growth. He contended that play between eighteen and twenty-four months shows new modes of thinking. Pretend play—where a child makes believe an absent toy is present or substitutes one toy for another—indicates the child has a mental image of the desired toy and is able to recall that image. A toddler uses small stones as a stand-in for the dog food that she serves to the stuffed animal that resides in her room.

The eighteen-month-old's increasing knowledge of ideas and words enriches pretend play, and then pretend play enriches language. Thus it's not surprising that pretend play is increasingly evident in toddlers' play repertoire at about the time they show a word spurt in vocabulary.

Increasingly during the eighteen- to twenty-four-month period, children become better able to deal with events and objects that are not present in the here and now. By twenty-four months the toddler will call up ideas about past events ("Yesterday we . . .") and the future ("Go when daddy home?"). Also during this time, toddlers are more sure of their sense of self and their distinctiveness and identity. I'll describe selfhood in more detail in the "Developmental Close-Up" at the end of this chapter.

In the social domain, research shows that toddlers are increasingly quick to realize that some problems and situations are too difficult for them and intentionally turn to another for assistance. They also now realize that if they want to show something to a parent, their message is more likely to be received if both of them are looking in the same direction. Overall, then, in the second half of the second year there is dynamic growth—cognitively, socially, linguistically, and personally—in behavioral maturity.

What about behavioral immaturity? Arnold Gesell, pediatrician and child psychologist, also described this age as a time rich in behavioral transformations. In contrast to Piaget, Gesell focused on the challenges confronting the eighteen-month-old in coordinating and integrating new behaviors. It is this integration that often leads to frustration and irritability. Consider this enigma for the child. Just when he has a good sense of who he is, what he looks like, the things he owns, and self-related achievements, he is increasingly confronted with requests to conform to family and social norms: ". . . no you can't run in the house, you need to get dressed now, you can't stand in the chair and eat, it's time to pick up your toys, you can't pull the dog's hair . . . ," and more. It's no wonder that one of Gesell's colleagues once remarked that children of this age walk a one-way street in the direction opposite to that desired by others and with headstrong single-mindedness. The toddler has to learn one of the great lessons of socialization: as a member of society we have to find the balance between our own desires and the values that society wants us to have and to follow.

Not surprisingly, eighteen-month-olds are overwhelmed from time to time and have difficulty dealing with the world outside their own sphere. In this context, it is understandable why seemingly trivial events and requests such as "Let me wipe your face," "Don't walk with the bottle," and "Please sit over here" sometimes lead to fretfulness and volcanic bursts of emotions. Of the ages described thus far, this is the one most apt to test a parent's patience.

Yet even at stressful times, the eighteen-month-old can be both loving and contrite. Ryan and his mother came to my developmental class one morning. As Ryan's mother described him to my students, she mentioned the previous evening's crisis. She seemed a little sad as she spoke. Ryan had forgotten a family rule and had run in the living room. He bumped into a small table that fell over, and a valuable lamp broke. Both were upset. Ryan listened intently while his mother talked to my students, then turning to her, he tugged at her skirt and urgently said, "Up, up." As his mother held him, he buried his face in her shoulder. The whole experience must have flashed before his eyes.

Ryan's actions in the classroom revealed prosocial (caring) behaviors, a sense of self and the wrong he had committed, and self-reproach for his actions. He also demonstrated some cognitive maturity: He clearly remembered the incident without requiring a visual hint such as a photograph, he understood some of the words spoken by his mother, and he anticipated the conclusion of the tale, responding to his mother's sadness and seeking her help to relieve his own distress. Ryan's behavior was direct and appropriate, a signal of developmental maturity.

Will Ryan consistently act so maturely at this age? Probably not. His ability to remember the event was aided by the fact that he and his mother had experienced a very emotional interaction in which both cared intensely about what specifically happened and how the other felt about the incident. The classroom reenactment provided them with another opportunity to play out their feelings. His mother's emotion-charged re-creation of the event reactivated Ryan's prosocial behaviors. Most of the time, of course, the eighteen-month-old doesn't dramatically reexperience events in this way. Ryan's cognitive skills and self-awareness are still fairly rudimentary, and his recollection of all the details of this complex event might be difficult for him to reconstruct without cues.

♦ IMAGES OF DEVELOPMENT

Motor Control

Occasionally, eighteen-month-olds run, jump, and climb blissfully, all within a minute or two, as if in love with their own athletic skills. Generally though, they are quieter and equally as entranced by play and fine-motor activities.

This month the biggest changes in gross-motor skills are improvements in balance. The eighteen-month-old strolls effortlessly on smooth surfaces, nimbly climbs on furniture, and can simultaneously wander about and pull a toy without losing his balance. A very noticeable change this month is that he is able to walk up stairs while holding onto a rail.

His fine-motor skills continue to improve. He picks up small pieces (a quarter inch or less) of bread or cracker smoothly without extraneous finger movements. He turns pages of books, tries to use a crayon to imitate lines on a sketchpad, and builds block towers that are three or four blocks high. He uses spoons for eating, although he often reverts to finger feeding since he is still much more successful with this technique.

Perception

Form perception now includes differentiation of round puzzle pieces from square ones, and the eighteen-month-old appropriately places some block forms into a puzzle board. He recognizes one or two colors by name.

Language

Comprehension. The eighteen-month-old continues to increase his understanding of word meanings. During a three-month period that begins at around eighteen months, toddlers usually learn the names of familiar persons; the labels given to everyday objects; action verbs such as *go, come,* and *bring*; and brief commands or statements such as, "Put the book on the shelf."

The eighteen-month-old also realizes that certain responses are required for specific phrases such as, "What's that?" or, "What do you say?" She recognizes a single word in a sentence and uses the word to infer the meaning of the entire sentence.

Despite her impressive growth in understanding, there are, of course, words the toddler does not know. So she makes "educated" guesses, sometimes successfully and other times not. Studies have shown that toddler guesses (about the names or labels for objects) are more likely to be correct if there's a cue. A parent might look at an object while naming it; the toddler sees the parent's direction of gaze and uses that as her cue. Suppose there's no cue. Then the toddler has a hit-or-miss situation; here's an example. One morning, an eighteen-month-old's mother, father, and aunt were chatting about the father going to work. The father was getting ready to leave the house for his workplace. The toddler was asked where her father "is going." "Work," she replies. That afternoon she is told her aunt has to leave. "Where is your aunt going?" she was asked. Solemnly she says, "Work." Later in the day, the toddler's mother realizes the family dog is not in the house. She asks her toddler daughter where the dog is. The toddler answers, "Work." What's going on? I think the child used the word *work* as a stand-in for the concept of *leaving the house.* In another example, an English-speaking toddler who has Italian grandparents picked up the Italian word *abri*, which means to open. She used *abri* to ask that objects be opened for her (a door, her mother's purse) and to describe opened objects (a book). Language studies do show that toddlers often continually use a word that is involved in a concept they are in the process of learning. If a child is learning about the concept of disappearance, he may say "Gone" when a toy disappears, when food is eaten, or when someone leaves the room.

Production. Word production at around eighteen months is highly variable, but for most children this is an age where production increases rapidly, often by 5 or 6 new words a week. In one study the range of vocabulary of twenty-month-old children was 1 word to over 400 words. The average was about 140 words. This represents about a threefold increase in production during the time since the end of the first year.

How often are words combined? In one of my studies, which was focused on children's compliance to requests, we were also somewhat curious about eighteen-month-olds' ability to produce sentences. Of the thirty children in our study, six routinely combined 2 or 3 words into a sentence. Four children (three of whom were boys) had no intelligible words. The rest, twenty toddlers, used only 1 word at a time. Some had vocabularies that consisted of 5 words, whereas others spoke 50 or more words clearly.

Overall, the most common words in the eighteen-month vocabulary are those used most in everyday interactions with people, objects, and events. Therefore, depending on their life experiences, two toddlers may produce the same number of words but the specifics of their vocabularies differ. Regardless of their individual rearing experiences, most eighteen-month-olds can identify and name one or two colors. They are also able to name a few pictures in their favorite books.

Several other interesting features of vocabulary growth may begin to occur at around eighteen months. Word play begins when a toddler becomes enchanted with his ability to produce a particular sound (a word, that is), although the meaning of the word is not fully understood. Andrew heard someone say "gorilla." He then said "rilla," he sang "rilla," and he called his truck "rilla." However, when he was shown a picture of a gorilla, he was surprised when it was called a "gorilla." Andrew had to work through the fact that the sound he loved, *rilla*, was actually a word that had a definite meaning.

New words demand psychic energy. For months Andrew had called his mother Mommy, his father Da, and his grandfather Poppa. One night when he was about eighteen months old, Andrew turned to give me a hug. Looking at me, he said, "Mommy." His face registered surprise. He looked at me again and said, "Poppa." His body stiffened; that wasn't right, either. His mother and I simultaneously called out "Grandma." That word was either too difficult to say, or he did not register that it was "my name." Weeks later he said "Gama" on his own.

Not unrelated to these language developments is the eighteen-month toddler's fascination with the word *no*. He says this word over and over again. This makes sense in the context of a concept he is learning, as well as a word he often hears. Granted, his own activities provide more than a few occasions when he hears the word "No!" Recognize, though, that sometimes your toddler does not really understand which of his activities are associated with a "No." On the plus side, some eighteen-month-olds are able to communicate what they do want by using words such as *want, like, mad*, and *sad*.

Other aspects of language growth at this age are more subtle. At around this age, toddlers are sometimes able to use a word in different contexts. This achievement is referred to as *decoupling*. One toddler's first decoupled word was *side*, which was her shorthand term for *outside*. On different occasions she used *side* to inform her mother of the whereabouts of the family pet ("Puppy side") and the family car ("Car side"). She also used it to announce her desire to go for a ride in the car when her mother had just told her it was naptime. She said, "Car side," ran from the room, and headed for the front door.

At this age, too, overgeneralization—use of one word to label related objects—is still common. One toddler used the word *jues* to indicate juice, water in his bottle, a small pond, and water that trickled from the garden hose. The word *puppy* covered the dinosaurs he saw on his socks, pictures of goats and lambs, and of course the neighbor's dogs.

An aspect of speech that eludes the toddler is word flexibility, that is, locating the right word to say or substituting one word for another. Thus the eighteen-month-old may find himself speechless in times of stress. Unrelated words may tumble out of his mouth as he struggles to find the right words to communicate his feelings. Of course, this happens to us as well.

Lastly, when eighteen-month-olds produce a two- or three-word sentence, the sentence usually includes a noun (or pronoun) and a verb and is delivered with an intonation that replicates the sentences of older children and adults. Two-word speech is often used descriptively about current actions ("Car go"), possession ("Mommy shoe"), location ("Doll gone"), disappearance and reappearance of an object or person ("Where ball?"), negation ("No sleep"), and emotional states ("Daddy mad"). The words in these short sentences are often slurred together (for example, "Poppatruck" or "Seeya"). Slurring also condenses words that have two or three syllables— "nana" for banana or "ple" for apple.

Cognition

This age period is associated with all kinds of learning, which I think is linked to the toddler's burgeoning language. Communicating with words helps solidify knowledge the child already has about people, objects, and events, a view repeatedly emphasized by the language researcher Katherine Nelson. Opportunities for new learning also occur when toddlers are exposed to new experiences and the words that parents use to describe the new experiences (trips to a heretofore unexplored zoo, store, town; introductions to new people). Then when parents take time to describe, for example, how one store differs from another store, the toddler has the opportunity to make comparisons—using words to represent ideas—and thus builds up a storehouse of knowledge about stores, in general. You're unlikely to "see" all the learning that is taking place in the mind of your eighteen-month-old, but it is happening.

I describe some examples of eighteen-month-olds' cognitive achievements in the following paragraphs. This is such an extraordinary age;

you're sure to notice similar examples of cognitive skills with your own toddler.

The toddler is able to devise new and complex forms of planning behavior when he begins to think in terms of ideas such as "if . . . , then" consequences, and then to consider solutions to problems. This level of reasoning may be more implicit than explicit, but it can get the job done. To wit, one eighteen-month-old discovered that a spring-loaded screen door slammed shut unless he held it open. He wanted a toy that was just inside the door, so he had to figure out a way to control the door so he could retrieve the toy. A possible solution: if I hold the door open, then I can get the toy. That was the toddler's approach: he held the door open with one hand and with the other reached inside the room. Toy in hand, he let go of the door.

There is improvement in recall memory this month, which is observed in a more complex variation of object-permanence tasks. This variation involves hiding a toy under one of several felt pads; the hiding is more complicated because of a complex series of toy moves that also challenge the toddler's attention and reasoning skills. I show the eighteen-month-old a toy, close my fist over it, and then randomly move my hand under and across three felt pads. I leave the toy under a pad and show the child my empty hand. Most eighteen-month-olds have no difficulty solving the task. Ignoring the intermediary actions of my hand, the toddler focuses on the final resting point of my hand, and concludes from my empty hand that I have placed the toy under the last pad. That's the one he typically goes to, to retrieve the toy.

Recognition memory is also more efficient and, increasingly, is used to remember everyday routines or scripts. Routines serve a crucial purpose for young children because they help focus their attention on one of their goals and the steps required to reach that goal. As the routine becomes more solidified, one or more cues can serve as memory reminders. An eighteen-month-old had been watching as a neighbor potted plants in the family's garden. Suddenly called away, the neighbor left tools, plants, pots, and soil in a corner. Upon his return, the toddler ran to him with a trowel and then ran back to a bag of planting soil trying to pull it toward an empty pot. Although the toddler incorporated only two steps of a longer routine, she clearly showed memory for the sequence of steps involved in planting.

At this age improved memory skills also result in transfer of knowledge. Tracy and her mom visited my class. Her mother told my students that one of Tracy's favorite activities was to pull a long-handled musical rolling toy. I showed Tracy a pull toy that consisted of a bear seated on a platform that had wheels. A colored string was attached to the platform. Tracy looked at the bear and studied the string. She picked up the string, glanced at it again while in her hand, and then tugged the string. The bear moved a few inches. Tracy then pulled the string so the bear followed her as she danced around the students. Tracy recognized that the long handle of the musical toy she pulled at home and the string attached to the classroom bear shared the common property of enabling a toy to be pulled.

The eighteen-month-old's keen observation skills help her learn about standards of "correctness" with respect to the world of objects. She is developing ideas about the way everyday objects ought to look. One toddler's father kept small treats for the family dog in a covered plastic jar. One day the toddler noted that the jar was lidless. Pulling her father over to see the jar, she jabbered to express her concern. Recognizing how physical things should be—jars should be *closed*—will also lead to dealing with how things should be in the social world. Equally as important, when the toddler learns the word that describes the way things ought to be the learning helps her organize her knowledge. Mommy *closes* her purse when she carries it. Daddy *closes* the car door before he starts the car. Mommy *closes* my jacket when she says it is cold outside.

Social Development

Toddlers of eighteen months are often delightfully caring with parents, siblings, and other familiar relatives and friends. They freely dispense hugs, kisses, and gentle pats and often react with prosocial responses when others show signs of hurt or distress. At the same time, toddlers increasingly seek out others' assistance, in contrast to the more passive-looking behaviors (social referencing) observed earlier. An eighteen-month-old struggles with a puzzle, frets a bit, and then takes the puzzle to her mother. Help is received, and she trots off happily to continue her play.

Toddlers often seek parents' help when they encounter a new situation, such as a first visit to the zoo or an introduction to unfamiliar age-mates. The toddler may briefly cling, fret, and avoid looking at the new surroundings or a strange child. Gradually she sneaks a few glances, furtively assesses the scene, acclimates to the situation, and eventually feels safe enough to venture forth. Knowing she can turn back to a caregiver gives her confidence.

The mobility of the eighteen-month-old means that parents increase their rules for safety, respect for possessions, and being nice. My research shows that by eighteen months or so most children do comply with a few rules; at this age parents generally report compliance to a very specific rule, such as "No going near a hot stove."

Children of this age often show rudimentary peer social skills by briefly maintaining play interactions with children of similar age in a meaningful sequence of behaviors. Two toddlers select a doll to play with. If one engages in feeding the doll, the other follows along. The children smile to each other and make eye contact. Verbalizations tend to be infrequent, though.

Emotions

The eighteen-month-old is frequently a happy child who laughs easily and shows delight in running and jumping, playing with his toy trucks and trains, and going to the playground with his parents. But his tolerance for frustration is low. If he can't move his train tracks into position, he frets, and he frets when someone has spilled sand all over the slide at the playground. The frets are signs of displeasure and pleas for help, and usually they last only a few seconds. Sometimes frets indicate a general state of restlessness in which the toddler cannot settle down and cannot get across what he wants or needs. One toddler of this age indicated he wanted to go swimming, so his grandfather took him to a nearby pool. But he fretted repeatedly, and his grandfather took him home. Thirty minutes later he whined repeatedly, tugged at his grandfather's hand, and said, "Pool, pool."

There are days when crying bouts are long and intense, perhaps related to fatigue or being especially hungry. A child in one of my studies wanted a pen belonging to a family friend. His mother said no and offered him a familiar toy. The toddler lay on the floor and kicked his legs, his face became flushed, and he wailed loudly. The tantrum lasted six long minutes.

On some occasions it is easy to identify the source of fretfulness but a solution is not readily forthcoming. One of my sisters cared for her eighteen-month-old grandson while his mother was in the hospital to give birth. The toddler had visited his grandparents many times and loved being with them. In turn, they doted on him. The first day of the mother's absence went well, with the usual number of brief upsets. The next morning the toddler woke up crying and whining, "Mommy, Mommy, Mommy." He was inconsolable for most of the morning. He cried when held by his grandmother and called out for Paulie, his favorite aunt, and Pah, his grandfather. When Paulie held him, he cried for Mah, his grandmother. When his grandmother took him again, he whined, "Mommy." Finally, despite miserable weather, the grandmother dressed him warmly and took him for a walk in his stroller. Eventually he fell asleep, and when he awoke his fretfulness had disappeared. But he was subdued for the rest of the day.

This is the age at which approximately 60 percent of toddlers turn to a *transitional object* as a means of securing comfort. These are soft and cuddly things like an old blanket that toddlers use for self-comforting. Linus's blanket in the *Peanuts* comic strip is an example. Adherents of psychoanalytic thinking suggest that a transitional object is a replacement for an unavailable mother. However, children become upset even when their mothers are present, and many a toddler chews on his favorite blanket while being held in his mother's arms. I think it's more useful to think of transitional objects as all-purpose soothers that effectively reduce tensions or emotional distress. Most children seem to find other ways to cope with upsets and turn away from their soothers between two and four years of age.

Sense of Self

Of all the developmental changes that occur at around eighteen months, none seems as wondrous as the child's burgeoning sense of selfhood. Self-recognition, self-consciousness, shyness, and a behavior that looks like shame all appear in a matter of weeks. The behaviors are so pervasive and come into view so suddenly that it seems as if a button labeled selfhood was pushed. Of course, there is no magic developmental button. The eighteen-month-old's awareness of her own personhood and identity is a logical derivative of cognitive advances, specifically those related to thinking and remembering.

The eighteen-month-old cares about her clothes, peers at her body parts, and gladly accepts a chore such as putting napkins on the table. She raises her arms to help when her mother puts on her sweatshirt. She stuffs her mouth with cookies, then opens her mouth to show her father what she has done.

Recognition and labeling of body parts increases, and toddlers often describe themselves in terms of physical characteristics: "Big girl," "Little boy." There is visual recognition as they regard themselves in a mirror. In a classic study, a researcher placed an eighteen-month-old in front of a mirror and let the child look at herself. Then he surreptitiously placed a bit of rouge on the child's nose and again placed her in front of the mirror. The toddler reacted negatively to her image with the spot. This study has been replicated many times, always with the same results. At eighteen months, but not much before, toddlers react with concern when their mirror image contains a violation of what they have come to expect.

I have observed behaviors that seem as if a toddler is somehow protecting his persona, another good indication of a developing self. Our grandson Andrew woke up terribly irritable one morning; he did not want breakfast. However, he took a cracker while standing near the kitchen table, whining all the while. He cried when encouraged to sit at the table next to his beloved grandfather. He then went behind a wooden chair, as if to hide from us. The back of the chair had slats so we could see him, and he could see us. It was as if he wanted to be alone, but yet physically near to us. After whining for a while longer, he went off to play with his trains.

The implications of self-development are profound. The way a child comes to think about her "self" affects her motivation to achieve, her feelings of worth, and the success of relationships with peers. I describe self-hood more fully in the "Developmental Close-Up" that follows.

Selfhood

Selfhood, the sense of an identity, looms large in toddlers' actions. Self-hood is at the root of the toddler's incessant push to be autonomous, that is, to do things on his own. Selfhood is also a major contributor to the toddler's negativity, which erupts when the toddler is told to do something or other. What is selfhood? It is a reflection of our personal identity. It is the knowledge each of us possesses about our bodies, the skills we know we have and those we wish we had, and how we feel about ourselves in relation to other people. Indeed, our selfhood in large part comes out of our social relationships.

Is selfhood present before the toddler period? Yes. Celia Brownell and I published our views about the primitive, implicit form of self that is present in the early months of life. This primitive self emerges from two sources: the baby's perceptual exchanges with his surroundings using his visual, auditory, and other sense systems; and the baby's social exchanges with others. The perceptual source is related to Ulric Neisser's "ecological self," in which the self consciously or not takes in information about the sights and sounds in the physical environment. In contrast, the self of social exchanges is Neisser's "interpersonal self," which is related to emotional rapport and communication that comes from the baby's interactions with others.

It is most likely that the primitive sense of self contributes to the two-month-old's attempt to make eye contact with others, the three-month-old's smile at a parent, the four-month-old's attempt to reach for and grasp a toy, and the six-month-old's tentative gestures. A more aware sense of a self-in-action contributes to the seven-month-old's rapt attention when he sees his own hands in a mirror; the ten-month-old's careful and systematic touching, rubbing, and even pinching parts of her body and careful observation of her own movements seen in a mirror; and the twelve-month-old's intentional actions to push away bothersome toys. At eighteen months, toddlers know what they should look like: they rub marks (surreptitiously placed by a researcher) on their noses or cheeks. This is called *self-recognition*.

We can summarize self-development during the first five or six years of life in terms of five interrelated paths. First is the self that reflects knowledge, even primitive knowledge, of one's physical body. The second is the sense of self-*efficacy*, the feeling of being capable of achieving a goal. For a baby, the goal might involve pushing a toy car along the floor. The third path reflects awareness of self-inspired action, such as the "I can . . . ," and the self-inspired knowledge of possession; this is "mine." The fourth strand of selfhood is the social and emotional one. This is the self that reminds one about ways to behave and the consequences of not following requests to behave in certain ways. This is also the self that begins to feel an elemental sense of guilt when one acts counter to others' wishes. The fifth path of selfhood is the reflective one; this is the evaluative self that consciously looks back at one's own actions and defines the actions based on goodness or badness. This definition most clearly reflects the self in relation to other people's opinions or views. The first four aspects of selfhood come into being during the first two years of life. The developmental changes that I've outlined suggests possible points of emergence.

Overall, the reason that selfhood is so important during the toddler years is that it reflects much of the toddler's sense of accomplishment, his feeling of importance, and his motivation. Much of this comes about in interactions with others, especially the toddler's parents. Later on, the sense of accomplishment, importance, and motivation forms an important part of the preschooler's self-identity, namely, feeling pride in who she is and what she can do. There's no better recipe for learning.

Twenty-One Months

- *applies ideas*

- *runs, squats, and throws*

- *understands me, my, mine, and I*

- *begins to understand meaning of yesterday, now, tomorrow*

- *uses words to describe self, feelings, desires*

- *replicates complex behavior sequences*

- *can be exacting and resistant*

This month, behavioral changes tend to be evolutionary rather than revolutionary. It's a pleasant period of relatively smooth growth in which both child and parents can collect themselves.

Steady growth is especially apparent in the size of the toddler's vocabulary and his use of short sentences, and it demonstrates the toddler's increased cognitive maturity. He understands a state of possession (mine), classes of objects (different kinds of clothing), conventional ways of greeting others ("hi," "bye"), and how to describe an action that is taking place ("train go bye").

Another subtle change is a modest decline in irritability and fretfulness, although it's too early for parents to breathe a sigh of relief. The twenty-one-month-old may cry less, but he is exacting, sometimes to the point of compulsiveness, in his wants and requests. One toddler wanted his breakfast waffles served whole; if they were cut, he would not eat them. His peas and carrots must not touch the piece of chicken on his plate; if they did, he perceived the food as contaminated and would not eat. He would only wear this shirt and not that one. His hands and his face must be washed right after he eats or he frets, "Dirty, dirty." "I hold milk," he insisted, even though the cup of milk is likely to spill.

This need for control reflects a growing sense of self and mastery. To exercise control, the toddler sometimes plans a course of action in terms of cause and effect. One twenty-one-month-old's mother has repeatedly told him he is not to pull at her glasses. But the little guy figured out that he could reach the forbidden eyeglasses when he was held. So he fretted until his mother picked him up, and as soon as he was in her arms, he reached out and snatched the glasses from her face. He laughed when she set him back on the floor. Clever little one, she smiled to herself. To her son she sternly said, "That's a no-no!" This toddler also knew that if he played with his mother's handbag, she would not be pleased. No problem, he reasoned; if she can't see me, she won't get mad. He hid behind the sofa and merrily explored the contents of her bag. The twenty-one-month-old's efforts to control a situation can be exasperating for parents. But at this age the toddler isn't purposely being contrary. Just remember to set limits on situations that are unacceptable to you.

There is a side benefit to efforts to exert control. Control over one's world demands close attention to other people and to their actions. Toddlers of this age tend to watch intently the things that happen in their miniworld. Their precise imitation of others' actions even days after the action has occurred shows that they can store and retrieve memories of all kinds of events. One morning not long after his dad had gone off to work, a toddler played quietly in a corner of the kitchen. Picking a small block from his toy basket, he began to rub it along each of his cheeks. Then he walked over to the sink and started to wash his face. He clearly remembered the actions of his father when he shaves and needed no cue to imitate this sequence of events. Along with attention and memory, this kind of imitation is important. It means that the child has worked out an understanding that a sequence of events has a beginning and an end.

At this age it is rare to see elaborate forms of imitation carried over to play with peers. Small groups of twenty-one-month-olds might play in brief episodes that involve physical activity: into the sandbox to fill buckets and dump them, over to the tunnel to explore, then inside to examine the new carpet for the play area. In their physical play they grunt and gesture to each other and laugh. If imitation occurs, it is immediate, one little parrot imitating another. Every so often a dispute breaks out over toys and crying results.

Children of twenty-one months also enjoy quiet times and spend short periods stacking blocks and knocking them down, putting objects into containers and taking them out, and stacking rings on a spindle. When another toddler comes by, one might hold out a toy to the visitor. But most of all, toddlers of this age tend to sit next to one other, looking at each other but playing alone. Verbal exchanges, if they occur at all, are brief. At this age producing extended conversations still demands so much energy and attention that it is difficult to play with a peer and simultaneously hold a conversation with him, especially when he too is not conversationally adept. Talk is out and gestures are in!

Overall, this month many toddlers slow down motorically, though they can hardly be described as quiet and prim. They still love to run and jump but they are also content to sit quietly and play with toys. You'll see examples of their ability to control their attention as they intently string beads or move toy trains along a track. Restlessness is clearly less of a problem than three months ago.

◆ IMAGES OF DEVELOPMENT

Motor Control

Balance is even better this month, and the toddler now routinely squats while playing. Now she sometimes walks down steps holding on with one hand. She is more comfortable this month walking up stairs by herself although she still holds onto the rail. She runs faster because her toddler gait is less pronounced. Her feet tend to point straight or even inward a bit, as opposed to the outward foot stance that characterizes the younger toddler. Although she can kick a large ball after watching her big brother kick strongly and forcefully, her kick is largely uncoordinated and somewhat unbalanced. The toddler is also better able to throw things this month. She seems to realize now that the whole arm, not just the wrist, is needed to throw. This throwing skill is not without its drawbacks. The twenty-one-month-old is not sure about what is throwable, so food and sand rank right up there with balls.

The twenty-one-month-old's hand control is increasingly precise. She clenches a crayon in her palm, and when presented a piece of paper, she uses the crayon to scribble. These fine-motor skills also lead to some explorations that increase safety risks. Electrical outlets seem to be made for things like paper clips. *Parents have to step up safety vigilance this month.*

Many toddlers enjoy showing how they do in everyday dressing activities. They wriggle out of clothes when it's time to undress—and sometimes when it's not time to undress. They successfully pull off socks and shoes and might work an arm out of a sweater or jacket. Some children of this age can partially zip up large zippers and unbutton large buttons. Much depends on how adept their fingers are; like adults, some toddlers are more adept than others.

Perception

Visual-form perception again shows improvement. The twenty-one-month-old not only recognizes the differences in shape of circular, square, and triangular puzzle pieces, she can also place them with assistance in a simple puzzle.

Most toddlers enjoy the feel of different textures and are fond of play that involves getting their hands into water, sand, cookie dough, and shaving cream. Mud is a different story. Many a twenty-one-month-old pleasurably wiggles her toes in mud but wouldn't dream of making mud pies: "Dirty!"

Language

Production shows growth in the number of new words the twenty-one-month-old has in her vocabulary and in her ability to construct two-word sentences. She also is better able to come up with the correct word label for an object or person. Sentences usually consist of a noun and a verb and do not include conjunctions such as *and*. Adjectives and adverbs are rarely used; however, sometimes toddlers use them to describe emotional states.

The way words are used expands considerably. Toddlers now use words intended to refer to themselves. At eighteen months the most common personal referents are *me* and *mine*; this month a small percentage of children also use *my* and *I*, as well as their own names. Being able to refer to herself in a variety of ways marks a profound change in the effectiveness of the toddler's communication with others. There is no mistaking the message in the statement "Me go" or "Mine doll," but there could have been a misinterpretation of the single-word sentences "Go" or "Doll" or "Mine."

In addition to labeling themselves and their possessions, toddlers of this age also use words to label their body parts. Nose, eye, hair, ears, and mouth are body parts that are most easily identified. Many little boys also use the label *penis*. It seems to be easier for boys to learn the label for their genitalia because the body part is so obvious. Little girls have a harder time with a term such as *vagina* because the body part is not visible to the child and the word is hard to pronounce.

Equally as important as being able to talk about possessions and wants is being able to talk about feelings. By twenty-one months, many toddlers can describe in a shorthand way their emotions and their internal states. It's not unusual to hear, "Me mad," "Head owie" (head hurt), "Me tired." Overall, toddlers of this age have so many more spoken words that the gap between comprehension and production is less of a problem for them.

For all the growth in speech skills at this age, toddlers have a difficult time with pronunciation of some letters and words. (Fully mastering pronunciation will take several more years.) Researchers who study language development suggest that young children need to simplify their language production in order to get their ideas across. It's as if their energy has to go into the communicative intent of their message rather than into correct pronunciation. At this age the toddler's vocal apparatus is developed enough to say full words and to use the right consonants, yet they don't. If a group of consonants appears in a word, one of the consonants tends to be dropped. "Street" becomes *treet*. Sometimes final consonants are dropped: "bring" becomes *brin*. The first consonant and vowel of some words are repeated to make up the word: "water" becomes *wawa*. In general, *g* and *k* sounds are difficult for toddlers. Fortunately, parents become expert at deciphering toddler language. More often than not, they get the right message from their toddler's fractured word or sentence.

Cognition

The toddler's grasp of ideas continues to evolve. Notions of past, present, and future are now part of his mental repertoire and are obvious in the toddler's word comprehension and speech. The twenty-one-month-old understands ideas in which words are a stand-in for events that will happen at a later time. Michael's father says, "We are going to Grandma's house" or "We have to buy some more soap," and Michael understands what his father means even though the words are about a distant event.

Twenty-one-month-olds can clearly remember two or three components of an activity, such as the individual events that involve getting ready to go somewhere. What this means is that ideas can be organized in terms of *scripts*. Developmental scientists define scripts as skeletal frameworks of everyday events. A script is not necessarily remembered in terms of words but rather in terms of a sequence of episodes that make up an event.

Scripts are similar to routines, which I described earlier. One difference is that a script captures an activity that repeatedly occurs: morning hygiene, going to the store. In contrast, a routine may occur only periodically; nonetheless, its critical feature is an organization of sequences to meet a goal. I view scripts as an important aid to memory retrieval, in contrast to routines, which represent an organized approach to solving a problem. Both scripts and routines are important learning tools for toddlers. And both benefit from brief parental remarks to toddlers about what they're doing and why.

A longtime colleague of Piaget described an example of a script. She observed a twenty-two-month-old boy at play accurately replicate a scene of his mother feeding the baby. His mother was not present; the only participants in the drama were the boy and his doll. Among the things he did was to carefully position the doll in the crook of his arm, hold the doll's bottle to visually inspect it, pull on the nipple to unclog it, and shake the bottle as if to enhance the flow of milk. This sequence of actions is a script rather than an imitation of a single act. The boy reproduced the skeletal framework of a real feeding in correct temporal sequence.

What does this example reveal about cognitive development? The boy's memory of the sequence of feeding events indicated some understanding of the temporal aspects of an event: A happens first, B is next, and then C occurs. His careful positioning of himself and his doll showed understanding of the spatial dimensions of an event: two people have to be positioned in a certain way in order for certain kinds of interaction to occur. The boy also showed awareness of cause and effect: milk will not flow through a nipple that is clogged.

Children of this age often devise scripts for events that occur repeatedly. When Andrew was around this age, he developed a morning script for overnight visits after we let him sleep in a bed rather than a crib. The first time he slept in the bed, he awoke in the morning, got out of bed, wriggled out of his wet diapers, found one of his books, came into our bedroom, and climbed into our bed. The script was the same for every overnight stay, for many years. Andrew's script probably evolved from the time he was a baby when I would take him out of his crib, change his diapers, and bring him to our bed. Andrew added wriggling out of his wet diapers and the book to his version of the script. Past the diaper stage, he'd go to the bathroom before joining us in bed.

At twenty-one months, toddlers also display ideas about the concepts of time and quantity. A toddler said to her mother: "Wan cookie now"; another, at the beach, said to his sister carrying a pail of sand: "Hurry!"; still another looking at two animal crackers said: "Two"; and another looked down at her shoes while her mother dressed her and said: "Two."

Some words represent categories of things: colors, chairs, stories, dresses, shirts. At this age, toddlers know that color is a category that stands for red, orange, blue, and so forth, which is another example of classification. When asked to find a shirt in the laundry basket, a toddler knows the meaning of *shirt* and goes to the clothesbasket to select one of his favorites.

Social Development

This month many toddlers show an increasing interest in social exchanges with their age-mates. One group of researchers who observed children of this age found all kinds of social exchanges: individual toddlers would attempt to join in another's play; they laughed and talked (at least briefly) to each other; they sometimes imitated each other; and they showed, offered, and gave toys. They also protested when a peer did something not to their liking. At least a third of the time the toddlers actively tried to engage another child in play.

Toddlers, however, are relatively inexperienced in dealing with their equals, even though they are skilled in social interactions with their parents, and to some extent with their siblings. Peer interactions have a different set of requirements and a different set of rules. Young children at play have to learn that a peer's bid to play requires a response and that the response needs to be directly related to the bid. A peer is unlike a parent; parents know or guess what toddlers mean, and—unasked—they often fill in the rest of incomplete sentences or help a toddler complete a task. About a third of the time, toddlers of this age do not understand each other's bids in play, so play ceases. Overall, then, peer play episodes at this age tend to be short because of difficulties in comprehension, speech production, and taking turns.

Both boys and girls enjoy dress-up play. However, gender separation tends to occur, as boys are more likely to dress up in order to play with trucks and large blocks whereas girls dress up to play with dolls. This preference takes place even when parents encourage gender-free toys. When it comes to gross-motor play such as running and jumping, girls are just as likely to run and chase as are boys.

Emotions

Toddlers of twenty-one months are mostly happy and pleasant to be with. They're often elated with their play and the little family chores they accomplish. They dance and sing to music.

They do get tearful when angered, when afraid, and when their wishes are not met. The frequency of tantrums varies considerably, but overall, fewer tantrums occur this month than at eighteen months. At this age there's more evidence of toddlers' actively trying to control their fear. They may talk about fear of an animal, seek a parent for support, or simply move away.

At this age, there's also evidence of self-conscious emotions akin to a sense of embarrassment. Many toddlers look for a refuge when an unfamiliar person comes close or makes a comment about the toddler's appearance. So here you can see a link between the developing self and an emotional response if the self seems threatened in some way.

Sense of Self

Autonomy and self-recognition continue to evolve. Sometimes a toddler will use descriptive evaluations when she refers to herself: "Bad girl, sticky hands." Once in a while she might lower her eyes in a nascent form of shame. In the morning she may greet her mother with "No cereal." One toddler unexpectedly found a visiting baby in her crib and immediately registered her displeasure about the intrusion into her space and her possession.

◆ DEVELOPMENTAL CLOSE-UP

Toilet Training

Parenting practices differ a great deal among families in the particular ways parents nurture, feed, and otherwise care for their babies. Some parents hold their babies to a fairly strict feeding schedule, and others feed their babies without regard to the clock. Amazingly, most babies adapt just fine to variations in parenting, provided, of course, the parenting is supportive, not harsh.

One of the most striking differences in parenting practices, I have found over the years, is in methods of toilet training toddlers. Some parents let it happen as a matter of course when the toddler indicates that he wants to sit on the potty. Other parents want to get the chore over with—the sooner the better. In a conversation I had with Dr. Benjamin Spock a long time ago, he revealed that he later changed some of the advice on toilet training he had given in the first edition of *Baby and Child Care*. In the first edition he suggested that mothers put off toilet training until children were close to three years old. Mothers complained bitterly to him telling him that toilet training should start earlier; enough of diapers! And so Dr. Spock modified his advice.

Freud and other psychoanalysts have long maintained that toilet training that was too severe led to the "anal" personality, a personality that is excessively compulsive. Alternatively, a child might rebel against rigid training by turning out to be excessively messy. Erik Erikson, a more modern interpreter of psychoanalysis, suggested that harsh toilet training could lead to feelings of shame and doubt among toddlers.

Following up on this theme, a number of years ago a husband-and-wife research team conducted a major study of child rearing in six different cultures around the world. These researchers were somewhat influenced by Freud's writings, so they thought important child-rearing issues for parents would include weaning babies from the breast, toilet training of toddlers, and gender training to teach young children appropriate sex roles. Years later, when all the observations and interviews had been analyzed, the researchers found that weaning was relatively unimportant, toilet training was rarely mentioned as a problem, and sex-role training actually took place during later childhood and adolescence.

What were parents concerned about? Aggressive acts (for example, fighting and hitting) and developing independence (for example, walking). These two common concerns were approached differently by parents. Some parents were more permissive and others were stricter about when training began and how regularly they enforced training.

What about today's parents? Is toilet training of great concern? Some of my own research findings shed some light on the question. We asked parents, primarily mothers, to respond to several child-rearing questions when their children were 13, 15, 18, 21, 24, 30, 36, 42, and 48 months of age. Particularly interesting to us were the answers to two questions: What do you prohibit your child from doing? What do you encourage your child to do on his/her own? As might be expected, safety issues (for example, touching electrical outlets), touching valuable household things, and hitting and biting were high on the prohibition list. As to encouraged independent behaviors, self-feeding, putting toys away, brushing teeth, and self-dressing were mentioned often. Only a few out of the hundreds of answers mothers gave to these questions mentioned toilet training! One mother of a 30-month-old said that she admonished her daughter for "peeing on the floor when her diaper was off"; another stated she had started potty training "but the results haven't been great"; and still another said, "He's old enough and we'll be more insistent." Three mothers, one of a 42-month-old and two of 48-month-olds, said they encouraged their children to use the toilet on their own. That was it.

This doesn't mean that toilet training doesn't matter to parents. There were two times that toilet training was an important issue for me. We lived in the East when our daughter was little. We bundled up and ventured out in all kinds of cold weather, but I was ill at ease knowing she was toddling around in the cold with wet diapers. When we moved west to the warmth of Southern California, toilet training became an issue for another reason. Our second child was ready for a few hours of preschool, but the director said he could be enrolled only if he was toilet trained. So we devoted ourselves to the task. By the time our third child was ready for preschool, that rule had been abolished. Toilet training just evolved naturally.

My suggestion is to do what feels comfortable for you, your schedule, and your child. Whenever you start toilet training, do it without threats and punishments. Some children are afraid of regular-sized toilets, so use a little potty. In general, parents who don't make a big issue of it often find toilet training is easier than teaching their child to put his toys away.

Twenty-Four Months

- often wants to assert self

- fantasy play; problem solving; creativity

- uses 2-, 3-, or 4-word sentences

- knows name, gender, some family roles

- likes consistency in family routines

- enjoys play with age-mates

- has a sense of humor

Two-year-olds are approaching the threshold of the preschool years. As with most major transitions, growth comes with some bumps. Let's look at skills first. Children of this age have the ability to

- think using ideas based on knowledge and recall memory
- understand basic categories such as boys, girls, shoes
- understand concepts such as broken, pretend
- speak in sentences, which are mostly grammatically correct
- move about with assurance
- remember everyday routines
- be partially independent in self-care such as helping dress themselves
- recognize and respond to others' moods

The two-year-old uses words and sentences in all kinds of conversations: "Grandma get up," "Doll go up," "Mommy go work," "Toy go there." Sentences grow in length and sometimes include prepositions that indicate cause-and-effect reasoning: "I put shoes on and go." Some children are able to incorporate "if" and "then" reasoning in their language: "If we go to store, I get candy."

The words of two-year-olds typically reveal their knowledge of different labels for objects that are similar, such as cup, mug, and bowl. Just a short time ago, they might have labeled all of these *cup*. The striking growth of language that often occurs between eighteen and twenty-four months has a cross-over effect on the young child's cognitive functioning. This can be observed in everyday memory for recent and longer-term events and in the richness and complexity of the child's pretend play.

Two-year-olds are smart! Two examples follow. The first occurred in my research laboratory and describes how a child handled a situation in which she was told to put toys away. The second deals with a child who sought to protect her possessions from an unwelcome peer and sometimes resorted to biting to do so.

Claire had been asked by her mother to put the lab toys away on the toy shelves. She responded to the request by neatly arranging a few toys on the top shelf. She then sat down in a chair near the shelves. Although her mother encouraged her to put more toys away, Claire sat unmoving. Her mother continued, "There are more shelves to be filled." Claire eyed the shelves and then moved the toys she had placed on the top shelf to the second shelf. Returning to the chair, she swung her feet and grinned. Her mother continued her prompting, at which point Claire responded, "Too tired, I watch you. Need to talk to you."

Claire used multiple skills—language, planning, and problem solving—to control a situation she did not like. Cleverly, she described herself as *tired* because she knew from past experience that invoking tiredness brought her mother's assistance. Claire's grin also suggested she enjoyed the verbal jousting with her mother, who by the way never lost her cool. Compare the sophistication of this resistant behavior to that of a younger toddler's exclamation of "No!"

The second episode, described by a grandparent, involved a two-year-old grandchild. Both had been talking about biting as an unacceptable behavior. It seems the grandchild had bitten a child who was new to a toddler playgroup; this child tended to take toys from other children. I can only presume the new toddler was trying to deal with assorted difficulties such as separation from parents or entry into a group that made her uneasy. In any event, the two-year-old's discussion with her grandparent included the following sentence: "I bit A [the new child] but I did not bite B [a favorite peer]."

This sentence is instructive because it reveals a young child's attempt to justify her behavior, and her presumed reasoning behind the justification. The child's biting was selective, and restricted to the child (A) who violated her possessions. She has never bitten the child (B) who has been her partner in a pleasurable relationship. Thus we're probably on target when we suspect this two-year-old's sense of well-being is being threatened by the toy-taking peer. Using language—"I bit . . . ," "I did not bite . . ."—the child clearly distinguished the vulnerability she experienced in the interactions with one peer and the feeling of comfort experienced with another.

In addition to language and cognitive growth, two-year-olds reveal their intense quest for autonomy and independence. Their motivation to do things on their own seems to swell almost daily and is often a sign of maturity that is welcome to parents. "I do it!" is frequent and might be said in relation to self-dressing, setting the dinner table, running an errand (in the house) for a sibling, and more. They recognize their own likes and dislikes and don't hesitate to tell their preferences to parents and others. It is fun to witness the blossoming of a genuine personality.

So, you might ask, "Where are the bumps?" There are a couple of big ones. One concerns selfhood and the chase for independence, which together sometimes lead to downright contrariness. There are days when two-year-olds don't comply with rules that are really important: They don't want to sit in a car seat without protest; they might look at a parent and then hit another child or walk across a sidewalk to the curb, look back to make sure a parent is watching, and then dangle a foot over the edge of the curb. Testing parents is sometimes done with considerable cleverness: one two-year-old, tempted by objects she was not supposed to touch, developed her own scripted answer if she was observed in the act. "This is for you," she would exclaim as she handed over the forbidden object.

Still these kinds of autonomy-related behaviors are not the kinds of acts you'll want to smile away. Issues concerning safety have to be dealt with without delay and repeatedly, if necessary. Explain to the child what's involved.

It's also in everybody's best interests to help the two-year-old respect possessions and the other dos and don'ts of family life. But there is a flip side here. It also helps to recognize that although two-year-olds' behaviors can be especially aggravating, often children of this age are simply attempting to understand more fully who they are, what they are capable of doing, and the kinds of behaviors others will accept and not accept. Most two-year-olds are not willfully disobedient. Help them learn, even though your patience is sometimes worn thin.

Another bump concerns their occasional helplessness in the face of frustration. Of course, toddlers are not alone in this regard. However, their resulting emotional storms can be tornado-size. It's interesting to consider the causes of tantrums at this age. Two examples follow: The first involves a child who wanted attention from her mother, and the second concerns a child who simply did not understand an event.

Esther, her twin brother, her mother, and her baby brother were walking outside after attending a religious service. The day was uncomfortably hot and all were tired. Esther said, "Birdie." Her mother didn't understand, and, besides, the baby needed attention. Fatigue, heat, and being ignored were just too much for Esther. She threw herself on the sidewalk and had a gigantic tantrum in full view of a parade of folks. Later that day as Esther and her mother talked about the tantrum, she told her mother she just wanted her to look at the birdie on a mailbox.

Then there was David, who was about to celebrate his second birthday with a midafternoon party for his playmates. At noontime his mother took him to a favorite ice cream store to buy the cake. David was beside himself with glee as he peered at the display case. After paying for the cake, David's mother started to leave, but David pulled and tugged at her, grunting and pointing to the case. "Cone!" he yelled. "Cone!" Clearly, she must have forgotten why they were there! His mother tried to explain that the cake was an ice cream cake and would be eaten later in the day. "No," David screamed, "ice creeeeem!" No ice cream now, says his mother. A dazzling temper tantrum followed. In hindsight, David's mother realized that he expected an ice cream cone because she had always bought him a cone when they were in the ice cream store. Besides, David did not know that birthday cakes can be made of ice cream.

To sum up, the two-year-old is a study in contrasts. He is an independent child who can be helpful, attentive, cooperative, and fun to be with. He uses language effectively and has a sense of humor. Sometimes reasoning is first-rate, and other times it is illogical. Sometimes frustrations lead to emotional breakdowns, and language skills are temporarily lost.

Parental patience, and more patience, is essential to keep the relationship on an even keel. Besides patience and a sense of humor, effective parenting also requires lots of age-appropriate cognitive and language stimulation to help the two-year-old's active mind keep growing. Don't hesitate to ask yourself, "What's going on?" if your two-year-old seems wound up too often or has many emotional meltdowns each day.

◆ IMAGES OF DEVELOPMENT

Motor Control

When a child reaches the age of twenty-four months, the toddler stance has almost disappeared. Besides walking adeptly, two-year-olds run, go up and down stairs, and squat for minutes at a time. They balance themselves on tiptoe. Two-year-olds also easily climb into chairs and seat themselves. Overall, most toddlers of this age love physical activity, and well they should. Not many months ago they struggled to get around. Now they seem to glide.

Hand coordination is generally good at this age, although there is occasional fumbling with very small toys. Turning pages, building a tower with blocks, and inserting rods into holes are easily accomplished. Fingers and thumb work well together when grasping an implement such as a spoon; mishaps occasionally happen because navigating a filled spoon from bowl to mouth is difficult. Many children of this age demonstrate preferential handedness.

The one disconcerting aspect of toddlers' motor agility is the hazards they create for themselves. They start to move and don't know how to stop. Andrew was bouncing up and down on the curb while his grandfather retrieved his jacket from the back of his red truck. Uncontrollably, Andrew bounced from the curb to the forbidden street. A frightened grandfather reacted with a spanking, followed by tears and hugs. Then there is the story told to me by a colleague whose nephew started to run and couldn't stop. He ended up against a wall with a broken leg, even though he had seen the wall.

Overall, be especially aware of the places that are risky for two-year-olds: the kitchen and bathroom, parking lots, and sidewalks.

Perception

At this age the toddler goes beyond recognition of two-dimensional illustrations. He now tries to copy a line. He tries to draw a vertical line by imitating one that has been drawn for him. He also tries to draw a circle. The
significance of copying is threefold. First, the child is adopting a tool (pencil, crayon) that others use to write and to draw with. Second, by copying
geometric shapes, he reinforces his knowledge of circles, squares, triangles,
and more. Third, he adds to his concept of his own competence when he
sees that he can use the tool and that he is capable of reproducing
another's mark.

Two-year-olds are occasionally fooled by their perceptions and precon-
ceptions. They have built up expectations about the ways objects should
look and the ways that events should occur. Compared to those of older
children, their reasoning abilities are still relatively immature. Thus they
are unable to work through unpredicted scenarios. Andrew sat in a restau-
rant with his grandfather and heard him ask the waiter for a glass of cola.
The waiter brought the soda, and Andrew asked for some. His grandfather
poured a small amount into an empty coffee cup, given there was no other
glass on the table. Andrew refused to drink from the cup, saying it contained coffee. No amount of persuasion could convince him otherwise.

Language

Comprehension. There is a steady increase in the number of categories of
objects the toddler identifies and in her knowledge of the specific items in
the group. She understands that rooms are parts of the house and goes to
the room called kitchen when her mother tells her that's where she's left
her toy. She knows the word *animal* and correctly points to pictures of different animals in her book.

Studies suggest that around this age children learn word definitions using
different kinds of strategies. One strategy is simply one-on-one. The parent
holds out a sock and says, "This is a sock." She teaches the word *sock* every
day for a week. More commonly, children learn words via indirect teaching
that occurs during the course of everyday interactions. However word
learning occurs, it requires attentiveness on the child's part—a point that
again reinforces the crucial role of attention in learning.

Word-learning strategies that come out of indirect teaching include the following. One involves using a combined visual-auditory cue for learning. In this
instance, a parent repeatedly looks at an object while talking about it. The
child has to be visually attentive to the parent's direction of attention, and
aurally attentive so she can identify the particular word that consistently
appears in the parent's conversation—when the object is in sight. This strat-

egy has some similarity to the younger child's propensity to link words with gestures and actions: a wave goes with "bye"; opening a door goes with "let's go." In any event, the visual-auditory strategy may be especially useful for word learning in the early years. Some researchers believe that young children are particularly receptive to word regularities in the content of parents' speech.

In another word-learning approach, the child utilizes salient perceptual features of objects. Cars and trucks have wheels, they are fairly similar in overall shape, they move, and they are ever present on roads and in media images. It's not surprising that *car* is a word that is understood early on in language development. Still another strategy involves the child's paying attention to an object's use. A parent uses a broom to sweep a floor, and that's just about the only function of a broom. Similarly, a cup is a container that typically holds liquid.

Word learning also occurs in combination with the child's imitation of a parent's everyday behaviors. Toddler Jane watches her father comb his hair in the morning. She gets a toy comb and combs her hair. Dad says something to the effect that he's using a comb, and Jane is using a comb. The object, comb, is consistently labeled by the father, and its function is visibly reinforced with use.

Toddler comprehension goes beyond learning words. Comprehension also involves learning the individual roles that family members assume (for example, work roles, caregiving roles, household-chore roles), and also understanding how family members fit into family schedules and activities. Here's a great example of learning that is "in process." When a toddler's mother told her it was time to eat, she ignored her mother even though she seemed hungry. When her mother asked for an explanation, the toddler said her sister was not yet home. The unspoken message was that her sister usually set the table: how could the family eat if the sister wasn't home to set the table and to eat with them?

In my view, talking to young children is a singularly important parenting activity. I don't mean fanciful, sophisticated talking but rather everyday conversations about activities, play, characters in books, and events that have taken place or will occur. Words become ideas. Ideas can be thought about and evaluated. Ideas open up untold vistas for young children.

Production. A two-year-old largely discards one-word sentences and uses two-word, three-word, and four-word sentences. One child's vocabulary during an afternoon in a toddler day-care program included sentences that reveal several kinds of knowledge:

"Finished juice already" (knowledge of the amount of time expected to complete a task)

"Oh, oh, dropped cracker" (past tense; knowledge that food is not to be dropped)

"I can't turn around" (knowledge of own limitations)

"I want tape" (self-related desires)

"Don't choke" (to a child eating corn) (awareness of a safety hazard related to things in mouth)

"Billy took play dough from Jill" (awareness of others' rights of possession).

Bear in mind, though, that there is considerable variability in children's language skills at this age. Some children speak in elaborate sentences that contain numerous words and complex ideas, and others still produce only single words. A few children, who have no physical or hearing problems, do not talk at all.

When a two-year-old speaks in sentences, the words are in the right grammatical order: "Doll go there," "Daddy go work," "Boy fell down." Most toddler sentences refer to immediate experiences and personal activities. The two-year-old correctly uses I, me, and you, although use of other pronouns is infrequent. Sentences rarely contain the, but they do sometimes include and, so, or 'cause. These words demonstrate command of cause-and-effect relations: "Open door so daddy come."

Despite the impressive growth in language, the two-year-old's speech is not always clear. It has been estimated that spoken words are incomprehensible one-third of the time. Sometimes toddlers are aware that they are not understood. One toddler talked to her father while he was driving. When she said something that was incomprehensible to him, he did not reply. The child repeated herself as if she knew that her father did not understand her words. "Honey, I still don't understand," he said. She accepted his comment and went on to talk about something else.

Studies show that twenty-four-month-old girls tend to be slightly more advanced in language production than boys, perhaps because they tend to be talked to more than boys. Toddlers with older siblings tend to talk earlier than only children. Children reared in families in which two or more languages are spoken tend to produce speech later than children reared in families in which one language is spoken; it seems as if they have to take time to sort out the words that go with each language. Most of the time this slight verbal hiccup has no discernible long-term consequences. In fact, research suggests that bilingualism has long-term cognitive benefits for children.

Overall, speech has become an extraordinary tool for twenty-four-month-olds. Words help them express needs, communicate intentions with adults and peers, offer affection, and control their negative emotions.

Cognition

One of the most notable cognitive achievements of this age is the development of insightful problem solving. In prior months toddlers figured out some cause-and-effect relations with objects and developed ideas about the functional use of objects. Now for the first time they are able to derive solutions for problems that involve nonconventional uses of an object. They are thinking both intelligently and creatively.

My colleagues and I studied insightful problem solving by adapting an idea from Jean Piaget. We used a prop that consisted of an opaque tube about six inches long that contained a cookie enclosed in a wad of tissue. Sitting at a table, the toddler was given the tube and a short toy rake and was told there was a cookie inside the tube. In order to retrieve the cookie, the child has to use the rake's handle to push the cookie out of the tube. In other words, success involves discovering that a rake can be used in an unconventional way. This is a thorny problem. Children younger than two years of age find it inordinately difficult to solve, even after the solution is shown to them. But at around two, a few come up with the solution on their own. And even if they don't solve the problem, they do reproduce the solution once it is demonstrated to them.

Another important cognitive activity at this age involves the elaboration of pretend play. A few months back, the pretend play of younger toddlers took the form of reproducing an everyday behavior. Now children may use objects and toys in ways that are unusual. They also take on roles of people outside the family. One child dragged a bench before a bush and used two of its branches to create a control wheel for an airplane cockpit. He became so absorbed in the activity he stopped to ask, "This is pretend, right?" As for assuming others' roles, this is the age when toddlers enjoy playing with a doctor's kit or wearing costumes that reflect spacemen, movie stars, and fairies. Language increasingly takes on a role in pretense. As Paul Harris has shown, two-year-olds talk about their pretend actions, they can identify a *missing action* in a pretend sequence that is shown to them, and they remember previously seen sequences.

Still another cognitive activity that emerges at around twenty-four months is a new form of self-management in situations that could cause emotional upheavals. Here, self-management means recruiting cognitive skills—control of attention, working memory, language—to control one's emotions. This is a lot to ask of two-year-olds.

This is the situation. We showed eighteen-month-, twenty-four-month-, and thirty-month-old children a bright red old-fashioned telephone and asked them not to touch the phone for a couple of minutes. We left the telephone on a table in front of the children and then disappeared behind a screen. The children's mothers sat nearby but were looking at magazines. By two years of age, but not before, more than half of the children did not touch the phone. Almost as soon as we made the request, some two-year-olds turned to their mothers and talked (one little girl talked about her nails needing nail polish), some sat on their hands, and some squirmed around in their chairs so as not to look at the telephone.

The children found ways to distract themselves so they did not have to look at the forbidden toy. This is the control side of attention. In similar-type research, Lisa Bridges and Wendy Grolnick found that more than one-third of two-year-olds turned away from potentially upsetting situations and actively sought ways to distract themselves. This is what we try to do, as adults, when confronted with things we should not do. My sense that working memory is involved in coping with delay relates to the fact that children had to remember the admonition about not touching the toy while figuring out a substitute behavior. Was this done at a conscious level? I don't know; my guess is that the children who were successful drew upon their implicit knowledge of behaviors that worked for them in the past.

Young children tend to be less successful in handling delays when they are asked to wait for a snack or if they have to wait for attention when a parent is talking on the telephone. In fact, in two different studies mothers reported it was rather difficult to teach their child not to interrupt when they were on the phone. This difficulty extended to children up to five years of age.

Going back to two-year-olds, there's another important point about cognitive functioning at this age. Within an instant, two-year-olds can size up a situation and realize when they are unable to do certain things such as solve a complicated four-piece puzzle. Without the least sign of frustration, they seek out assistance. In addition, they offer help or solace quickly. Overall, they process information both more rapidly and more effectively than even two months ago. Again, my sense is that increasing language skills promote thinking about their own needs and another person's distress.

Social Development

Two-year-olds are generally good company. They run simple errands (get Mommy's purse) and are often interested in helping with routine tasks. They are getting better at complying with family rules, particularly those that have to do with safety and not touching prohibited objects. However, they tend to have trouble with not interrupting, not yelling in the house, and putting toys away. They're also not quite ready to generalize from one situation to another: rules they learn in one context don't seem to apply to another. Why should Mommy's warning, "Don't run," in the grocery store have anything to do with how to act in a clothing store?

Often children of this age do not understand why certain rules are imposed, and many think that the best way to get clarification is to check out a parent's reaction. In spite of having been admonished to put his shoes in the closet after taking them off, my son Paul used to stand in front of the toilet bowl with a shoe in hand looking at me. Did he really think little brown shoes belonged in the toilet bowl? Who knows? It's helpful for sighing parents to know that one researcher found that, on average, children of this age commit five rule infractions an hour!

Two-year-olds increase their play with other children and at times show genuine cooperation for several minutes. This is impressive because they're not highly skilled in planning a play script with each other. Nonverbal imitation is still a popular play activity (if he runs, she runs), but children also coordinate their behaviors with each other. They sometimes take turns and occasionally talk to each other while they play. Their fights primarily involve heated disputes over possessions, which can lead to grabbing toys, pushing, or hitting. Sometimes two-year-olds are content to sit next to each other and play alone. It's a way for them to rest from social challenges and to replenish their energy.

A two-year-old tends to be very accepting of other children who differ in some way, such as skin color, garbled speech, or a physical handicap. Mostly the difference just doesn't matter.

Emotions

There is no mistaking the emotional intensity of the two-year-old in displays of pleasure (exuberance or elation) as well as dismay. "Wow! Wow!" one child exclaimed each time he visited a friend's house and saw a train set. Contrarily, one afternoon this boy stood in front of the family's refrigerator and whined and whined. "Milk, apple juice, orange juice? What?" asked his mother. He stood there and kicked at the refrigerator door, tears running down his face.

At this age, frequent causes of crying include fatigue, hunger, parents' departure for a job or an evening, and loss of a possession (a toy) to a peer. Children of this age also get upset if major changes are made in their lives and routines. Thus, when a major change occurs, such as moving to a new house, the birth of a sibling, or even a new daytime baby-sitter, the two-year-old perceives a violation of his sense of control and a disruption of the consistency in his life.

Some changes in routines are unavoidable. And it may be difficult to find a solution that works for the two-year-old. A couple with young children found it necessary to make frequent trips to visit a seriously ill parent. They decided it would be less stressful for their young children (including the two-year-old) to take them along on these trips rather than exposing them to repeated separations. However, the tension and the travel required too much adaptation from the children. Whining, crying, and sleep problems resulted. Unfortunately, given all of their worries, the children's parents did not immediately realize the cause of their children's emotional turmoil.

In addition to the negative emotions that result from fear, hurt, anger, and uncertainties, the two-year-old shows emotions that are precursors to shame and embarrassment. When caught in the act, they cry, hang their heads, and bite their lips. Clearly they don't understand the meaning of shame, but they do realize that they have behaved in a way a parent does not like. Children do not show shame until they have a mature sense of self and how that self is supposed to act; this sense evolves with cognitive growth.

Interestingly, at this age emotional distress can come from dreams. The mother of a two-year-old girl described this dream episode. One Sunday the mother and her husband entertained relatives who had two preschool age boys. The boys were rough and appropriated the little girl's toys. She watched and was unusually quiet. The family left. That night the two-year-old woke up screaming in terror. Between heaving sobs, she told her mother that the boys were still in the house and were taking her toys. She was frantic and would not believe the boys were gone until her mother carried her from room to room to show her that they were empty. The dream was reality for the child.

Yes, two-year-olds are a reservoir of emotions. However, they are getting better at emotion control. And they get even better: studies show that preschoolers work out all kinds of ways to handle some of their frustrations.

Sense of Self

Two-year-olds refer to themselves by name. They also talk about themselves using such verbs as *can, can't, hurt, know, like, want,* and *need.* When they use words such as these, they are telling us they understand the everyday definition of the words, and they know how to apply the definition of a particular word to themselves: "I want cookie." They also realize that we know the definition of words they use, and therefore we can respond to wishes/dislikes/abilities in the "right" way.

You'll find occasions when your two-year-old finds it necessary to assert herself while not understanding the limits of her abilities. She declares, "I do it," even when it is impossible. "Mine," she says, when clearly it is not. Sometimes she uses the word *mine* when she actually wants to say yours!

At this age, children recognize their gender. They also recognize some of the attributes and roles little girls share with their mothers or other females, and little boys share with fathers or other males. *Girlness* and *boyness* are learned through observation, play with other children, and stories.

◆ DEVELOPMENTAL CLOSE-UP

Parenting: Commitments

Each time I teach a course in infant development, I organize it in the same way. The first few sessions cover the meaning of development, two or three classes discuss prenatal life, and the rest of the classes are devoted to infant and toddler development. I invite my students to ask friends and relatives who have babies and toddlers to join us in class for about half an hour. Fortunately, there is always a good supply of mothers and fathers who are willing, and we can usually arrange their visits to coincide with the age group we are studying. I encourage the visiting parents to talk about themselves as parents and to describe life with their babies. I want my students to understand that babies do not grow up in a social vacuum. Parents get this message across effectively.

During one class, two mothers visited the class during the week we were talking about prenatal development. Each came on a separate day. These two mothers were remarkable; even I, who have seen hundreds and hundreds of parents over the years, was awed by their special qualities. Both women were mothering young children who placed extraordinary strains and demands on them, yet they accepted their responsibilities with a grace and commitment that were compelling. Each also unhesitatingly mentioned her own frailties and mistakes.

One mother—I'll call her Maddy—loves children, and she and her husband plan to have as many as they can. She came to class with her fourth baby, who was about a year old. Maddy told the class about her pregnancy, which had not gone well, the week before the baby's birth when she came down with a serious case of the flu, and the unexpected cesarean section she had to undergo while she still had the flu. A baby girl was born prematurely who was very, very sick, and Maddy knew she might not survive. Spellbound, we listened as Maddy told us about her inability to cope with the baby's birth because of her own illness; although she felt guilty, her own pain and misery were overpowering. Fortunately, Maddy told us, she soon began to feel better. Somewhat more slowly the baby improved and was well enough to go home at three weeks. However, for six months the baby was constantly attached to a special respiratory monitor because she could stop breathing at any time. Either Maddy or her husband kept watch, but it was mostly Maddy's responsibility because her husband had a business to run. Maddy hardly slept for six months, but as she matter-of-factly told my class, "You do what you have to do." And she did. And the baby was doing fine.

The second mother—we'll call her Deanne—came to class with her little boy, who was three years old and had spina bifida, a condition that has its origins early in the prenatal period. At birth, the baby's spinal tissue was exposed right above the buttocks. In medical terms, there was risk of paralysis below the lesion; the boy might not have use of his legs and might not have control of his bladder and bowel. The physicians told the parents that the baby would be severely impaired.

Deanne brought us pictures of the baby at the time of his birth, after his surgery, and while he was an infant, and she brought articles and books about spina bifida for my students to read. Almost from her son's birth,

Deanne arranged for her baby to receive special therapy routinely. She also worked with him at home, and he began to thrive. Later on, he even began to walk on his misshapen feet. In time, Deanne found a toddler class for him and eventually a preschool. The boy dazzled us with his play and language, the affection he had for his mother, and the affection he had for a friend of the family who had come along. Deanne told us she still did not know if her son would have bladder and bowel control, but she would face that in time. For now her concerns were to provide a good developmental start for her son. Clearly, she was doing just that.

Not all parents must deal with the strains of an early birth or severe physical impairment. Nevertheless, sleeplessness, crying, sickness, and child negativism are stresses every parent faces. Weathering these developmental challenges requires commitment from parents. The fundamental strategy is to find effective ways to deal with stresses, so that you can provide the sensitivity and responsiveness that go along with good parenting.

Because infants and very young children are captive audiences for their parents and substitute caregivers, they are particularly susceptible to good or bad rearing influences. Because babies are naturally attracted to people, it stands to reason that very early on parents begin to exert influences on their child's development. These influences become easier to recognize as the baby begins to identify familiar caregivers, and they attain progressively greater import as the young child learns to distinguish emotions, comprehend words, and imitate behaviors. In times of distress, the baby looks to familiar people for affection, play, and solace. If a baby's distress signals are consistently ignored, there can be negative effects including increases in overall arousal and disturbances in physiological and psychological regulatory mechanisms.

One of the most important research findings that has come out of studies of parents and children is that parents' unrealistic expectations about development can lead to harsh punishment and abuse. Young babies cry, sometimes for reasons that we do not understand. But their cries are not merely a ploy to annoy us. They cry because something is bothering them. It is up to us to make them feel better. Similarly, the exploring toddler is not willfully disobedient; he is seeking to know his world. It is a fact that some explorations are bothersome for us or unsafe for him. That he needs to be monitored is a certainty; that he should not be assaulted is also a certainty.

Research has also repeatedly found that parent knowledge and education are invariably linked to children's developmental outcomes. Many factors are involved here. As one example, educated parents in our country generally have larger and more complex vocabularies than parents whose education ceased at high school or earlier. Not surprisingly, educated parents tend to talk a lot to their children. They explain and reason with their children, play games that involve words and songs, and read books to them. These young children grow up surrounded by a verbal environment. They enter school more verbally adept than children whose early years were spent in relatively impoverished verbal settings. So often in our society, language skills are linked to educational and social competencies.

It is also true that the more educated the parent, the more likely it is that he or she tries to obtain information about developmental trends and attempts to learn what children of one or another age can or cannot do. Parent education also plays an important role in ensuring that babies and young children get good starts in their intellectual growth. Parents who realize that cognition is important for a child's academic success, social-skill development, emotion control, and self-concept will facilitate child learning with age-appropriate playthings, books, excursions, and informal lessons.

Researchers have studied the influence of parents on child development in a variety of contexts. Among the research questions that have immediate application for helping parents become more competent are: How do parents respond to their babies' irritability? What are parents' beliefs about good and not-so-good babies? How do parents feel about punishment for young children? For older children? What characteristics make some parents truly effective? I have touched upon a few of these themes. For example, in the seven-month close-up regarding day care, the effect of separation from parents on a child's attachment and the influence of attachment on social adjustment were discussed. The impact of differences in parenting patterns—the degree of routine in babies' lives, the amount of time parents read to their young child, the extent to which parents participate in social games—has been emphasized throughout this book.

One research team described various kinds of parent influences. There is an influence that provides emotional security for children, and another influence that, for example, involves providing good role models for being kind to others (prosocial behaviors). Still other influences come from the way parents give rewards for good behavior and discipline for unacceptable behaviors. Discipline that is restrained (for example, time-outs) as opposed to discipline that is harsh (for example, repeated spankings) leads to fewer childhood fights and less aggression. Still other influences derive from the way parents provide opportunities for learning, such as trips to zoos, local supermarkets, and the like. Trips provide new inputs for learning.

The point is that a child's social motivation and social behavior skills are affected by all of these parental acts. At a practical level, this means that children do better when their parents set good behavior examples, praise children when they do well and reprimand them when they err, take time to explain what is expected, and make their children feel they have someone to turn to if things go awry. That's a pretty tall order for parents. The goal for parents is not to reach a state of perfection, which is all but impossible, but rather to approach parenting with sensitivity, knowledge, patience, humor, and commitment. Of course, sometimes parenting just seems too demanding. When this happens, find ways to get away—even for an hour or two.

DEVELOPMENTAL ALERTS:

Eighteen Months, Twenty-Four Months

Eighteen Months: Seek Help If Your Child

- is not interested in parents or toys
- cannot stand without assistance
- does not remember any routines
- does not understand any words
- cannot distinguish a circle from a square
- does not combine toys in play
- does not comply with any safety rules
- does not show attachment to anyone
- is mostly irritable

Twenty-four Months: Seek Help If Your Child

- does not walk
- does not group any objects together
- does not show any kind of imitative behavior
- does not show functional play
- does not use jargon
- does not identify himself/herself in any way
- does not show any pleasure with own accomplishments
- is mostly noncompliant with your requests
- is mostly irritable

SHARPENING OUR FOCUS

PARENTING AND STRESSES

The wedding of the thirtyish couple was outdoors, high on a bluff overlooking the city. Puffy white clouds floated in the azure blue sky. Nearby tennis courts were empty. A dozen or so well-dressed guests wore minibackpacks: I soon learned they were parents of toddlers who were carrying all sorts of toys, clothes, and snacks.

A few minutes into the ceremony, the toddlers broadcast their presence. They squirmed. They cried. One exclaimed, "Go"; another asked for a pacifier. By the ceremony's midpoint, a parade of parents and toddlers headed to the tennis court or elsewhere, then back to their seats, only to take off again. Later during lunch, toddlers periodically scampered by our table followed by a chasing parent. Still later, as guests headed for their cars, I saw four of the couples with their toddlers in tow. All of the parents looked exhausted: it had been a tough three hours.

Let's face it, parenting a toddler is hard work and can be more challenging than caring for a baby, which, as you well know, demands lots of time and energy. Despite charm, exuberance, and cleverness, toddlers often seem to be in perpetual motion, can be assertive, are sometimes heedless of their own safety, scream "No!" in a blink, and have awesome temper tantrums. These behaviors are bothersome enough when they occur at home, but are downright troublesome in public places. It's no wonder that parents of toddlers are at times physically and emotionally weary.

It's also not surprising that some researchers have written about *developmentally related stresses*. (Of course, recognize that stress for parents can arise anytime.) However, developmentally related stresses are those that steadily accumulate as parents attempt to deal with the ever changing landscape of child skills. Just consider the second year. Within a twelve-month period, toddlers start to walk and suddenly can't be left alone for a minute; they begin to talk, and before long are saying "no," "want," "mad," and so on; they discover their self-identities and begin to shrug off assistance and emphatically declare, "I," "mine," and "my." Toddlers are constantly asking parents to adapt! Given that flexibility and patience are demanded of parents of toddlers, it's not surprising that stresses mount up. They tend not to decrease until young children are more physically and behaviorally responsive to parents—often at about three years. Please be aware that I'm not equating the day-to-day stresses that arise when caring for a toddler to those stresses that come about as a result of major personal catastrophes (death of a loved one, serious illness, divorce, job loss, destruction of a home). Parenting stresses are usually not comparable to personal upheavals. They are more like day-to-day hassles, which Keith Crnic describes as a type of ongoing annoyance or irritation.

However we define developmentally related parent stresses—as a series of minor stresses that reflect adaptations made by parents to the toddlers' burgeoning abilities or as hassles—the fact is that parenting-related stresses can also have adverse effects on the young child. Both parent and child can be at risk.

What is the risk for parents? Crnic suggests risks include decreased feelings of well-being, an increase in negative attitudes toward children, and decreases in effectiveness in parent and child interactions. Some readily identifiable stress-related symptoms include poor sleep habits, becoming short-tempered with the slightest of provocations, eating too much, and feeling out of sorts and run down.

Parental stress holds potential risks for young children. Parents who are chronically stressed tend to monitor their children less often and less effectively. In addition, these parents are less sensitive to the child's own stress experiences and thus often unavailable to the child as a protective resource. It is not surprising that research findings indicate that toddlers of stressed parents tend to be more aggressive and irritable than toddlers of nonstressed parents.

Before you—as a parent of a toddler—push the proverbial panic button, let's step back and consider stress in more detail.

+ Stress is not always easy to define and to measure, albeit most of us know when we feel stressed. There are, of course, major individual differences in the perception of stress and our ability to cope with it. The kinds of events that cause us stress also vary. One person can feel intense stress because of a spouse's expensive hobby, but another (of similar economic means) simply shrugs it off.

+ The stresses that we perceive range from mild to particularly intense. Moreover, some of our stresses are relatively brief (e.g., a work-related deadline), whereas others extend into months and years. Examples include the illness or death of a spouse that is exacerbated by a substantial decline in one's standard of living, and disasters (a natural disaster such as an earthquake or hurricane, or conflicts and wars) that markedly disrupt the usual flow of family life. Often, it is the negative, intense, long-term stressors that are most disruptive of an individual's physiological and behavioral well-being.

+ Parents can experience stress because of events that are unrelated to their children, but they can also experience stress because of the challenges directly related to child rearing. This is the kind of stressor that I focused on in my description of toddlers and their parents at the outdoor wedding. Whatever the cause of a parent's stress, if it is intense and chronic, the outcomes for the child can be jeopardized.

- For the most part, the stresses that arise from parenting are thought to be relatively universal, and less intense than many other stress-causing experiences. This decreased intensity is one of the reasons that Crnic uses the term *hassles* to identify the stresses that arise in the day-to-day challenges of parenting.
- The stresses related to parenting, however they are labeled, are developmental. By developmental I mean that during the course of children's development some age periods are more demanding of parents than other age periods. Toddlerhood is one such period, and adolescence is another. Some research findings suggest parental stress increases during toddlerhood and then decreases, with a similar pattern for the overall period of adolescence.
- It is important to recognize that even for an age period known for its heightened parental challenges, the experience of stress varies among parents. This variation can also be observed between fathers and mothers within the same family.
- Research suggests that parents' use of support systems is an effective way to reduce stress.

Are there solutions for feelings of stress that are related to your toddler's behavior? Yes. An important first step is recognizing that parenting, especially the parenting of toddlers, can be stressful at times. One workable solution is to obtain some personal time for yourself by turning to informal support systems. Possibilities include exchanging baby-sitting with local parents, calling on grandparents or other relatives who have some free time, joining neighborhood gyms that have child care, and taking a part-time job that allows paying for child care.

In addition, you can turn to community agencies that support child-rearing information programs specifically geared to parents of toddlers. Perhaps changing some of your parenting approaches will lead to stress reduction for you. Still another strategy involves approaching your toddler's pediatrician for an intervention referral for you and your child. In this case, a trained specialist can provide specific advice tailored to your needs and those of your child.

Help yourself as a parent, and you help your toddler. You'll both be better for it.

THE CHILD AND THE CHIMP

Geneticists tell us that approximately 98 percent of our genetic material is similar to that of chimpanzees. Does this mean that chimpanzees are likely to develop a humanlike civilization? Not likely, although we now know that chimpanzees and other primates have rich social traditions, think intelligently, act creatively, make and use simple tools, and communicate intentionally. These and other behaviors have evolved in the course of chimpanzee adaptation to various kinds of living conditions and to their social organization. So, too, our brains, minds, and bodies have evolved over many thousands of years—sometimes adapting to forces similar to those faced by other primates, which likely included forming kinship groups and family ties for mutual support as well as the means to communicate with others.

It's long been obvious, though, that baby chimpanzees (and closely related nonhuman primates) and human babies—before the onset of speech—display behaviors that are quite similar. A number of researchers have looked closely at these behaviors: some point out subtle differences, others argue for the extraordinary skills of nonhuman primates, and some imply that the skills of human babies are not so special. There is, of course, no single explanation or interpretation that suits everyone. At the end of this section I summarize a few recent perspectives on these issues.

I've long believed that a good case study serves as a fine starting place to latch onto developmental arguments and issues, whatever their focus. So, here is a summary of a remarkable case study of a child and chimp who were reared together for close to a year.

The time was the late 1920s, the years when psychologist John Watson's behaviorism included a mission to identify *the* environmental conditions that led to behavior. During this decade there were increasing reports of children reared in wretched conditions, some of whom were later placed with supportive caregivers. In general, the children never fully adapted to more humane social interactions, and their language and social skills were poor. Was early deprivation the cause? Was it possible that the children were abnormal at birth? What was the role of the environment and the influence of biology?

A psychology-faculty member, W. Kellogg, believed that environmental influences could be evaluated by trying to *overcome* biological endowments. One way this could be accomplished would be to rear a nonhuman primate as parents might rear their own human child. If the primate became more humanlike because of the rearing process, then it could be said that the environment has a unique and powerful role in development. By extension, one could then infer that grossly deprived children did not talk because they lacked adequate rearing experiences. Professor Kellogg decided he wanted to raise a baby chimp along with his baby son. His wife was not enthusiastic but eventually agreed.

Donald Kellogg was 10 months old when Gua, at 7½ months, joined the household. Gua came from a university-sponsored primate compound. The Kelloggs dressed the babies in similar clothes, fed them the same foods, put both of them in training walkers, and gave them comparable playthings. Both were exposed to the same daily training routines, including potty training. They both received the same punishments in the form of time-outs when they were naughty (running in the house, pilfering forbidden food, or banging on walls and furniture).

Donald and Gua immediately took to each other. Soon they played together with exuberance and affection. Chasing each other, they also climbed over furniture together, and in Gua's case, climbed up curtains and drapes. Toys were shared and then fought over, just like other toddler pairs.

Both also established warm and affectionate social and emotional relationships with Donald's parents. Whereas Donald often turned to his mother for nurturance, Gua was partial to Professor Kellogg. Her attachment to him was particularly intense. During one weeklong separation from him, she was mostly inconsolable and could find relief only by huddling around an old pair of his pants.

Sometimes the Kelloggs' training routines led to marked proficiency in Gua's skills. At times, she was a more apt pupil than Donald. Gua was potty trained first, learned to skip earlier than Donald, and was more proficient in using a spoon to feed herself. She was also terrified of loud noises that were barely noticed by Donald.

After nine months, Gua was sent away and the family unit changed. Perhaps the workload was too much for Donald's parents. There's also an unconfirmed rumor that Donald began to imitate Gua's behaviors too frequently. An eighteen-month-old toddler is enough of a handful for most parents; can you imagine one that tries to swing from the living-room drapes or attempts to fling himself across a room from chair to chair? How did Gua react to her loss? How did Donald react? We do not know.

✧ The Kelloggs' detailed descriptions of Donald's and Gua's skills provide intriguing insights into behavioral differences that became obvious across the nine-month period. Donald's actions illustrate the psychological energy and curiosity of human toddlers as they try to understand their surroundings. Donald enjoyed manipulating playthings and paid rapt attention to his own activities. He showed interest in different kinds of objects and carefully explored each before going on to the next. His play was rich and elaborate and contained multiple sequences of simulated events. Donald also began to imitate the everyday activities of his parents. His imitation included use of a hairbrush, a broom, and other household items. Donald watched Gua intently and imitated some of her behaviors, as well. He observed her pulling pillows from a couch and joined her in the activity; he imitated her grunts, and once picked up an object with his mouth (which she did most of the time). Donald's social skills also moved forward. He became increasingly aware of the pleasures of shared social activities. He would bring toys to his parents so they could look at them with him. He learned and participated in social games such as pat-a-cake. Donald's observational skills extended to family activities: while watching his mother sort oranges, he spontaneously joined her in the task.

Donald's attentiveness, play, and imitation were rarely part of Gua's behavior. Whereas Donald's play focused on exploring objects and figuring out what they could or could not do, Gua's play preferences were largely dictated by an object's most obvious physical attributes. She was drawn to things that were hard, portable, novel, and did not make noise. She might pick up any nearby object, glance at it briefly, and then move on to something else. Sometimes she was innovative in play, as when she discovered her breath condensed on a windowpane, and she made marks on the pane as if scribbling. Other times her play was boisterous and destructive; she enjoyed picking up a light piece of furniture, holding it over her head, and dropping it while she ran away. In general, Gua's fine-motor play lacked intense interest, and her attention span tended to be brief. Gua seldom imitated Donald or either of the Kelloggs. She did not initiate joint social activities with the adults nor did she ever learn social games common to parents and infants.

Gua was physically adept when it came to climbing but she could not match Donald's fine-motor skills. Gua's grasp of small objects was awkward, given that chimpanzees' hands are not designed to pick up very small things. Their hands are most useful for picking up large objects such as a tree branch and for stripping leaves from a branch. Gua was clever, though, and learned to adapt to human toys by using her lips as a pickup tool. This strategy helped but only partially: when she grasped a toy with her lips, she had to transfer it to her hands in order to see it clearly and to play with it. Even then her long primate fingers were not nimble. The kinds of exploration that Donald routinely engaged in must have been difficult for her, and probably were a factor in her brief exploratory play episodes.

Lastly, Donald began to understand words and phrases and to speak, but his spoken-language skills were of course unattainable for Gua. However, she did use gestures to communicate, and she understood and responded appropriately to many commands. That Gua understood as much as she did is impressive. But Donald's use of words would broaden the gulf between them. He would be able to talk about himself, his needs, others' needs, yesterday and tomorrow, and all the other topics of little children's interests. Gua could only grunt.

Decades later, other researchers would replicate some of the Kelloggs' research and in other instances would show a far more complicated comparative picture of human and nonhuman primate infant performance. As one example, recounted by Tomasello and Call, chimpanzees do not in general show high levels of creative problem solving *unless* they are reared in human environments. Sue Parker notes that nonhuman primates can stack blocks in play but only human babies stack blocks, push one block with another, hammer blocks one against another, and pretend to nail blocks together. Indeed, humans are the only species that can use two tools simultaneously (holding a wood chisel and hammering on its head) or sequentially (using a drill to make a hole, then using a screwdriver to screw a nail in place). Human babies are endlessly engaged in trial-and-error learning, but chimpanzees do not routinely explore this way. Nonhuman primates rarely engage in imitation.

With respect to language, Kanzi (a captive-born bonobo, a primate in the chimpanzee family) has comprehension skills that far exceed those of Gua. Kanzi, studied extensively by Sue Savage-Rumbaugh, was the recipient of many learning experiences provided by human teachers. Tomasello suggests that the three-year-old Kanzi and a two-year-old human child have relatively similar comprehension abilities, and both understand more language than they could produce (for the bonobo, using lexigrams). However, other studies reveal that nonhuman primate communication is often less spontaneous and less complex than the communication of human babies, who by the time they are a year of age have elaborate gestures, including pointing to show, giving, waving bye-bye, and hugging a toy to the chest to signify possession.

Thus, research findings show us that in early life, human infants and chimpanzees have key similarities. In fact, during a short period of time, human babies and chimps are more alike in some ways than human babies and their parents. There is a powerful biological/evolutionary force that provides a template for early behavioral development. However, primary differences are found in the degree of immaturity at birth, the degree of flexibility in learning, and the length of the socialization period.

Human babies are not *better* than nonhuman primate infants. Each species has adapted to meet the requisites of survival in their own surroundings, and each species may respond to some forms of environmental stimuli in very different ways. However, there is another point worth considering, that has to do with training. The fact that nonhuman primates, such as Gua, can be trained to accomplish human tasks is not surprising. However, the end result does not mean that the trained behavior means the same thing to the animal and to the human. When Gua was encouraged to walk upright, the behavior became an end point but not a means to an end. By that I mean, she could not easily use this skill as a stepping-stone to other achievements. In contrast, when a human baby walks, the walking prepares the way for more learning and subsequent achievements. Even at first, walking frees the baby's hands so he can hold a toy and study it visually while he moves around to take it from one place to another. The potential to build one skill on top of another is largely responsible for our ability to become highly adaptive.

In the end then, although we share genetic material and some behaviors with other species, it is the human baby's steps that lay the developmental foundation for the relationships and skills that we cherish. Parents, families, researchers, clinicians, and policy makers owe our young the very best experiences for the very best foundations.

Is My Child Okay?

It's the rare parent who hasn't wondered, "Is my baby okay?" Maybe the baby didn't roll over on schedule, or for a while she was slow in focusing her eyes on toys, or he didn't say words when all the other toddlers his age were talking. Most of the time, parents' worries dissolve because, given a little time, the baby is fine.

There are, however, situations when month after month parents feel that the baby's behaviors show consistent differences when compared to other babies' behaviors. Perhaps parents were alerted this might happen: the mother had a serious infection during pregnancy; the baby was born very early; the newborn was very ill. Sometimes there is no clue at all. What should parents do? Where should they seek help? What are the implications of development that does not seem right?

If you feel that something is not developmentally all right with your baby or toddler and your concerns have been growing over time, make an appointment with your child's pediatrician so you can discuss your concerns. You'll be better prepared to share your worries if you bring the pediatrician your written observations of your child's behavior and development. As parents, you see your child every day and thus have the best opportunity to observe and make notes. And your observations can be invaluable resources should you and your child be referred to other specialists. You can record your child's development in any number of ways, but at the end of this section, I provide a few suggestions for organizing your concerns.

The baby's pediatrician might decide to schedule additional appointments to observe your baby during the next few weeks or even a month or two. After detailed examinations, she might tell you that the baby is doing fine. What you see as a developmental concern is just a minor variation in development. Examples are a three-month-old whose visual attention to faces is a bit unsteady; an eighteen-month-old whose head size is at the 15th percentile, but who is developmentally on target in all domains; a twenty-four-month-old who is not speaking, but who understands words and phrases at age level and whose play is age-appropriate.

Alternatively, the pediatrician might suggest it is time to refer you to other specialists such as audiologists, ophthalmologists, pediatric neurologists, or a physician who deals with genetic-based developmental disorders such as Fragile X syndrome. The pediatrician might also request a detailed developmental evaluation. It is the developmental evaluation that I focus on here.

The purpose of a careful evaluation of the baby's developmental status is not simply to obtain a test score. A developmental evaluation should include an analysis of the baby's behavioral strengths (for example, he is very social), possible problem areas (for example, he is eight months old and hasn't yet rolled from back to tummy), and the developmental implications of these behaviors.

I wish I could assure parents that evaluating a baby's or toddler's developmental status is an exact science. In the absence of gross physical impairments or major signs of developmental deviation, making a judgment about developmental problems can sometimes be difficult. To begin with, as I have repeatedly emphasized, there is a good deal of variability in normal development. Infants naturally differ from one another in their rates of growth and their behavioral styles. One language-precocious baby who said five hundred words when she was a year old did not walk on her own until she was close to seventeen months old. This is an age that approaches the far side of the curve for the normal onset of walking.

Second, as I noted above, some key features of development relate not only to the presence of a specific behavior but also to the quality of the behavior. I once evaluated a sturdy nine-month-old whose overall developmental-test capabilities were clearly within the normal ranges. If I had paid attention only to his test profile, I could have concluded that he was fine. But there was something about his behaviors that was clearly inappropriate. The baby's smile was inconsistent and wan; he made sounds, but rarely, and took no delight in this accomplishment; and he just didn't seem to care whether people were around or not. These developmental signs were indeed worrisome. It turned out that he was the last baby in a very large family and was not receiving much attention or being talked to enough. I was impressed with the baby's ability to sustain his development as well as he had, but his relative isolation and his lack of interest in other people did not bode well for his long-term language or social development.

Also know that professionals differ in how they evaluate babies' development. I'll explain the way I go about doing an evaluation, but bear in mind that other approaches work just as well. My developmental evaluations usually have four components: a parent interview, my informal observations of the child, administration of one or more standardized developmental or clinical assessments, and my clinical judgment. I try to answer several basic questions. For this age, what constitutes the developmental norm for each domain of behavior? What do I consider a developmental deviation for this age? Are some of the baby's behaviors okay? Which are not? Why do I think a behavior is questionable? If I observe deviations from developmental norms, are they major or minor deviations? Do the baby's behaviors reflect organization or disorganization? What are the implications of developmental deviations for the baby's overall ability to play, to be social, to learn? Are there detectable ramifications for long-term competencies? I try not to draw firm conclusions until I've had a chance to see the baby and his parents on two or three separate occasions. At that point I might feel confident about stating that a baby is developmentally normal, has developmental delays, or shows signs of development that are troubling.

While my multistep process of evaluation is comprehensive, I know that there are no precise rules for determining when a baby's behaviors signify developmental delay. Good clinical judgment is essential. I also tend to be cautious about making definitive statements of either delayed or suspect development early in infancy. For one thing, labeling a young baby as having a developmental problem can be a risky proposition: labels can lead to social interaction patterns that reinforce deficiencies at just the time a more supportive environment might put the baby's development back on course. Second, there are strong self-corrective mechanisms in development, and although a baby may seem delayed early on, he may be fine six or eight months later. Third, our standardized infant-development tests are not precise tools. Thus the information obtained from them has to be used cautiously.

Many parents are familiar with intelligence and achievement tests. However, evaluations of infants and toddlers are very different. They do not consist of straightforward, programmed question-and-answer sessions. Young babies do not talk, and older babies do not talk well. Younger and older babies have limited comprehension. Also, babies are blithely unconcerned about the goals of adults; they have their own agendas. A developmental evaluation has to be done by a sensitive clinician. A famous psychologist once commented that the perfect test takes place when the ever moving, squalling baby becomes relatively quiet, attentive, and responsive. Obviously, perfection is not easy to achieve.

Always keep in mind, though, that nobody sees your baby as often as you do. If there's something not quite right with your baby's development, be active in discussions with your pediatrician and other specialists, and take an active role in securing the kind of assistance that seems most likely to help you and your baby. Work closely with professionals, and don't hesitate to speak your mind.

✦ RECORDING WORRISOME DEVELOPMENT

These ideas represent one strategy for you to identify your developmental concerns about your baby or toddler. Freely adapt the ideas so they best suit your style and needs and your baby's behaviors. Write your developmental notes when you're not tired and things are relatively quiet in your household. Don't try to complete your documentation in one sitting. Indeed it would be better if you made notes over a week or two so you can review your notes and revise them should you wish. You might want to make separate notes on different occasions. As you record your concerns, be sure to keep in mind the wide variability that exists among babies for almost all facets of development. No baby marches along exactly.

- ✦ Using notebook-sized paper, record the date and your baby's age at the top of the page. Summarize in a few sentences your overall developmental concerns about your baby. You'll use the columns that I describe below to provide documentation about your concerns.
- ✦ Draw a column on the left side of the page, and then list the child behaviors that are appropriate for his/her age. List the behaviors by developmental domain. As a resource, use the developmental guidelines from this book or other reputable sources.
- ✦ Draw a second column. Now make a note of the behaviors that your child routinely shows, again listing them by developmental domain. *At eight months: the baby sits when propped; reaches and grasps toys; smiles, etc.*
- ✦ Draw a third column, and now list the behaviors you haven't seen, but think you should see. Again list them by developmental domain, but now be very specific as to the exact behavior you are concerned about. *The baby is eight months old, but rarely makes sounds.*
- ✦ In a fourth column, list the behaviors you observe that are age-appropriate but do not seem coordinated or are inappropriate to a situation. *The baby is eight months old, and the occasional sound that he makes is not directed to other people.*

- In a fifth column, list the behaviors that you observed previously but that you haven't observed recently. *At four months, the baby smiled at her parents, but now at seven months she does not smile at all.*
- At the bottom of the page, or on another page, write a few additional comments. Try to add further examples of your baby's or toddler's behavior that worry you.

My version of this kind of chart follows. Yours could look quite different and be equally useful. The point is to document your concerns about your child in a systematic way.

An example of an approach to thinking about your baby's development, if you have concerns. Italicized entries are examples of comments made to me by parents about a variety of their concerns.

MY BABY/TODDLER'S DEVELOPMENT

My Baby/Toddler _____ Date of Birth _____

Age _____ Date of my observations _____

Behaviors appropriate for my baby/toddler's age	Behaviors my baby/toddler routinely shows	Behaviors I expect to see, but haven't as yet	Behaviors I see, but am not sure if OK	Behaviors observed before, don't see now, and am concerned
Motor: Gross motor: Fine motor:		*She's 15 months, but not walking.*	*She drags one leg. Her hands are fisted.*	
Cognitive: Attention: Perception: Memory: Problem solving: Play:		*He shows no interest in toys, but he should now that he's fourteen months old.*	*My five-month-old does not look at me.* *She loses interest in toys.*	

Language:
Comprehension:
Production:
  Words
 	
  Sentences
		She's twenty-two months, but doesn't talk.		*She used to say words, but doesn't anymore.*

Social:
Interactions
  with me (us),
  other adults,
  children
Family norms
			She doesn't listen to me.
			He hits and bites other children all the time.
				She used to hug and kiss us, but doesn't anymore.

Emotional:
Pleasure;
  distress; fear;
  anger; self-
  consciousness
			He's never affectionate with anyone.
			She mostly cries during the day.	

Self-awareness: Mastery behaviors Self-awareness Autonomy seeking			*He won't listen, just does what he wants.*	

My baby/toddler's typical style:

Sleep patterns: _____*"my ten-month-old is up four times a night"*_____

Ease of feeding: _____

Temperament: _____*"my eighteen-month-old is kind of irritable"*_____

References

SENSORY SYSTEMS, PERCEPTUAL AND COGNITIVE DEVELOPMENT, AND COGNITIVE NEUROSCIENCE

Aslin, R. N. (1987). Visual and auditory development in infancy. In J. D. Osofsky (Ed.), *Handbook of infant development.* Vol. 2. New York: John Wiley & Sons.

Aslin, R. N., Jusczyk, P. W., and Pisoni, D. B. (1998). Speech and auditory processing during infancy: Constraints on and precursors to language. In D. Kuhn & R. Siegler (Eds.), *Handbook of child psychology: Cognition, perception, and language.* 5th ed. Vol. 2, pp. 147–98. New York: John Wiley & Sons.

Axia, G., Bonichini, S., and Benini, F. (1999). Attention and reaction to distress in infancy: A longitudinal study. *Developmental Psychology* 35: 500–504.

Baillargeon, R. (1994). How do infants learn about the physical world? *Current Directions in Psychological Science* 3: 133–40.

Baillargeon, R. (1999). Young infants' expectation about hidden objects: A reply to three challenges. *Developmental Science* 2: 115–32.

Bell, M. A. (1998). Frontal love function during infancy: Implications for the development of cognition and attention. In J. Richards (Ed.), *Cognitive neuroscience of attention: A developmental perspective.* Mahwah, N.J.: Lawrence Erbaum Associates.

Bauer, P. J. (1996). What do infants recall of their lives? Memory for specific events by 1- to 2-year olds. *American Psychologist* 51: 29–41.

Bauer, P. J., Schwade, J. A., Wewerka, S. S., and Delaney, K. (1999). Planning ahead: Goal directed problem solving by two-year-olds. *Developmental Psychology* 35: 1321–37.

Bauer, P. J., Wenner, J. A., Dropik, P. L., Wewerka, S. S. (2000). Parameters of remembering and forgetting in the transition from infancy to early childhood. *Monographs of the Society for Research in Child Development* 65 (4, Serial No. 263).

Bjorkland, D. F. (1997). The role of immaturity in human development. *Psychological Bulletin* 122: 153–69.

Blair, C. (2002). School readiness: Integrating cognition and emotion in a neurobiological conceptualization of children's functioning at school entry. *American Psychologist* 57: 111–27.

Bremner, G. (1997). From perception to cognition. In G. Bremner, A. Slater, and G. Butterworth (Eds.), *Infant development: Recent advances,* pp. 55–74. East Sussex, Eng.: Psychology Press.

Bremner, G., Slater, A., and Butterworth, G. (Eds.) (1997). *Infant development: Recent advances.* East Sussex, Eng.: Psychology Press.

Calvin, W. H. (1996). *How brains think.* New York: Basic Books.

Caron, A. J., Caron, R., Roberts, J., and Brooks, R. (1997). Infant sensitivity to deviations in dynamic facial-vocal displays: The role of eye regard. *Developmental Psychology*, 33: 802–13.

Church, J. (1996). *Three babies: Biographies of cognitive development*. New York: Random House.

Collis, G. M., and Schaffer, H. R. (1975). Synchronization of visual attention in mother-infant pairs. *Journal of Child Psychology and Psychiatry* 16: 315–20.

Colombo, J. (1995). On the neural mechanisms underlying developmental and individual differences in visual fixation in infancy: Two hypotheses. *Developmental Review* 15: 97–135.

Colombo, J. (2001). Visual attention in infancy. In S. T. Fiske, D. L. Schacter, and C. Zahn-Waxler (Eds.), *Annual Review of Psychology* 52: 337–67. Palo Alto, Calif.: Annual Reviews.

Colombo, J., McCollam, K., Coldren, J. T., et al. (1990). Form categorization in 10-month-olds. *Journal of Experimental Child Psychology* 49: 173–88.

Courage, M. L., and Howe, M. L. (2002). From infant to child: The dynamics of cognitive change in the second year of life. *Psychological Bulletin* 128: 250–77.

Crook, C. K. (1978). Taste perception in the newborn infant. *Infant Behavior and Development* 1:52–69.

Crook, C. K. (1979). The organization and control of infant sucking. In H. W. Reese and L. P. Lipsitt (Eds.), *Advances in child behavior and development*. Vol. 14. New York: Academic Press.

Dawson, G., Ashman, S., and Carver, L. (2000). The role of early experience in shaping behavioral and brain development and its implications for social policy. *Development and Psychopathology* 12: 695–712.

DeCasper, A. J., and Fifer, W. P. (1980). Of human bonding: Newborns prefer their mothers' voices. *Science* 208: 1174–76.

Derryberry, D., and Reed, M. (1996). Regulatory processes and the development of cognitive representations. *Development of Psychopathology* 8: 215–34.

Diamond, A. (2000). Close interrelation of motor development and cognitive development and of the cerebellum and prefrontal cortex. *Child Development* 71: 44–56.

Elman, J. L., Bates, E. A., Johnson, M. H., Karmiloff-Smith, A., Parisi, D., and Plunkett, K. (1996). *Rethinking innateness: A connectionist perspective on development*. Cambridge, Mass.: MIT Press/Bradford Books.

Fagen, J. W., and Ohr, P. S. (2001). Learning and memory in infancy: Habituation, instrumental conditioning, and expectancy formation. In L. T. Singer and P. S. Zeskind, (Eds.), *Biobehavioral assessment of the infant*, pp. 233–92. New York: The Guilford Press.

Gauvain, M. (2001). *The social context of cognitive development*. New York: The Guilford Press.

Gibson, E. J. (1970). The development of perception as an adaptive process. *American Scientist* 58: 98–107.

Gibson, E. J., and Spelke, E. S. (1983). The development of perception. In J. H. Flavell and E. M. Markman (Eds.), *Handbook of child psychology*. Vol. 3, *Cognitive development*. 4th ed. New York: John Wiley & Sons.

Gopnik, A., Meltzoff, A. N., and Kuhl, P. K. (1999). *The scientist in the crib*. New York: William Morrow & Company.

Gottfried, A. W., Rose, S. A., and Bridger, W. H. (1978). Effects of visual, haptic, and manipulatory experiences of infants' visual recognition memory of objects. *Developmental Psychology* 14: 305–12.

Haith, M. M. (1980). *Rules that babies look by: The organization of newborn visual activity*. Hillsdale, N.J.: Lawrence Erlbaum Associates.

Haith, M. M. (1994). Visual expectations as the first step toward the development of future-oriented processes. In M. M. Haith, J. B. Benson, J. Roberts, and B. F. Pennington (Eds.), *The development of future-oriented processes*, pp. 11–38. Chicago: The University of Chicago Press.

Haith, M. M., and Benson, J. B. (1998). Infant Cognition. In J. H. Flavell and E. M. Markman (Eds.), *Handbook of child psychology*, Vol. 3, *Cognitive development*. 4th ed. New York: John Wiley & Sons.

Hanna, E., and Meltzoff, A. N. (1993). Peer imitation by toddlers in laboratory, home, and day-care contexts: Implications for social learning and memory. *Developmental Psychology* 29: 701–10.

Hood, B., Carey, S., and Prasada, S. (2000). Predicting the outcomes of physical events: Two-year-olds fail to reveal knowledge of solidity and support. *Child Development* 71: 1540–54.

Johnson, M. H. (1997). *Developmental cognitive neuroscience*. Cambridge, Mass.: Blackwell Publishers.

Johnson, M. H. (1998). The neural basis of cognitive development. In D. Kuhn and R. Siegler (Eds.), *Handbook of child psychology: Cognition, perception, and language*. 5th ed. Vol. 2, pp. 1–50. New York: John Wiley & Sons.

Johnson, M. H. (2000). Functional brain development in infants: Elements of an interactive specialization framework. *Child Development* 71: 75–81.

Kahan-Kalman, R., and Walker-Andrews, A. S. (2001). The role of person familiarity in young infants' perception of emotional expressions. *Child Development* 72: 352–69.

Kalverboer, A. F., and Gramsbergen, A. (2001). Brain-behavior relationships in the human: Core issues. In A. F. Kalverboer and A. Gramsbergen (Eds.), *Handbook of brain and behavior in human development*, pp. 3–10. Boston: Kluwer Academic Publishers.

Karmiloff-Smith, A. (1992). *Beyond modularity: A developmental perspective on cognitive science*. Cambridge, Mass.: MIT Press.

Kellman, P. J., and Arterberry, M. E. (1998). *The cradle of knowledge: Development of perception in infancy*. Cambridge, Mass. and London: MIT Press.

Kellman, P. J., and Banks, M. S. (1998). Infant visual perception. In D. Kuhn and R. S. Siegler (Eds.), *Handbook of child psychology: Cognition, perception, and language*. 5th ed. Vol. 2, pp. 103–46. New York: John Wiley & Sons.

Kellogg, W. N., and Kellogg, L. A. (1933). *The ape and the child*. New York: Whittlesey House, McGraw Hill Book Company, Inc.

Kuhn, D. (2000). Does memory development belong on an endangered topic list? *Child Development* 71: 21–25.

Lyon, G. R., and Krasnegor, N. (Eds.) (1996). *Attention, Memory, and Executive Function*. Baltimore: Brookes Publishing.

Madole, K. L., and Cohen, L. B. (1995). The role of object parts in infants' attention to form function correlations. *Developmental Psychology* 31: 637–48.

Mandler, J. (1997). Development of categorization: Perceptual and conceptual categories. In G. Bremner, A. Slater, and G. Butterworth (Eds.), *Infant development: Recent advances*, pp. 163–89. East Sussex, Eng.: Psychology Press.

Mandler, J. (1998). Representation. In D. Kuhn and R. S. Siegler (Eds.), *Handbook of child psychology: Cognition, perception, and language*. 5th ed. Vol. 2, pp. 255–308. New York: John Wiley & Sons.

Melzoff, A. N. (1988). Infant imitation and memory: nine-month-olds in immediate and deferred tests. *Child Development* 59: 217–25.

Melzoff, A. N. (1995). Understanding the intentions of others: re-enactment of intended acts by 18-month-old children. *Developmental Psychology* 31: 838–50.

Melzoff, A. N. and Gopnik, A. (1993). The role of imitation in understanding persons and developing a theory of mind. In S. Baron-Cohen, H. Tager-Flusberg, and D. J. Cohen (Eds.), *Understanding other minds: Perspectives from Autism*, pp. 335–66. New York: Oxford University Press.

McCune, L. (1995). A normative study of representational play at the transition to language. *Developmental Psychology* 31: 198–206.

Mondloch, C. J., Lewis, T. L., Budreau, D. R., Maurer, D., Kannemiller, J. D., Stephens, B. R., and Kleiner-Gathercoal, K. A. (1999). Face perception during early infancy. *Psychological Science* 10: 419–22.

Munakata, Y., McClelland, J. L., Johnson, M. H., and Siegler, R. S. (1997). Rethinking infant knowledge: Toward an adaptive process account of successes and failures in object permanence tasks. *Psychological Review* 104: 686–713.

National Research Council and Institute of Medicine (2000). *From neurons to neighborhoods: The science of early childhood development*. Washington, D.C.: National Academy Press.

Neisser, U. (2000). Memory: What are the important questions? In U. Neisser and I.E. Hyman (Eds.), *Memory observed: Remembering in natural contexts*, pp. 3–18. 2d ed. New York: Worth Publishers.

Nelson, C. (1994). Neural correlates of recognition memory in the first postnatal year of life. In G. Dawson and K. Fisher (Eds.), *Human behavior and the developing brain*, pp. 269–313. New York: The Guilford Press.

Nelson, C. (1995). The ontogeny of human memory: A cognitive neuroscience perspective. *Developmental Psychology* 31: 723–38.

Nelson, C. (1999). Neural plasticity and human development. *Current Directions in Psychological Science* 8: 42–45.

Nelson, C.A. and Webb, S.J. (in press). A cognitive neuroscience perspective on early memory development. In M. de Haan and M.H. Johnson (Eds.), *The cognitive neuroscience of development*. London: Psychology Press.

Nelson, K. (1986). *Event knowledge: Structure and function in development*. Hillsdale: N.J.: Lawrence Erlbaum Associates.

Nelson, K. (1996). *Language in cognitive development: Emergence of the mediated mind*. New York: Cambridge University Press.

NICHD Early Child Care Research Network (2000). The relation of child care to cognitive and language development. *Child Development* 71: 958–78.

Oakes, L.M., and Madole, K.L. (2000). The future of infant categorization research: A process-oriented approach. *Child Development* 71: 119–26.

Parker, S.T., and Gibson, K.R. (Eds.) (1990). *"Language" and intelligence in monkeys and apes*. New York: Cambridge University Press.

Pinker, S. (1997). *How the mind works*. New York: W.W. Norton & Co.

Posner, M.I., and Raiche, M.E. (1994). *Images of mind*. New York: Scientific American Library.

Richards, J.E. (Ed.) (1998). *Cognitive neuroscience of attention: A developmental perspective*. Mahwah, N.J.: Lawrence Erlbaum Associates.

Rogoff, B. (1990). *Apprenticeship in thinking: Cognitive development in social context*. New York: Oxford University Press.

Rovee-Collier, C. (1997). Dissociations in infant memory: Rethinking the development of implicit and explicit memory. *Psychological Review* 104: 467–98.

Ruff, H.A., and Rothbart, M.K. (1996). *Attention in early development: Themes and variations*. New York: Oxford University Press.

Ruff, H.A., Saltarelli, L.M., Capozzoli, M., and Dubiner, K. (1992). The differentiation of activity in infants' exploration of objects. *Developmental Psychology* 28: 851–61.

Siegler, R.S. (1996). *Emerging minds: The process of change in children's thinking*. New York: Oxford University Press.

Slater, A., and Butterworth, G. (1997). Perception of social stimuli. In G. Bremner, A. Slater, and G. Butterworth (Eds.), *Infant development: Recent advances*, pp. 223–46. East Sussex, Eng.: Psychology Press.

Smith, B.A., and Blass, E.M. (1996). Taste-mediated calming in premature, preterm, and full-term human infants. *Developmental Psychology* 32: 1084–89.

Stigler, J.W. (2001). Breakthroughs in using individual differences to study learning: Comments. In J.L. McClelland and R.S. Siegler (Eds.), *Mechanisms of cognitive development: Behavioral and neural perspectives*, pp. 149–55. Mahwah, N.J.: Lawrence Erlbaum Associates.

Thelen, E., and Smith, L.B. (1994). *A dynamic systems approach to the development of cognition and action*. Cambridge, Mass.: MIT Press.

Tomasello, M. (1999). *The cultural origins of human cognition*. Cambridge, Mass.: Harvard University Press.

Tomasello, M., and Call, J. (1997). *Primate cognition*. New York: Oxford University Press.

Wakeley, A., Rivera, S., and Langer, J. (2000). Can young infants add and subtract? *Child Development* 71: 1525–34.

Wellman, H.M., Phillips, A.T., and Rodriguez, T. (2000). Young children's understanding of perception, desire, and emotion. *Child Development* 71: 895–912.

Welsh, M. C. (2001). The prefrontal cortex and the development of executive function in childhood. In A. F. Kalverboer and A. Gramsbergen (Eds.), *Handbook of brain and behavior in human development*, pp. 767–89. Boston: Kluwer Academic Publishers.

Woodward, A. L. (1999). Infants' ability to distinguish between purposeful and non-purposeful behaviors. *Infant Behavior and Development* 22: 145–60.

Zeifman, D., Delaney, S., and Blass, E. M. (1996). Sweet taste, looking, and calm in 2-and 4-week-old infants: The eyes have it. *Developmental Psychology* 32: 1090–99.

LANGUAGE DEVELOPMENT AND COMMUNICATION

Baldwin, D. A., and Moses, L. J. (2001). Links between social understanding and early word learning: Challenges to current accounts. *Social Development* 10: 309–29.

Bloom, L. (1998). Language acquisition in its developmental context. In D. Kuhn and R. S. Siegler (Eds.), *Handbook of child psychology: Cognition, perception, and language*. 5th ed. Vol. 2, pp. 309–70. New York: John Wiley & Sons.

Bloom, L. (2000). Commentary: Pushing the limits on theories of word learning. *Monographs of the Society for Research in Child Development* 65 (3, Serial No. 262).

Bloom, L., and Tinker, E. (2001). The intentionality model and language acquisition. *Monographs of the Society for Research in Child Development* 66 (4, Serial No. 267).

Camaioni, L., Castelli, M. C., Longobardi, E., and Volterra, V. (1991). A parent report instrument for early language assessment. *First Language* 11: 345–59.

Fenson, L., Dale, P. S., Reznick, J. S., Bates, E., Thal, D. J., and Pethick, S. J. (1994). Variability in early communicative development. *Monographs of the Society for Research in Child Development* 59 (5, Serial No. 242).

Fernald, A., and Kuhl, P. (1987). Acoustic determinants of infant preference for motherese speech. *Infant Behavior and Development* 10: 279–93.

Golinkoff, R. M., and Hirsh-Pasek, K. (1999). *How babies talk: The magic and mystery of language in the first three years of life*. New York: Penguin-Putnam.

Greenfield, P. M., and Savage-Rumbaugh, E. S. (1990). Grammatical combination in *Pan paniscus*: Processes of learning and invention in the evolution and development of language. In S. T. Parker, and K. R. Gibson (Eds.), *"Language" and intelligence in monkeys and apes: Comparative developmental perspectives*, pp. 540–78. New York: Cambridge University Press.

Hollich, G. J., Hirsh-Pasek, K., and Golinkoff, R. M. (2000). Breaking the language barrier: An emergenist coalition model for the origins of word learning. *Monographs of the Society for Research in Child Development* 65 (3, Serial No. 262).

Jusczyk, P. W. (1997). *The discovery of spoken language*. Cambridge, Mass.: MIT Press.

Kemler, D. G., Russell, R., Duke, N., and Jones, K. (2000). Two-year-olds will name artifacts by their function. *Child Development* 71: 1271–88.

Messer, D. (1997). Referential communication: Making sense of the social and physical worlds. In G. Bremner, A. Slater, and G. Butterworth (Eds.), *Infant development: Recent advances*, pp. 291–309. East Sussex, Eng.: Psychology Press.

Nelson, K. (1989). Monologue as representation of real-life experience. In K. Nelson (Ed.), *Narratives from the crib*, pp. 27–72. Cambridge, Mass.: Harvard University Press.

Nelson, K. (1996). *Language in cognitive development: The emergence of the mediated mind*. New York: Cambridge University Press.

Nelson, K., and Kessler Shaw, L. (2002). Developing a socially shared symbolic system. In E. Amsel and J. P. Byrnes (Eds.), *Language, literacy, and cognitive development: the development and consequences of symbolic communication*, pp. 27–57. Mahwah, N.J.: Lawrence Erlbaum Associates.

Oller, D. K., Eilers, R. W., Basinger, D., Steffens, M. L., and Urbano, R. (1995). Poverty and speech precursor development. *First Language* 15: 167–88.

Pinker, S. (1994). *The language instinct*. New York: William Morrow & Company.

Savage-Rumbaugh, E. S., Murphy, J., Sevcik, R. A., Brakke, K. E., Williams, S. L., and Rumbaugh, D. M. (1993). Language comprehension in the ape and child. *Monographs of the Society for Research in Child Development* 58 (3–4, Serial No. 233).

Shatz, M., Gelamn, S. A., Behrend, D., and Ebeling, K. S. (1996). Color term knowledge in two-year-olds: Evidence for early competence. *Journal of Child Language* 23: 177–99.

Waxman, S. R., and Markow, D. B. (1998). Object properties and object kind: Twenty-one-month-old infants' extension of novel adjectives. *Child Development* 69: 1313–29.

Werker, J. F., and Desjardins, R. N. (1995). Listening to speech in the 1st year of life: experiential influences on phoneme perception. *Current Directions in Psychological Science* 4:76–81.

Woodward, A. L., Markman, E. M., and Fitzsimmons, C. M. (1994). Rapid word-learning in 13- and 18-month-olds. *Developmental Psychology* 30: 553–66.

Woodward, A. L., and Markman, E. M. (1998). Early word learning. In D. Kuhn and R. S. Siegler (Eds.), *Handbook of child psychology: Cognition, perception, and language.* 5th ed. Vol. 2, pp. 371–420. New York: John Wiley & Sons.

MOTOR AND PHYSICAL DEVELOPMENT

Adolph, K. E., Vereijen, B., and Denny, M. A. (1998). Learning to crawl. *Child Development* 69: 1299–1312.

Connolly, K. J., and Dalgleish, M. (1989). The emergence of tool using skill in infancy. *Developmental Psychology* 25: 894–912.

Freedland, R. L., and Bertenthal, B. I. (1994). Developmental changes in interlimb coordination: Transition to hands-and-knees crawling. *Psychological Science* 5: 26–32.

Gesell, A., and Ames, L. B. (1940). The ontogenetic organization of prone behavior in human infancy. *Journal of Genetic Psychology* 56: 247–63.

Lockman, J. L. (2000). A perception-action perspective on tool use development. *Child Development* 71: 137–44.

McCarty, M. E., Clifton, R. K., and Collard, R. R. (1999). The beginnings of tool use by infants and toddlers. *Infancy* 2: 233–56.

McGraw, M. B. (1943). *The neuromuscular maturation of the human infant.* New York: Columbia University Press.

Mittlemann, E. (1954). Motility in infants and adults: Patterning and psycho-dynamics. *Psychoanalytic Study of the Child* 9: 142–77.

Newman, C., Atkinson, J., and Braddick, O. (2001). The development of reaching and looking preferences in infants to objects of different sizes. *Developmental Psychology* 37: 561–72.

Paine, R. S., Brazelton, T. B., Donovan, D. E., Drorbaugh, J. E., Hubbell, J. P., Jr., and Sears, E. M. (1964). Evolution of postural reflexes in normal infants and in the presence of chronic brain syndromes. *Neurology* 14: 1036–48.

Prechtl, H. F. R. (2001). Prenatal and early postnatal development of human motor behavior. In A. F. Kalverboer and A. Gramsbergen (Eds.), *Handbook of brain and behavior in human development,* pp. 415–27. Boston: Kluwer Academic Publishers.

Rochat, P., and Goubet, J. (1995). Development of sitting and reaching in 5- to 6-month-old infants. *Infant Behavior and Development* 18: 53–68.

Rushworth, G. (1961). On postural and righting reflexes. *Cerebral Palsy Bulletin (Developmental Medicine and Child Neurology)* 3: 535–54.

Thelen, E. (1995). Motor development: A new synthesis. *American Psychologist* 50: 79–95.

Thelen, E. (2001). Dynamic mechanisms of change in early perceptual-motor development. In J. L. McClelland and R. S. Siegler (Eds.), *Mechanisms of cognitive development: Behavioral and neural perspectives,* pp. 161–84. Mahwah, N.J.: Lawrence Erlbaum Associates.

Thelen, E., and Ulrich, B. D. (1991). Hidden skills: A dynamic systems analysis of treadmill stepping during the first year. *Monographs of the Society for Research in Child Development* 51 (1, Serial No. 223).

Van der Meer, A. L. H., van der Weel, F. R., and Lee, D. N. (1995). The functional significance of arm movements in neonates. *Science* 267: 693–94.

von Hofsten, C. (1990). A perception-action perspective on the development of manual movements. In M. Jeannerod (Ed.), *Attention and performance.* Hillsdale, N.J.: Lawrence Erlbaum Associates.

DEVELOPMENTAL PROBLEMS

Diamond, A., Prevor, M., Callender, G., and Druin, D. P. (1997). Prefrontal cortex cognitive deficits in children treated early and continuously for PKU. *Monographs of the Society for Research in Child Development* 62 (4, Serial No. 252).

Hagerman, R. J. (1999). *Neurodevelopmental disorders: Diagnosis and treatment.* New York: Oxford University Press.

Seifer, R. (2001). Conceptual and methodological basis for understanding development and risk in infants. In Singer, L. T., and Zeskind, P. S. (Eds.) (2001), *Biobehavioral assessment of the infant*, pp. 18–39. New York: The Guilford Press.

Singer, L. T., and Zeskind, P. S. (Eds.) (2001). *Biobehavioral assessment of the infant.* New York: The Guilford Press.

EMOTION, SELF, AND SOCIAL DEVELOPMENT; TEMPERAMENT

Adamson, L. B., and Bakeman, R. (1984). Mothers' communicative acts: Changes during infancy. *Infant Behavior and Development* 7: 467–78.

Ainsworth, M. D. S., Blehar, M. C., Waters, E., and Wall, S. (1978). *Patterns of attachment: A psychological study of the strange situation.* Hillsdale, N.J.: Erlbaum.

Ainsworth, M. D. S. (1967). *Infancy in Uganda: Infant care and the growth of love.* Baltimore: The Johns Hopkins University Press.

Barr, R. G. (1990). The "colic" enigma: Prolonged episodes of a normal predisposition to cry. *Infant Mental Health Journal* 11: 340–48.

Barr, R. G., and Gunnar, M. (2001). Colic: The "transient responsivity" hypothesis. In R. G. Barr, B. Hopkins, and J. Green (Eds.), *Crying as a sign, a symptom, and a signal: Clinical, emotional, and developmental aspects of infant and toddler crying.* New York: McKeith.

Barrett, K. C., Zahn-Waxler, C., and Cole, P. M. (1993). Avoiders vs. amenders: Implications for the investigation of guilt and shame during toddlerhood. *Cognition and Emotion* 7: 481–505.

Bates, J. E. (1989). Applications of temperament concepts. In G. A. Kohnstamm, J. E. Bates, and M. K. Rothbart (Eds.), *Temperament in childhood*, pp. 321–55). Chichester, Eng.: John Wiley & Sons.

Belsky, J., Campbell, S. B., Cohn, J. F., and Moore, G. (1996). Instability of infant-parent attachment security. *Developmental Psychology* 32: 921–24.

Blair, C. (2002). School readiness: Integrating cognition and emotion in a neurobiological concept of children's functioning at school entry. *American Psychologist* 57: 111–27.

Bowlby, J. (1951). *Maternal care and mental health.* Geneva: World Health Organization Monograph Series (2).

Bowlby, J. (1958). The nature of the child's tie to his mother. *International Journal of Psycho-analysis* 41: 89–113.

Bowlby, J. (1969). *Attachment and loss.* Vol 1: *Attachment.* New York: Basic Books.

Brazelton, T. B. (1962). Crying in infancy. *Pediatrics* 29: 579–88.

Brazelton, T. B. (1969). *Infants and mothers: Differences in development.* New York: Delacorte Press.

Braungart, J., and Stifter, S. (1991). Regulation of negative reactivity during the Strange Situation: Temperament and attachment in 12-month-old infants. *Infant Behavior and Development* 14: 349–64.

Bretherton, I., Fritz, J., Zahn-Waxler, C., and Ridgeway, D. (1986). Learning to talk about emotions: A functionalist perspective. *Child Development* 57: 529–48.

Bridges, L. J., and Grolnick, W. S. (1995). The development of emotional self-regulation in infancy and early childhood. In N. Eisenberg (Ed.), *Social Development*, pp. 185–211. Vol. 15. Thousand Oaks, Calif.: Sage Publications.

Bridges, L., Grolnick, W., and Connell, J. (1997). Infant emotion regulation with mothers and fathers. *Infant Behavior and Development* 20: 47–57.

Brownell, C. A., and Kopp, C. B. (1991). Common threads, diverse solutions: Concluding commentary. *Developmental Review* 11: 288–303.

Calkins, S. D. (1994). Origins and outcomes of individual differences in emotion regulation. *Monographs of the Society for Research in Child Development* 59 (2–3, Serial No. 240).

Calkins, S. D., and Johnson, M. C. (1998). Toddler regulation of distress to frustrating events: Temperamental and maternal correlates. *Infant Behavior and Development* 21: 379–95.

Campos, J. J., Campos, R. G., and Barrett, K. C. (1989). Emergent themes in the study of emotional development and emotion regulation. *Developmental Psychology* 25: 394–402.

Camras, L. A. (1992). Expressive development and basic emotions. *Cognition and Emotion* 6: 269–83.

Caspi, A. (1998). Personality development. In N. Eisenberg (Ed.), *Handbook of child psychology: Social, emotional, and personality development.* Vol. 3, pp. 311–88. New York: John Wiley & Sons.

Caspi, A., Henry, B., McGee, R. O., and Moffitt, T. E. (1995). Temperamental origins of child and adolescent behavior problems: From age three to fifteen. *Child Development* 66: 55–68.

Chao, R. K. (1994). Beyond parental control and authoritarian parenting style: Understanding Chinese parenting through the cultural notion of training. *Child Development* 65: 1111–19.

Crnic, K., and Acevado, M. (1999). Everyday stresses and parenting. In M. H. Bornstein (Ed.), *Handbook of parenting: Biology and ecology of parenting*, pp. 277–97. Mahwah, N.J.: Lawrence Erlbaum Associates.

Davidson, R. J., and Fox, N. A. (1989). Frontal brain asymmetry predicts infants' responses to maternal separation. *Journal of Abnormal Psychology* 98: 127–31.

Davidson, R. J., Jackson, D. C., and Kalin, N. H. (2000). Emotion, plasticity, context, and regulation: Perspectives from affective neuroscience. *Psychological Bulletin* 126: 890–909.

Dawson, G. (1994). Frontal electroencephalographic correlates of individual differences in emotion expression in infants: A brain systems perspective on emotion. *Monographs of the Society for Research in Child Development* 59 (2–3, Serial No. 240).

DeHaan, M., Gunnar, M. R., Tout, K., and Stansbury, K. (1998). Familiar and novel contexts yield different association between cortisol and behavior among 2-year-olds. *Developmental Psychobiology* 31: 93–101.

Demos, V. (1986). Crying in early infancy: An illustration of the motivational function of affect. In T. B. Brazelton and M. W. Yogman (Eds.), *Affective development in infancy*, pp. 39–73. Norwood, N.J.: Ablex.

Denham, S. A. (1998). *Emotional development in young children.* New York: Guilford Publications.

Derryberry, D., and Rothbart, M. K. (1988). Arousal, affect, and attention as components of temperament. *Journal of Personality and Social Psychology* 55: 958–66.

Derryberry, D., and Rothbart, M. K. (1997). Reactive and effortful processes in the organization of temperament. *Development and Psychopathology* 9: 633–52.

Dunn, J., Bretherton, L., and Munn, P. (1987). Conversations about feeling states between mothers and young children. *Developmental Psychology* 23: 132–39.

Dunn, J., and Munn, P. (1987). Development of justification of disputes with mother and sibling. *Developmental Psychology* 23: 791–98.

Dunn, J., Brown, J., and Beardsall, L. (1991). Family talk about feeling states and children's later understanding of others' emotions. *Developmental Psychology* 27: 448–55.

Eisenberg, N. (1998). Introduction in N. Eisenberg (Ed.), *Handbook of child psychology: Social, emotional, and personality development.* Vol. 3, pp. 1–24. New York: John Wiley & Sons.

Eisenberg, N., and Fabes, R. A. (1992). Emotion, regulation, and the development of social competence. In M. S. Clark (Ed.), *Emotion and social behavior.* Vol. 14, pp. 119–50. Thousand Oaks, Calif.: Sage Publications.

Emde, R. N., Biringen, Z., Clyman, R. B., and Oppenheim, D. (1991). The moral self of infancy: Affective core and procedural knowledge. *Developmental Review* 11: 251–70.

Emde, R. N., Plomin, R., Robinson, J., Corley, R., DeFries, J., Fulker, D., Reznick, J. S., Campos, J. J., Kagan, J., and Zahn-Waxler, C. (1992). Temperament, emotion, and cognition at fourteen months: The MacArthur Longitudinal Twin Study. *Child Development* 63: 1437–55.

Escalona, S. (1953). Emotional development in the first year of life. In M. Senn (Ed.), *Problems of infancy and childhood*, pp. 11–92. New York: Josiah Macy, Jr., Foundation.

Escalona, S. (1963). Patterns of infantile experience and the developmental process. In F.

Eissler, A. Freud, H. Hartman, and M. Kris (Eds.), *The psychoanalytic study of the child.* Vol. 18, pp. 197–244. New York: International Universities Press.

Escalona, S. (1968). *The roots of individuality.* Chicago: Aldine.

Feinman, S. (1982). Social referencing in infancy. *Merrill-Palmer Quarterly* 28: 445–70.

Fox, N. A. (1994). Dynamic cerebral processes underlying emotion regulation. *Monographs of the Society for Research in Child Development* 59 (2–3, Serial No. 240).

Fox, N. A., Calkins, S. D., and Bell, M. A. (1994). Neural plasticity and development in the first two years of life: Evidence from cognitive and socioemotional domains of research. *Development and Psychopathology* 6: 677–96.

Frank, L. K. (1957). Tactile communication. *Genetic Psychology Monographs* 56: 209–55.

Garcia Coll, C. T., Meyer, E. C., Brillon, L. (1999). Ethnic and minority parenting. In M. H. Bornstein (Ed.), *Handbook of parenting: Biology and ecology of parenting.* Vol. 2, pp. 189–209. Mahwah, N.J.: Lawrence Erlbaum Associates.

Goldberg, S. (2001). Attachment assessment in the Strange Situation. In L. T. Singer and P. S. Zeskind (Eds.), *Biobehavioral assessment of the infant,* pp. 209–29. New York: The Guilford Press.

Goldsmith, H. H., Buss, K. A., and Lemery, K. S. (1997). Toddler and childhood temperament: Expanded content, stronger genetic evidence, new evidence for the importance of environment. *Developmental Psychology* 33: 891–905.

Gralinski, J. H., and Kopp, C. B. (1993). Everyday rules for behavior: Mothers' requests to young children. *Developmental Psychology* 29: 573–84.

Grolnick, W. S., Bridges, L. J., and Connell, J. P. (1996). Emotion regulation in two-year-olds: Strategies and emotional expression in four contexts. *Child Development* 67: 928–41.

Gross, J. (1998). The emerging field of emotion regulation: An integrative review. *Review of General Psychology,* Special Issue: *New Directions in Research on Emotion* 2: 271–99.

Harris, P. L. (1994). The child's understanding of emotion: Developmental change and the family environment. *Journal of Child Psychology and Psychiatry* 35: 3–28.

Kagan, J. (1998). Biology and the child. In W. Damon (Series Ed.) and N. Eisenberg (Vol. Ed.), *Handbook of child psychology.* Vol. 3, *Social, emotional, and personality development,* pp. 177–236. 5th ed. New York: John Wiley & Sons.

Kagan, J., Arcus, D., Snidman, N., and Feng, W. Y. (1994). Reactivity in infants: A cross-national comparison. *Developmental Psychology* 30: 342–45.

Karen, R. (1994). *Becoming attached.* New York: Warner Books.

Kelley, S. A., Brownell, C. A., and Campbell, S. B. (2000). Mastery motivation and self-evaluative affect in toddlers: Longitudinal relations with maternal behavior. *Child Development* 71: 1061–71.

Klimes-Dougan, B., and Kopp, C. B. (1999). Children's conflict tactics with mothers: A longitudinal investigation of the toddler and preschool years. *Merrill-Palmer Quarterly* 45: 226–41.

Klinnert, M. D. (1984). The regulation of infant behavior by maternal facial expression. *Infant Behavior and Development* 7: 447–65.

Kochanska, G. (1995). Children's temperament, mother's discipline, and security of attachment: Multiple pathways to emerging internalization. *Child Development* 66: 597–615.

Kochanska, G. (1997). Multiple pathways to conscience for children with different temperaments: From toddlerhood to age 5. *Developmental Psychology* 33: 228–40.

Kochanska, G., and Aksan, N. (1995). Mother-child mutually positive affect, the quality of child compliance to requests and prohibitions, and maternal control as correlates of early internalization. *Child Development* 66: 236–54.

Kopp, C. B. (1982). The antecedents of self-regulation: A developmental perspective. *Developmental Psychology* 18: 199–214.

Kopp, C. B. (1989). Regulation of distress and negative emotions: A developmental view. *Developmental Psychology* 25: 343–54.

Kopp, C. B. (1994). Infant assessment. In C. Fischer and R. Lerner (Eds.), *Applied Developmental Psychology.* New York: McGraw-Hill.

Kopp, C. B. (2001). Self-regulation, in childhood. In N. Eisenberg (Section Ed.), N. Smelser and P. Baltes (Eds.), *International encyclopedia of social and behavioral sciences.* Oxford, Eng.: Elsevier Science Ltd.

Kopp, C. B. (2002). Commentary: The codevelopments of attention and emotion regulation. *Infancy* 3:199–208.

Kopp, C. B., Neufeld, S. J. (in press). Emotional development during infancy. In R. J. Davidson, L. Scherer, and H. Goldsmith (Eds.), *Handbook of affective sciences*. Oxford, Eng.: Oxford University Press.

Kopp, C. B., Regalado, M., Neufeld, S. J., Coulson, S., Lafean, K., and Wishner, J. (2000). *Appraisals of parenting, parent and child interactions, parenting styles, and children. An annotated bibliography*. New York: Commonwealth Fund.

Kopp, C. B., and Wyer, N. (1994). Self-regulation in normal and atypical development. In D. Cicchetti and S. Toth (Eds.), The self and its disorders. *The Rochester Symposium on Developmental Psychopathology*. Hillsdale, N.J.: Lawrence Erlbaum Associates.

Lagattuta, K. H., and Wellman, H. M. (2002). Differences in early parent-child conversations about negative versus positive emotions: Implications for the development of psychological understanding. *Developmental Psychology* 38: 564–80.

LeDoux, J. E. (1993). Emotional networks in the brain. In M. Lewis and J. M. Haviland (Eds.), *Handbook of emotions*, pp. 109–18. New York: The Guilford Press.

Lehtonen, L., Gormally, S., and Barr, R. G. (2000). "Clinical pies" for etiology and outcome in infants presenting with early increased crying. In R. G. Barr, B. Hopkins, and J. Green (Eds.), *Crying as a sign, a symptom, and a signal: Clinical, emotional, and developmental aspects of infant and toddler crying*. New York: McKeith.

Lemery, K. S., Goldsmith, H. H., Klinnert, M. D., and Mrazek, D. A. (1999). Developmental models of infant and childhood temperament. *Developmental Psychology* 35: 189–204.

Lewis, M. (1993). Self-conscious emotions: Embarrassment, pride, shame, and guilt. In M. Lewis and J. M. Haviland (Eds.), *Handbook of emotions*, pp. 563–573. New York: The Guilford Press.

Lewis, M., Alessandri, S. M., and Sullivan, M. W. (1990). Violation of expectancy, loss of control, and anger expressions in young infants. *Developmental Psychology* 26: 745–51.

MacLean, P. D. (1993). Cerebral evolution of emotion. In M. Lewis and J. M. Haviland (Eds.), *Handbook of emotions*, pp. 67–83. New York: The Guilford Press.

MacTurk, R. H., McCarthy, M. E., Vietze, P. M., and Yarrow, L. J. (1987). Sequential analysis of mastery behavior in 6- and 12-month-olds. *Developmental Psychology* 23: 199–203

Mangelsdorf, S. C., Shapiro, J. R., and Marzolf, D. (1995). Developmental and temperamental differences in emotion regulation in infancy. *Child Development* 66: 1817–28.

Matheny, A. P., Wilson, R. S., and Nuss, S. M. (1984). Toddler temperament: Stability across settings and over ages. *Child Development* 55: 1200–11.

Mosier, C. E., and Rogoff, B. (1994). Infants' instrumental use of their mothers to achieve their goals. *Child Development* 65: 70–79.

NICHD Early Child Care Research Network (1997). The effects of infant child care on infant-mother attachment security: Results of the NICHD Study of Early Child Care. *Child Development* 68: 860–79.

NICHD Early Child Care Research Network (1999). Child-care and mother-child interaction in the first 3 years of life. *Developmental Psychology* 35: 1399–1413.

Park, S-Y., Belsky, J., Putnam, S., and Crnic, K. (1997). Infant emotionality, parenting, and 3-year inhibition: Exploring stability and lawful discontinuity in a male sample. *Developmental Psychology* 33: 218–27.

Parke, R. D., and Buriel, R. (1998). Socialization in the family: Ethnic and ecological perspectives. In N. Eisenberg (Ed.), *Handbook of child psychology: Social, emotional, and personality development*. Vol. 3, pp. 463–552. New York: John Wiley & Sons.

Pedlow, R., Sanson, A., Prior, M., and Oberklaid, F. (1993). Stability of maternally reported temperament from infancy to 8 years. *Developmental Psychology* 29: 998–1007.

Plomin, R., DeFries, J. C., and Fulker, D. W. (1988). *Nature and nurture during infancy and early childhood*. New York: Cambridge University Press.

Plomin, R., Emde, R. N., Braungart, J. M., Campos, J., Corley, R., Fulker, D. W., Kagan, J., Reznick, J. S., Robinson, J., Zahn-Waxler, C., and DeFries, J. C. (1993). Genetic change and continuity from fourteen to twenty months: The MacArthur Longitudinal Twin Study. *Child Development* 64: 1354–76.

Robinson, N.S., & Garber, J. (1995). Social support and psychopathology across the life span. In D. Cicchetti and D.J. Cohen (Eds.), *Developmental psychopathology: Risk, disorder, and adaptation*. Vol. 2, pp. 162–209. New York: John Wiley & Sons.

Rothbart, M.K., and Bates, J.E. (1998). Temperament. In N. Eisenberg (Ed.), *Handbook of child psychology: Social, emotional, and personality development*. Vol. 3, pp. 105–76. New York: John Wiley & Sons.

Rothbart, M.K., Posner, M.I., and Hershey, K. (1995). Temperament, attention, and developmental psychopathology. In D. Cicchetti and D.J. Cohen (Eds.), *Developmental psychopathology: Risk, disorder, and adaptation*. Vol. 1, pp. 315–40. New York: John Wiley & Sons.

Rothbart, M.K., Ziaie, H., and O'Boyle, C.G. (1992). Self-regulation and emotion in infancy. In N. Eisenberg & R. Fabes (Eds.), *Emotion and its regulation in early development*. New directions for child development, No. 55: The Jossey-Bass education series, pp. 7–23. San Francisco: Jossey-Bass.

Rubin, K.H., Hastings, P.D., Stewart, S.L., Henderson, H.A., and Chen, X. (1997). The consistency and concomitants of inhibition: Some of the children, all of the time. *Child Development* 68: 467–83.

Saarni, C. (1999). *The development of emotional competence*. New York: Guilford Publications.

St. James Roberts, I., Bowyer, J., Varghese, S., and Sawdon, J. (1994). Infant crying patterns in Manali and London. *Child: Care, Health, & Development* 20: 323–37.

St. James Roberts, I., Conroy, S., and Wilsher, K.(1995). Clinical, developmental and social aspects of infant crying and colic. *Early Development and Parenting* 4: 353–76.

Salzarulo, P., Giganti, F., Fagiolo, I., and Ficca, F. (2001). Development of state regulation. In A.F. Kalverboer and A. Gramsbergen (Eds.), *Handbook of brain and behavior in human development*, pp. 725–42. Boston: Kluwer Academic Publishers.

Schaffer, H.R. (1996). *Social development*. Oxford, Eng.: Blackwell Publishers.

Shore, A.N. (1994). *Affect regulation and the origin of the self*. Hillsdale, N.J.: Lawrence Erlbaum Associates.

Sroufe, L.A. (1996). *Emotional development: The organization of emotional life in the early years*. New York: Cambridge University Press.

Stifter, C.A., and Braungart, J.M. (1995). The regulation of negative reactivity in infancy: Function and development. *Developmental Psychology* 31: 448–55.

Stipek, D.J. (1995). The development of pride and shame in toddlers. In J.P. Tangney and K.W. Fischer (Eds.), *Self-conscious emotions: The psychology of shame, guilt, embarrassment, and pride*, pp. 237–54. New York: The Guilford Press.

Stipek, D.J., Gralinski, J.H., and Kopp, C.B. (1990). Self concept development in the toddler years. *Developmental Psychology* 26: 972–77.

Stipek, D.J., Recchia, S., and McClintic, S. (1992). Self-evaluation in young children. *Monographs of the Society for Research in Child Development* 57 (1, Serial No. 226).

Tangney, J.P., and Fischer, K.W. (1995). *Self-conscious emotions: The psychology of shame, guilt, embarrassment, and pride*. New York: Guilford Publications.

Thomas, A., Chess, S., and Birch, H. (1963). *Behavioral individuality in early childhood*. New York: New York University Press.

Thompson, R.A. (1994). Emotion regulation: A theme in search of a definition. *Monographs of the Society for Research in Child Development* 59 (2–3, Serial No. 240).

Thompson, R.A. (1998). Early sociopersonality development. In N. Eisenberg (Ed.), *Handbook of child psychology: Social, emotional, and personality development*. Vol. 3, pp. 25–104. New York: John Wiley & Sons.

Tronick, E.Z. (1989). Emotions and emotional communication in infants. *American Psychologist* 44: 112–19.

Vaughn, B.E., and Bost, K.K. (1999). Attachment and temperament: Redundant, independent, or interacting influences on interpersonal adaptation and personality development? In J. Cassidy and P.R. Shaver (Eds.), *Handbook of attachment: Theory, research, and clinical applications*, pp. 198–225. New York: The Guilford Press.

Vaughn, B.E., Kopp, C.B., and Krakow, J.B. (1984). The emergence and consolidation of self-control from 18- to 30-months of age: Normative trends and individual differences. *Child Development* 55: 990–1004.

van den Boom, Dymphna, C. (1995). Do first-year intervention effects endure? Follow-up during toddlerhood of a sample of Dutch irritable infants. *Child Development* 66: 1798–1816.

van den Ijzendoorn, M. H., Juffer, F., and Duyvesteyn, M. G. C. (1995). Breaking the intergenerational cycle of insecure attachment: A review of the effects of attachment-based interventions on maternal sensitivity and infant security. *Journal of Child Psychology and Psychiatry* 36: 225–48.

Wolff, P. H. (1969). The natural history of crying and other vocalizations in early infancy. In B. M. Foss (Ed.), *Determinants of infant behavior*, pp. 81–108. London: Methuen.

Zahn-Waxler, C. (1998). From the enlightenment to the millennium: Changing conceptions of the moral sentiments. *Developmental Psychologist: Division 7/APA* (Fall): 1–7.

Zahn-Waxler, C., Radke-Yarrow, M., Wagner, E., and Chapman, M. (1992). Development of concern for others. *Developmental Psychology* 28: 126–36.

Zeanah, C. H. (1993). *Handbook of infant mental health*. New York: The Guilford Press

PHYSIOLOGICAL DEVELOPMENT AND REGULATION; REGULATORY PROCESSES; STRESS RESPONSES

American Academy of Pediatrics, Task Force on Infant Sleep Position and Sudden Infant Death Syndrome (2000). Changing concepts of infant sudden death syndrome: Implication for infant sleeping environment and sleep position. *Pediatrics* 105: 650–56.

Anders, T. F. (1982). Biological rhythms in development. *Psychosomatic Medicine* 44: 61–72.

Blass, E., and Ciaramitaro, V. (1994). A new look at some old mechanisms in human newborns: Taste and tactile determinants of state, affect, and action. *Monographs of the Society for Research in Child Development* 59 (1, Serial No. 239).

Boyce, W. T., and Jemerin, J. (1990). Psychobiological differences in childhood stress response. I: Patterns of illness and susceptibility. *Journal of Developmental and Behavioral Pediatrics* 11: 86–94.

Calkins, S. (1997). Cardiac vagal tone indices of temperamental reactivity and behavioral regulation. *Developmental Psychobiology* 31: 125–35.

Chrousos, G. P., and Gold, P.W. (1992). The concepts of stress and stress system disorders. *Journal of the American Medical Association* 267: 1244–52.

Cicchetti, D., & Tucker, D. (1994). Development and self-regulatory structures of the mind. *Development and Psychopathology* 6: 533–49.

Dahl, R. E. (1996). The regulation of sleep and arousal: Development and psychopathology. *Development and Psychopathology* 8: 3–27.

Gunnar, M. R. (1992). Reactivity of the hypothalamic-pituitary-adrenocortical system to stressors in normal infants and children. *Pediatrics* 90: 491–97.

Gunnar, M. R., and Nelson, C. A. (1994). Event-related potentials in year-old infants: Relations with emotionality and cortisol. *Child Development* 65: 80–94.

Gunnar, M. R., and White, B. P. (2001). Salivary cortisol measures in infant and child assessment. In L.T. Singer and P. S. Zeskind (Eds.), *Biobehavioral assessment of the infant*, pp. 167–89. New York: The Guilford Press.

Lewis, M., and Ramsay, D. S. (1995). Developmental change in infants' responses to stress. *Child Development* 66: 657–70.

Lipton, E.L., Steinschneider, A., and Richmond, J. (1960). Autonomic function in the neonate: Physiologic effects of motor restraint. *Psychosomatic Medicine* 22: 57–65.

McEwen, B. S., and Sapolsky, R. M. (1995). Stress and cognitive function. *Current Opinion in Neurobiology* 5: 205–16.

Stansbury, K., and Gunnar, M. R. (1999). Adrenocortical activity and emotion regulation. *Monographs of the Society for Research in Child Development* 59 (2–3, Serial No. 255).

Stifter, C. A., and Braungart, J. M. (1995). The regulation of negative reactivity in infancy: Function and development. *Developmental Psychology* 31: 448–55.

Stifter, C. A., and Fox, N. A. (1990). Infant reactivity: Physiological correlates of newborn and 5-month temperament. *Developmental Psychology* 26: 582–88.

Wishner, J. (2002). Parenting stress: Developmental trends and individual differences. Unpublished.

adaptation, 5
affection:
  expansion of social network, 188–89, 203
  for specific individuals, 159, 169, 202–3
  see also caring behaviors
affectionless child, 127
Ainsworth, Mary, 129–30
amygdala, 59
anger, 57, 59, 204, 258
  biological basis for, 17–18
anticipation, 89–90, 96, 113
arm symmetry, 53, 63
Arterberry, Martha, 135
Aslin, Richard, 142
assertiveness, 198
assistance, turning to others for, 238, 245, 270
associations, 56, 62–63, 157–58, 177
  of sound of words and objects, 167
  of words with objects and people, 186, 187
attachment, 16, 152, 233, 275
  day-care settings and, 131–33
  developmental close-up, 128–33
  emotional ties to others, 227
  multiple attachments, 203
  "proximity seeking," 129
  Strange Situation (SS) measure of, 130–31, 132, 216
  temperament and, 216–17
  see also separation
Attachment and Loss (Bowlby), 129
attention, 2, 13, 56, 197, 270
  to color, 14
  coordinates with reach and grasp, 14
  crying for, 96
  development of, chart, 14
  examining, in, 156
  joint, 15, 117, 152, 162
  to landmarks, 14
  multiple tasks, ability to distribute among, 165
  sustained, 14, 156, 199, 238, 253 14,
  visual, *see* visual attention
  vocalizations to gain, 103
  whining for, 112

auditory abilities, *see* hearing
autonomy, *see* independence and autonomy
awareness of others, growing, 67–69

babbling, 126, 143–44, 158, 167
  canonical, 116, 143
Baby and Child Care (Spock), 258–59
balance, 113, 166, 228, 240, 253, 265
Bates, Jack, 213, 214, 217
Bauer, Patricia, 73, 75, 78, 171
Bayley, Nancy, 108
behavior domains, 10–19
  integration and organization of, 19–20
  see also specific domains, e.g., cognition; motor control
Benson, Janette, 136
birth to three months, 25–85
  developmental hints and alerts, 60
  preview, 25–26
  see also newborns; early weeks; one month; two months; three months
Blair, Clancy, 6
blankets, self-comforting with, 223, 246–47
Blass, Elliott, 47
Bloom, Lois, 138, 141, 208, 209
body:
  baby's learning about and recognizing his own, 102, 159–60, 169, 190, 247
  body control, 63
  labeling of body parts, 247, 255
  memory, 172
boredom, 62, 96
  crying and, 46
Bost, Kelly, 216
Bowlby, John, 127, 128, 130
brain:
  ability to learn and development of, 6–7
  cortical neurons and pathways, 3, 31, 63, 71
  early development of, 70–73
  chart, 72
  experience and development of, 73
  frontal lobes, increasing activation at twelve months at, 201
  language's demands on the, 138
  limbic system and emotions, 57, 59

brain (*cont'd*)
  neuronal connections, 70–71
  pruning of synapses, 71
  sleep and maturation of, 37
  subcortical neurons and pathways, 3, 31, 71
Bremner, Gavin, 135
Bridges, Lisa, 270
Brownell, Celia, 248
Buriel, Ray, 192

Call, J., 282–83
Calvin, William, 165
Campos, Joe, 180–81
Camras, Linda, 58
canonical babbling, 116, 143
caring behaviors, 231–32, 239, 245, 275
categorizing, *see* classification
cause-and-effect, awareness of, 168, 231, 252, 268
chairs, climbing into, 265
change, development and, 2–3
Chao, Ruth, 191
Chess, Stella, 213, 217
child care:
  day care, 131–33
  at gyms, 189, 279
chimpanzee babies, comparison of human babies and, 279–84
Chinese cultural patterns, parenting and, 191
Chomsky, Noam, 209
Church, Joseph, 221, 227
clapping hands, 156, 157, 160
classification, 228–29, 252, 257, 261, 266
  overgeneralization, 243
  using sounds to identify similar objects and events, 175
climate, adaptation to, 5
climbing, 228, 240
clinging, 233
clothing, *see* dressing
cognition:
  at one month, 45
  at two months, 56
  at three months, 65–66
  at four months, 96
  at five months, 105
  at six months, 115–16
  at seven months, 126
  at eight months, 158–59
  at nine months, 168
  at ten months, 178
  at eleven months, 188
  at twelve months, 201–2

  at fifteen months, 230–31
  at eighteen months, 243–45
  at twenty-one months, 255–57
  at twenty-four months, 262–63, 268–70
  behaviors classified as, 13
  cause and effect, understanding of, 68, 231, 252, 268
  knowledge, implicit, explicit, 135
  learning, 13
  overview, 13–15
  play (functional, pretend), representative of cognition, 201–2, 230–31
  problem-solving, *see* problem-solving skills
  trial and error learning, 231
colic, 48
Colombo, John, 13
colors:
  preferences, 95, 104, 135
  recognition by name, 240, 242
  visual ability to distinguish, 64
comforting others, *see* caring behaviors
commitment of parenting, 272–75
comprehension, 13, 140, 144–45, 186, 200, 267
concentration, 152
consolidations of behaviors, 10
contingent responsiveness, 68
contrariness, 263–64
control, desire to exert, 252–53
cooing, 66, 95, 143
"correctness" of objects, understanding standards of, 245
coughing, 28
crawling, 102, 123, 127, 155, 156
  developmental close-up, 107–9
creeping, 9, 155, 156, 176
  developmental close-up, 107–9
cribs, 185
Crnic, Keith, 277, 278, 279
cross-modal processing, 115
crying:
  early weeks, 35, 46
  at four months, 96
  by toddler, 203, 271
  colic, 48
  developmental close-up, 45–49
  on hearing others cry, 203
  intense and prolonged, 48–49
  nighttime waking and, 37
  parental intervention, 46, 47, 274
    nighttime waking, 37
  to resist parents' request, 235
  soothing techniques, 47, 56
  teething and, 90
  when left alone, 68

cultural differences, 21
  developmental norms and, 7–8
  parenting and, 190–93
curiosity, 102, 168, 226

Davidson, Richard, 70
day care, attachment research and, 131–33
decoupling of words, 242–43
deferred imitation, 170–71
deletions of behaviors, 9–10
Denham, Susanne, 58, 206
depth perception, 104, 114, 135
detail, attention to, 175
development:
  chart for recording concerns about, 288–90
  concerns about, 285–90
    chart for recording, 288–90
    consulting pediatrician about, 285–86
    specialists, evaluation by, 286–88
  interpreting the research, 134–36
  meanings of, 2
  miniguide to early, see miniguide to early
    development
  norms, 7–8
  parent knowledge and education about,
    274–75
  patterns of:
    consolidations of behaviors, 10
    deletions of behaviors, 9–10
    growth patterns, 9
    growth rates, 8
    refinement of behaviors, 10
  variability in, see variability, individual
  ways of thinking about:
    adapt, ability to, 5
    biological behaviors of newborns, 3–4
    biology and experience working
      together, 4–5
    individual variability, 5–6
    limitations on malleability of babies,
      6–7
developmental hints and alerts:
  birth to three months, 60
  four to seven months, 133
  eight to twelve months, 207
  eighteen months, 276
  twenty-four months, 276
developmentally related stresses of
    parenting, 277–79
discipline, 275
displeasure, 67
  learning to control, 68
    see also emotions and emotional
      development, controls over
dolls, functional play with, 231
do's and don'ts, see safety; socialization

drawing, 266
dreams causing emotional distress, 272
dressing, 247, 254
  awareness of appearance, 233
dress-up play, 257
Dunn, Judy, 206

early development, miniguide to, see
    miniguide to early development
early weeks, 33–39
  emotional development, 80–81
  hearing in, 35–36
  motor reflexes in, 38–39
  sleep and wakefulness in, 36–38
  snapshot, 34–35
  vision in, 34, 35, 135
education, parent, 274–75
eighteen months:
  cognition at, 243–45
  developmental alerts, 276
  emotions at, 84–85, 246–47
  language comprehension and production
    at, 241–43
  motor control at, 240
  perception at, 240
  sense of self at, 247–49
  snapshot, 238–40
  social development at, 245
eight months:
  cognition at, 158–59
  emotions at, 82–83, 159
  hearing at, 157
  motor control at, 155–56
  sense of self at, 159–60
  snapshot, 154–55
  social bids, 154, 161–62
  social development at, 159
  social play, 154, 160–61
  vision at, 154, 156–57
  vocalizations and language at, 157–58
eight to twelve months, 149–219
  developmental hints and alerts, 207
  preview, 151–52
  see also eight months; nine months; ten
    months; eleven months; twelve
    months
eleven months, 183–93
  cognition at, 188
  culture and parenting, 190–93
  emotions at, 82–83, 189–90
  language comprehension and production
    at, 185, 186–87
  motor control at, 185–86
  sense of self at, 190
  snapshot of, 184–85
  social development at, 188–89

embarrassment, 258, 271–72
emotions and emotional development, 152
  at two months, 56–59
  at three months, 62, 66–67
  at four months, 80–81, 92, 97
  at five months, 106
  at six months, 117
  at seven months, 82–83, 127–28
  at eight months, 159
  at nine months, 169
  at ten months, 175, 179
  at eleven months, 189–90
  at twelve months, 203–6
  at fifteen months, 232–33
  at eighteen months, 246–47
  at twenty-one months, 258
  at twenty-four months, 84–85, 264,
    271–72
  ability to talk about, 255
  with biological roots, 17–18
  chart of, 79–85
  cognition and, 127
  control over, 80–85, 204–6, 223, 269–70
    blankets and cuddly objects used to
     aid, 223, 246–47
  developmental close-up, 57–59
  emotion-focused conversations, 206
  expressions, 80–85
  jealousy, 203
  learning opportunities and, 58–59
  limbic system and, 57, 59
  matching, to emotions of others, 117
  mood swings, 221
  negative emotions, 81, 83, 222, 239, 246,
    264
  of mothers, contingent responsiveness
    and, 68–69
  overview of, 17–18
  positive emotions, 62, 66–67, 80–81, 83,
    97, 117
  primary, 57–58
  self-conscious (social) emotions, 18, 58,
    83–85, 223–49, 258, 271–72
  understanding, 80–85
Erikson, Erik, 259
Escalona, Sybil, 113
examining, 156
expectations, 56
  role of routines and schedules in
    developing, 118–19
experience(s):
  development as combination of biology
    and, 4–5
  learning new words and new, 243
explicit knowledge, 135
explicit memory, see memory, explicit

exploration, 152, 176, 178, 196, 226
  four to seven months, 89, 92, 102
  trial-and-error, 202

faces, 54, 135
  baby's facial expressions, emotion and,
    58, 105, 127, 169
  discrimination of different facial
    expressions, 97, 123, 124, 232
  distinguishing between male and female,
    124
  remembering, 124
  of strangers, see strangers, reaction to
  visual ability to discern, 31, 35, 44, 64
Fantz, Robert, 30
fear, 57, 59, 127, 204, 258
  biological basis for, 17–118
  trying to control, 258
feeding:
  associations and, 56, 62–63
  baby's feeding herself, 169, 186, 190,
    240
  at one month, 45
  compulsiveness in wants and requests,
    252
  resistance behaviors, 107
fifteen months:
  cognition at, 230–31
  emotions at, 84–85, 232–33
  language comprehension and production
    at, 229–30
  motor control at, 228
  perception at, 228–29
  sense of self at, 233
  snapshot, 223, 226–28
  social development at, 231–32
  socialization to everyday standards of
    behavior, 233–36
fingers, 64, 104
  playing of baby with his, 62
  pointing, see pointing
  probing objects with, 165, 178
  see also hands
five months, 102–9
  cognition at, 105
  emotions at, 80–81, 106
  hearing at, 104–5
  motor control at, 103–4
  pushing, pivoting, crawling, and
    creeping, 107–9
  sense of self at, 107
  snapshot, 102–3
  social development at, 102–3, 106
  vision at, 104
  vocalizations and language at, 103, 105
flexibility, 123

form perception, 64, 240, 254
four months, 91–99
    cognition at, 96
    emotions at, 80–81, 92, 97
    grasping abilities at, 97–99
    hearing at, 95
    motor control at, 93–94
    snapshot, 92–93
    social development at, 96–97
    vision at, 92, 93, 94–95
    vocalizations and language at, 95–96
four to seven months, 87–147
    developmental hints and alerts, 133
    preview, 89–90
    see also four months; five months; six
        months; seven months
Fox, Nathan, 70
Fragile X syndrome, 286
fretting, 46, 239, 252
Freud, Sigmund, 259
frustration, 102, 106, 222, 239, 246, 264
functional play, 201–2, 230–31

games, 122, 154, 160–61, 161–62, 275
    baby-initiated, 97
    control over social, 203
    dropping, 126
    see also specific games
Gauvain, Mary, 182
gazing following another person's gaze, 106
gender:
    differences:
        in language production, 268
        in play, 188, 257
    recognition of, 272
geographical adaptations, 5
Gesell, Arnold, 108, 239
gestures, 103, 137, 156, 178, 197, 229, 282
    waving goodbye, 122, 157
goals, understanding of, 168, 178
Goldsmith, Hill, 214, 215
Golinkoff, Roberta, 96, 125, 145, 208
grammar (language), 139–40, 211, 268
Gramsbergen, A., 70
grasping, 8, 94, 103–4, 114, 122–23, 124,
        151, 166–67, 199, 228, 240
    development close-up, 97–99
    with fingertips, 98–99
    holding toys and implements by the
        handle, 176
    one-handed, 124
    reflex, 28, 38, 39, 43, 53, 98
    releasing and, 99, 167, 184–85, 199
    see also reaching
Grolnick, Wendy, 270
Gross, James, 204

grouping items, see classification
Gua (chimpanzee), 280–82, 283
guilt, 18, 58, 223

Haith, Marshall, 74, 136
handedness, 176
hands, 63, 172
    clapping, 156, 157, 160
    communication, see gestures
    control, increasingly precise, 254
    coordination, 265
    dirty, preoccupation with, 233
    -eye coordination, 158
    fingers, see fingers
    grasping, see grasping
    handedness, 176
    investigation with, 96
    learning, role in, 115
    reaching, see reaching
    as tools, 176, 197
    transferring objects between, 104
    see also touch, sense of
hand-to-mouth movement of newborns,
        28–29
Harris, Paul, 269
head control, 11, 42, 52, 53, 63, 92, 93
head shaking, 178–79, 184, 187
head-turning response, 3–4, 38–39
health problems, serious, 273–74
hearing:
    of newborns, 29, 135
    early weeks, 35–36, 135
    at one month, 42, 44
    at two months, 54–55
    at three months, 64–65
    at four months, 95
    at five months, 104–5
    at six months, 115
    at seven months, 125
    at eight months, 157
    at twelve months, 200
    distinguishing male and female voices,
        112, 115
    fine-tuning of, to speech sounds of
        family's language, 115, 142, 200
    intonations, 44, 54–55, 157
    localization, 35–36
    loudness (intensity) of sounds, 141
    overview, 12
    perception of sounds, 141–42
    physical limitations on babies', 7
    sound frequencies, 141
    speech, responsiveness to, 44, 142
    vocal signatures, identifying, 115
heritability of temperament, 214–15
Hirsh-Pasek, Kathy, 96, 125, 145, 208

"horsey" (social game), 122, 161
How Babies Talk (Golinkoff and
        Hirsh-Pasek), 208

ideas, thinking using, 238, 244
identity, *see* self
imagination, 238
"I'm gonna getcha!" (social game), 122, 161
imitation, 78, 227, 253, 271, 281, 283
    of body actions, 179
    deferred, 170–71
    imitative learning, 201–2
    intentional, onset of, 152
    social, 117
    vocal tennis, 66
    word learning and, 267
implicit knowledge, 135
implicit memory, *see* memory, implicit
independence and autonomy, 169, 184,
        196, 222, 234, 248, 263, 265
inside and outside, concept of, 178
intelligence, 152
    defined, 14, 161
    emergence of, at nine months, 164–65
    media reports on infant behavior,
        interpreting, 134–36
    social, 174
intentionality, 113
interactions with others
    and emotions, 80–85
    and social development, 80–85
interrupting, 270
interruptions, handling of, 102
intonations, 139
    hearing, 44, 54–55, 157
    learning to produce sounds the mimic
        intonations of family's, 116, 126,
        143
    of toddler's two- and three-word
        sentences, 243
    vocalizations, 55, 115, 126
irritability, 42, 90, 93, 166, 239, 252
    see also temperament

jack-in-the-box (play), 166
jealousy, 203–4
Johnson, Mark, 73
joint attention, 15, 117, 152, 162
jump-start responses (newborn period), 4
Jusczyk, Peter, 125
just born, *see* newborns
justifying of behavior, toddler's, 263

Kalverboer, A. F., 70, 280
Karen, Robert, 129
Kellman, Philip, 135

Kellogg, Donald, 280–82
Kellogg, W., 280–82
kicking a ball, 254
kisses, throwing, 122, 245
knowledge, implicit and explicit, 135
    see also cognition

Lagattuta, Kristen, 206
language, 5, 136–47, 222, 282
    at two months, 55
    at three months, 66
    at four months, 95–96
    at five months, 105
    at six months, 115–16
    at seven months, 126
    at eight months, 157–58
    at ten months, 177
    at eleven months, 185, 186–87
    at twelve months, 200–201
    at fifteen months, 229–30
    at eighteen months, 241–43
    at twenty-one months, 254–55
    at twenty-four months, 262, 263, 265,
        266–68
    babbling, 126, 143–44, 158, 167
    bilingualism, 268
    brain, demands on the, 138
    canonical babbling, 116, 143
    components of development of, 140–46
        comprehension of others' words,
            144–45
        learning to produce words and
            learning labels, 145–47, 208–12,
            241, 254–55, 262
        perception of sounds, 141–42
        vocalizations, 143–44
    comprehension, 144–45, 151
        at eleven months, 186–87
        at twelve months, 200
        at fifteen months, 229
        at eighteen months, 241
        at twenty-four months, 266–67
    decoupled words, 242–43
    fine-tuning of hearing to speech sounds
        of family's, 115, 142, 200
    first words, 145–46, 151, 201, 208–11
    individual differences in language
        development, 147
    learning the family's, 116, 137, 139, 143
    morphemes, 139
    nonspecific or protolanguage, 144
    overview of development of, 16–17
    parental actions the influence baby's
        learning of, 137–38
    phonemic rules of, 139, 142
    pragmatic rules of, 140

pronunciation difficulties, 255
rules of (grammar), 139–40, 211, 268
self-awareness, 211–12
semantic rules, 139–40
sentence production, 145, 146–47, 210,
    211, 229–30, 241–42, 243, 252,
    254, 267–68
speech acquisition, theories of, 209–11
spurts in learning of, 138
syntactic rules of, 140
variability in speech among children of
    similar age, 210, 241, 268
vocabulary, 137, 138, 151, 187, 201,
    210–11, 229, 230, 241, 252, 254–55
    word-learning strategies, 266–67
    word spurt, 146–47
vocalizations, *see* vocalizations
word flexibility, 243
word play, 242
word recognition, 125
word segmentation, recognition of, 125
Language Instinct, The (Pinker), 209
larynx, 45
laughter, 97, 106, 127, 172, 203
learning and ability to learn, 13
    brain development and, 6–7
    see also cognition
localization, 35–36

MacLean, Paul, 57
Mandler, Jean, 170
mastery motivation, 172
mature behavior, inconsistent, 240
Meltzoff, Andrew, 171
memory, 13, 73–79, 202, 238, 253
    body, 172
    cross-modal, 75
    explicit, 73, 74, 126
        diagram, 77
        proto-, 75
    implicit, 73–75
        conditioned, 74–75
        diagram, 76
        expectant, 74
    multiple strategies to aid, 201
    object permanence, 158–59, 170
    recall, 244
        developmental close-up of, 170–72
    recognition, 75, 105, 172, 244
        cross-modal, 202
    at three months, 62, 65
    selfhood, 171
    transfer of knowledge and, 244–45
    ways in which we use, 171
    working, 78
        diagram, 77

miniguide to early development, 1–21
    behavior domains, 10–19
        definitions of development and change,
            2–3
        integration and organization of the
            behavior domains, 19–20
        patterns of development, 8–10
        using this book, 20–21
        ways of thinking about development,
            3–8
mirror:
    smiling at self-image, 107
    understanding one's reflection in the,
        179–80, 247
mirrors, 172
mobiles, 65
Mommy & Me programs, 189
mood swings (parenting) 221, 232
Moro reflex, 39
morphemes, 139
"motherese," 55
motor control:
    early weeks, 38–39
    at one month, 43
    at two months, 53
    at three months, 63–64
    at four months, 93–94
    at five months, 103–4
    at six months, 113–14
    at seven months, 122–24
    at eight months, 155–56
    at nine months, 166–67
    at ten months, 176
    at eleven months, 185–86
    at twelve months, 198–99
    at fifteen months, 228
    at eighteen months, 240
    at twenty-one months, 253–54
    at twenty-four months, 265
    fine motor skills, 11, 89, 176, 184, 186,
        199, 240, 254, 282
        examining, 156
    gross motor skills (generally), 11, 89
    overview, 10–11
    sequence to overall pattern of
        development, 11
mouth:
    bringing objects to the, 114, 155, 176
    hand to mouth of newborn, 28–29
    putting foot and toes in the, 102, 123
    safety and, 114
movement, fascination with, 104, 184
moving objects, visually following, 62
    outside line of vision, 105
music, swaying to, 126
myelin sheath (brain), 71

negotiation by toddler, 235
Neisser, Ulric, 171
Nelson, Charles, 73
Nelson, Katherine, 146, 243
nesting objects, 188, 202
newborns, 27–31
   snapshot, 28–29
   vision of, 30–31, 135
   see also birth to three months; early weeks
nine months:
   cognition at, 168
   emotions at, 82–83, 169
   intelligent behavior at, 164–65
   motor control at, 166–67
   recall memories, 170–72
   sense of self at, 169
   snapshot, 164–65
   social development at, 168–69
   vision at, 167
   vocalizations and language at, 167
"no," 235, 238, 242
   head shaking and, 178–79, 184, 187
   to keep baby safe, 203, 277
nonspecific language, 144
norms, developmental, 7–8, 21

object permanence, 158–59, 169, 202, 244
Oller, Kim, 143
one month, 41–49
   cognition at, 45
   crying, 45–49
   emotional development, 80–81
   hearing at, 42, 44
   motor control at, 43
   snapshot, 42–43
   social development at, 45
   vision at, 42, 43–44
   vocalizations, 44–45
options, understanding of multiple, 168
outside and inside, concept of, 178
overgeneralization, word use and, 243
overstimulation, 46, 93, 96

palmomental reflex, 38
parenting:
   books on child rearing, 191, 258–59
   commitments of, development close-up
      on, 272–76
   cultural differences, 190–93
   importance of, 21
   knowledge and education, 274–75
   parental soothing, 47, 56
   parents as role models, 275
   parents' interventions for crying, colic,
      45–49
   parents' roles, 192

reading, 274–75
schedules and routines, 118–20
socializing children, 233
stresses of, developmentally related,
   277–79
time-outs, 275
see also affect, to parents; attachment;
   specific topics relating to parenting
Parke, Ross, 192
Parker, Sue, 283
pat-a-cake (social game), 122, 126–27, 154,
   157, 160, 161, 282
pediatrician, consulting your, 285–86
peekaboo (social game), 97, 126, 161
peers:
   accepting differences in, 271
   play with, 189, 245, 253, 257, 271
   social exchanges with, 257
perception:
   at fifteen months, 228–29
   at eighteen months, 240
   at twenty-one months, 254
   at twenty-four months, 254
   defined, 12
   hearing, see hearing
   vision, see vision
persistence, 218
personality, temperament compared to,
   213
phonemic rules of language, 139, 142
photographs, 172
physiological regulation, 25
Piaget, Jean, 152, 238, 269
Pinker, Steven, 136, 138, 209
pivoting, 107, 108
play:
   baby's bringing others into their, 197
   dress-up, 257
   functional, 201–2, 230–31
   gender differences, 188
   with peers, 189, 245, 253, 271
   pretend, see pretend play
   quiet, 253
   see also games; toys, playing with
playpens, 185
pleasure, 57, 67, 97, 106
   learning to control overexcitement, 68
pointing, 165, 175
Posner, Michael, 70, 199
possession, understanding, 252, 255
possessions, socialization to respect, see
   socialization, to everyday standards
   of behavior
possessiveness, 198
pretend play, 222, 223, 238, 269
pride, 18, 58

primitive self, 248
problem-solving skills, 13, 158, 197, 201, 263, 268–69
  "if . . . then" consequences and, 244
  proto-explicit memory and, 75
prohibitions, *see* safety; socialization
prosocial behaviors, 231–32, 239, 245, 275
protolanguage, 144
psychological beings, babies at, 63
pushing-away hand movements, 107
puzzles, 175, 240, 254, 270

quantity, concept of, 257

reaching, 63–64, 92, 94, 99, 103, 166, 199
  one-handed, 124
  see also grasping
reading to your children, 274–75, 275
recognition, seeking, 197
recognition memory, 75, 105, 172
refinement of behaviors, 10
reflexes, developmental, 9–10, 28, 38
  see also individual reflexes, e.g., sucking reflex
releasing (grasp), 99, 167, 184–85, 199
repetition, 226, 233
  of specific sequences, 178
resistance behaviors, 107
restlessness, 238
Rogoff, Barbara, 112–13
role models, parents as, 275
role playing, 269
rolling over, 93–94, 97, 103, 112
rooting reflex, 39
Rothbart, Mary, 13, 70, 199, 213, 214, 217
routines, 66, 244, 275
  developmental close-up, 118–19
  distinguished from schedules, 118
  language of, 119
  scripts compared to, 256
  upset at major changes in, 271
Rubin, Kenneth, 217
Ruff, Holly, 13, 199
rules of behavior, socialization to, *see* socialization

Saarni, Carolyn, 206
safety, 226, 228, 265
  baby-proofing the house, 123, 156, 207, 254
  do's and don'ts, 203, 227, 234, 236, 245, 259
  putting objects in the mouth and, 114
  routines and, 119
  teaching baby about, 166
  of walking baby, 198

Scarr, Sandra, 57
schedules, 66, 267
  developmental close-up, 118–19
  distinguished from routines, 118
scripts, 244, 256–57
second year, 219–84
  developmental alerts, 276
  preview, 221–24
  see also fifteen months; eighteen months; twenty-one months; twenty-four months
self, 8, 67
  at five months, 107
  at six months, 117–18
  at seven months, 128
  at nine months, 169
  at ten months, 179–80
  at eleven months, 190
  at twelve months, 204
  at fifteen months, 233
  at eighteen months, 247–49
  at twenty-one months, 258
  at twenty-four months, 272
  autonomy, 222, 258, 263
    exert control, 252–53
  developmental close-up, 248–49
  justification of behavior, 263
  knowledge of body parts, 190
  negativism, 263–64
  overview of, 19–20
  primitive self, 248
  referring to oneself by name, 272
self-conscious emotions (e.g., shame, guilt), 18, 58, 85, 223, 249, 258, 271–72
self-efficacy, 248
self-language, 255, 272
self-recognition, 248
semantic rules of language, 139–40
sensation, defined, 12
  see also perception; *individual senses*
sense of humor, 223, 265
separation, 115–16, 128–29, 189, 275
  see also attachment
seven months, 122–33
  attachment, developmental close-up of, 128–33
  cognition at, 126
  emotions at, 82–83, 127–28
  hearing at, 125
  motor control at, 122–24
  sense of self at, 128
  snapshot, 122–23
  social development at, 122, 123, 126–27
  vision at, 124–25
  vocalizations and language at, 126
shame, 18, 58, 271–72

shape constancy, 64
sharing, 162, 231, 232
siblings:
  caring behaviors with, 245
  prosocial behaviors with, 232
SIDS (Sudden Infant Death Syndrome),
    38, 53
sitting, 94, 103, 155, 166
  at six months, 112, 113
  at seven months, 124
  getting into seated position, 155–56, 166
six months, 112–19
  cognition at, 116–17
  developing expectations, role of
      schedules and routines in, 118–19
  emotions at, 80–81, 117
  hearing at, 115
  motor control at, 113–14
  sense of self at, 117–18
  snapshot, 112–13
  social develpment at, 117
  vision at, 114–15
  vocalizations and language at, 113, 115–16
sleep and wakefulness:
  early weeks, 34
  at one month, 42–43
  at two months, 52
  at nine months, 166
  co-sleeping, 38
  developmental close-up, 36–38
  dreams causing emotional distress, 272
  Sudden Infant Death Syndrome,
      position of baby and, 38, 53
smell, sense of:
  early weeks, 34
  of newborns, 29
  memory of scents, 73
smiling by baby, 45, 56, 62, 66–67, 96–97
  responding to, 62
  at successful achievements, 127
sneezing, 28
social bids, 154, 161–62
social development, 152
  at one month, 45
  at two months, 55–56
  at three months, 66–67
  at four months, 96–97
  at five months, 102–3, 106
  at six months, 117
  at seven months, 122, 123, 126–27
  at eight months, 159
  at nine months, 168–69
  at ten months, 178–79
  at eleven months, 188–89
  at twelve months, 202–3
  at fifteen months, 231–32

  at eighteen months, 245
  at twenty-one months, 257
  at twenty-four months, 270–71
  in relation to emotions, 80–85
  overview, 15–16
social games, see "I'm gonna getcha,"
      pat-a-cake, peek-a-boo
social imitation, 117
social intelligence, 174
socialization, 123
  to everyday standards of behavior, 227,
      233–36, 239, 270
    do's and don'ts, 203, 227, 234, 236,
      245, 259, 264
  generalizing rules, 270–71
  routines' role in, 119
  social referencing and, 174–75, 180, 181
  starting, 233
  ways toddlers find to resist parents'
      wishes, 235, 263–64
social play, 154, 160–61, 203
  see also games; specific forms of social play
social referencing, 174, 180–82, 245
  as cultural apprenticeship, 182
sound:
  fascination with objects that produce, 165
  hearing, see hearing
  language, see language
  vocalizations, see vocalizations
spanking, 275
spatial perception, 14, 64, 125
speech, see language; vocalizations
spina bifida, 273–74
Spock, Benjamin, 258–59
Sroufe, L. Alan, 127
standing, 155, 166, 176
  assisted, 112, 113–14, 123, 155
  rising from sit to, 228
Stone, Joseph, 221
strangers, reaction to:
  at five months, 106
  at eight months, 154, 159
stresses of parenting, dealing with, 272–75
sucking reflex, 9, 28, 38, 39
Sudden Infant Death Syndrome (SIDS),
    38, 53
swaddling, 38
synapses, 70, 71
  pruning of, 71
synaptic space, 71
syntactic rules of language, 140

tantrums, 223, 239, 246, 258, 264, 277
taste, sense of:
  early weeks, 34
  of newborns, 29

teasing, 161–62, 223, 227, 235
teething, 90, 155
telephone, learning to wait until Mom gets
    off the, 235, 270
temperament, 212–18
    attachment and, 216–17
    definitions of, 214
    heritability and, 214–15
    measurements of, 214
    personality compared to, 213
    response to unfamiliarity and, 159
    separation and reunions and, 131
    stability and, 217–18
ten months, 82–83, 173–82
    cognition at, 178
    emotions at, 179
    motor control at, 176
    sense of self at, 179–80
    snapshot, 174–76
    social development at, 178–79
    social referencing, 190–92
    vision at, 177
    vocalizations and language at, 177
texture, recognizing differences in, 95,
    254
Thomas, Alexander, 213, 217
Thompson, Ross, 131, 181
Three Babies (Church), 227
three months, 61–69
    becoming aware of others at, 67–69
    cognition at, 65–66
    emotions at, 80–81
    hearing at, 64–65
    motor control at, 63–64
    snapshot, 62–63
    social interactions and emotions at, 62,
        66–67
    vision at, 64
    vocalizations and language at, 66
throwing, 254
thumb sucking, 204
tickling, 97
time-outs, 275
time (sense of past, present, and future),
    255–57
toddlers, see fifteen months; eighteen
        months; twenty-one months;
        twenty-four months; second year
toilet training, 258–60
Tomasello, Michael, 152, 227, 282–83
tonic neck reflex, 39, 43, 63
tool use, 283
touch, sense of:
    of newborns, 29
    coordination of vision and, 115
    investigation with, 96

toys, playing with, 197, 281–82
    banging, 125, 158
    bringing two toys together, 125
    coordinated release and, 184–85
    dropping toys from a height, 126
    gender differences, 188
    joint play activities with parents, 172
    mouthing toys, 155, 176
    nesting, 188, 202
    pushing along a smooth surface, 125
    putting toys away, 270
    systematic exploration, 178
    transfer of knowledge in, 244–45
    trial-and-error exploration, 202
transitional objects, securing comfort in,
    223, 246–47
trial-and-error learning, 202, 230, 233, 283
Tronick, Ed, 68
turtle frustration fret, 106
twelve months, 195–206
    cognition at, 201–2
    emotions at, 82–83, 203–6
    hearing at, 200
    language comprehension and production
        at, 200–201
    motor control at, 198–99
    sense of self at, 204
    snapshot, 196–98
    social development at, 202–3
    vision at, 199
twenty-four months, 261–76
    cognition at, 262–63, 268–70
    developmental alerts, 276
    emotions at, 84–85, 264, 271–72
    language at, 262, 263, 265, 266–68
    motor control at, 265
    parental commitment, 272–76
    perception at, 266
    sense of self at, 272
    snapshot, 223–24, 262–64
    social development at, 270–71
twenty-one months, 251–60
    cognition at, 255–57
    emotions at, 84–85
    language at, 254–55
    motor control at, 253–54
    sense of self at, 258
    snapshot, 223, 252–53
    social development at, 257–58
    toilet training, 258–60
two months, 51–59
    cognition at, 56
    emotions at, 56–59, 80–81
    hearing at, 54–55
    motor control at, 53
    snapshot, 52

two months (*cont'd*)
  social development at, 55–56
  vision at, 54
  vocalizations and language at, 55

values, socialization to accept, *see*
     socialization
variability, individual, 2, 5–6, 113, 286
  developmental norms and, 7–8
  factors that may account for, 5–6
  in the second year, 222
  in speech acquisition, 210
Vaughn, Brian, 216
vision:
  of newborns, 29, 30–31, 135
  early weeks, 34, 35, 135
  at one month, 42, 43–44
  at two months, 52, 54
  at three months, 64
  at four months, 92, 93, 94–95
  at five months, 104
  at six months, 114–15
  at seven months, 124–25
  at eight months, 154, 156–57
  at nine months, 167
  at ten months, 177
  at twelve months, 199
  at twenty-one months, 254
  coordination of touch and, 115
  overview, 12
visual attention, 3, 14, 42, 52, 92, 93,
     94–95, 124–25, 177, 199
visual pursuit, 105, 106
vocabulary, *see* language, vocabulary
vocalizations, 16–17, 137, 143–44, 197
  at one month, 44–45
  at two months, 55

at three months, 66
at four months, 95–96
at five months, 103, 105
at six months, 113, 115–16
at seven months, 126
at eight months, 157–58
at nine months, 167
at ten months, 177
babbling, *see* babbling
consonants, 95–96, 105
dependent on speech heard by baby, 105
intonations, 55, 115
vocal volley, 55
vocal signatures, identifying, 115
vocal tennis, 66
von Hofsten, Claes, 98

wait, learning to, 234–35, 270
wakefulness, *see* sleep and wakefulness
walking, 151, 176, 184, 196, 198–99, 265,
     283
  gait, 198, 228, 254
  monitoring baby's wanderings, 196
  stairs, 253–54
  transition to, 198–99
wants, ability to send messages about,
     112–13
Watson, John, 280
waving good-bye (gesture), 122, 157
weight gain, 156
Wellman, Henry, 206
Werker, Janet, 142
"where are you?" (social game) 122
wiggling, 107
words, *see* language
working memory, 78
  diagram, 77

About the Author

Dr. Claire B. Kopp is an acclaimed developmental psychologist. She has been a professor at Claremont Graduate University and has also taught at UCLA. *Baby Steps* is the result of her over three decades of work with children and parents, as well as her own experiences as a mother and grandmother.